Stigmata

Stigmata brings together Hélène Cixous's most recent essays for the first time in any language. It is a collection of *texts that get away* – escaping the reader, the writer, the book – by one of the greatest authors and intellectuals of the modern world.

Signifying through a tissue of philosophical metaphor, poetic power, critical insight and disarming lightness, Cixous's writing is taken up in a reading pursuit, chasing across borders and through languages on the heels of works by authors such as Stendhal, Joyce, Derrida, Lispector, Tsvetaeva, and Rembrandt, da Vinci, Picasso – works that share an elusive movement in spite of striking differences.

Along the way these essays explore a broad range of poetico-philosophical questions that have long been circulating in the Cixousian universe: love's labours lost and found, feminine hours, autobiographies of writing, animal–human family ties, the prehistory of the work of art . . . woven into a *performance* of writing at the intersection of contemporary Western history and a singularity named Hélène Cixous.

Evoking her 'origins', the economy of a departure from Algeria (so as) never to arrive, and the psychomythical events that are engraved as fertile wounds into the body's many bodies, this book is an extraordinary writer's testimony to our lives and times.

Stigmata

Escaping texts

Hélène Cixous

London and New York

First published 1998 by Routledge
11 New Fetter Lane, London EC4P 4EE

Simultaneously published in the USA and Canada
by Routledge
29 West 35th Street, New York, NY 10001

Typeset in Garamond by M Rules
Printed and bound in Great Britain by T J International Ltd,
Padstow, Cornwall.

British Library Cataloguing in Publication Data
A catalogue record for this book is available from the British Library

Library of Congress Cataloging in Publication Data
Cixous, Hélène, 1937–
    [Essays. English. Selections]
    Stigmata: surviving texts/Hélène Cixous.
        p.   cm.
    Includes bibliographical references and index.
    I. Title.
PQ2663.I9A27   1998
844'.914—dc21   98–17127 CIP

ISBN 0–415–17978–5 (hbk)
ISBN 0–415–17979–3 (pbk)

Contents

From my menagerie to Philosophy   173

Illustrations

Reading in painting

1 Bathsheba or the interior Bible

Translated by Catherine A.F. MacGillivray

I've taken twenty-four steps in the direction of Bathsheba.

1. To what degree it is not about 'a nude,' behold why, between all the magic ones, I first said that one.

From her, I want to receive the secret messages.

This female nude is not a nude.

She is not made – not painted – to be seen nude. Precisely her – Bathsheba. She who was seen. Should not have been seen. She who is perceived. From afar.

She whom we see is not the mortal object.

Not the object of desire, and of murder.

It is Bathsheba in truth.

The non-nude nudity. Not denuded. Not undressed. Clean, characteristic.

Absolute Bathsheba. Without a man. Can we imagine seeing her: 'David and Bathsheba'? (The name Bathsheba invokes David – but not this woman, here, no.)

2. This is Bathsheba. The dark surroundings must be what's left of David. This sort of blackness? . . . If there is a couple, a pair in the painting, indeed it would be day and night.

(I say blackness, and not: black. Blackness isn't black. It is the last degree of reds. The secret blood of reds. There are so many blacks . . . Twenty-four, they say.)

I said 'without a man.' I mean to say without a 'visible' man. I mean

'Bethsabée ou la Bible intérieure' was first published in *FMR* 43, 1993 (April): 14–18; this translation (of a different version) first appeared in *New Literary History* 24, 4, 1993: 820–37.

Figure 1.1 Rembrandt, *Bathsheba bathing*, 1654. Paris, Musée du Louvre.

to say without an interior man. Inside herself. Without . . . preparation, without rigidity. This woman is not erect.

(And Rembrandt? – Ah! Rembrandt's sex –
Nothing to do with Rubens's sex of flourishes, nothing to do with da Vinci's mirror. Rembrandt is without ostentation.
The Rembrandt('s) sex is matrical.)

3. Why wouldn't Freud have anything to say about Rembrandt? Because there is no family scene, one sees no menace, no transference, no projection, there's no dependence, no authority, no cruel attachment.
Look at Titus. Titus is not 'a son,' he's a boy. This is a young man. This young man is.

This old woman is not maternalized. This old man is not venerabilized. The old man is old.

The wars of appurtenance, of appropriation, that rage in families: no. No violence. Only insistence and profundity. And to each, his or her profound destinal mission: becoming human.

4. What there is not in Rembrandt: there is no da Vinci.

Not the smile. Not the look that takes or the smile that flees.

There is no smile: no exterior. No face that lets itself be looked at. That knows it is looked at. No face. No surface. No scene. Everything is in the interior. No representation.

The passivity of Bathsheba. The despondency.
The imminence. Drooping over her somber heart.

5. There is no Vermeer.

No walls, no painting on the walls, no window, no panes, no curtain, no nautical map on the wall, no cupboard,

In Vermeer, light enters by the window on the left and draws. Everything is in the cell. The outside knocks on the windowpanes. The exterior enters the interior.

(The *camera obscura*, the machine for seeing gives us: photographic vision, from foreground to background.)

Here: no objects in the foreground, no fruits. No spools of thread. Here, no exterior, no era, no city.

Vermeer takes us to Delft. To the Lacemaker's. Eternal Reconstitution.

Where does Rembrandt take us? To a foreign land, our own.

A foreign land, our other country.

He takes us to the Heart.

6. One must penetrate into the country (– says Van Gogh – stay in the Midi, until, by penetration, you become it).

Sharpen one's eye on the land.

Cézanne being absolutely from the very land, he knows it so intimately, one must make the same calculation internally in order to arrive at tones like this (Firm tones).[1]

Rembrandt's very land? Neither the city, nor the countryside. The interior land: 'the landscape of the interior Bible.' I say the Bible, that is to say, the land of the most ancient passions, it is a land without landscape, without monuments. But not without form and without inhabitants.

How to get there? How to get inside a star, Van Gogh wondered? The fastest method of transportation is not the train, it's death.

And to get inside the interior Bible? One must take the stairs, and plunge into the flesh. Down to the farthest memory.

7. It's dark here. We're down below. We're here.
In the breast. Immediately. Such an absence of exterior!
The country is a room of palpitating folds.
What I feel: this obscurity. It is the troubled air of our secrets, those that govern us and that we're not really aware of. We (Bathsheba) are in the secret. The secret surrounds us. Bathsheba is seated in our room, in our breast, like a luminous heart. She contains the light. The light doesn't spill out.
The Body: bread of light.
I verify: where is the light coming from? The shadow of the ribbon on Bathsheba's skin tells us that a strong light is coming from the left. But the pearly luster of the triangular lining under the servant's cap tells us that a stream of light must be rising up from the right.
The source of the light is cut off. The light remains. The secret fire that emanates from the flesh.

8. Of what secret lights are we made?
Of what densities?
What Rembrandt gives back to us: the dough, the depth, the tactile, that which we lose, which we have lost, we who live flat, without density, in silhouettes on a screen: the interior radiance.
– A scene by Rembrandt (let's take a family scene, or a scene like this one, a scene of 'corporation'), what gives it its force – by which it takes us, pushes us, pinches us, caresses us, is, beyond courtly war exchanges – beyond pretenses, codes . . .
– that it always occurs at the same time in the cellar in the cave or in the forest, in these great and somber prehistoric cathedrals where our colors, our drawings stir, where attraction and repulsion shine, like lanterns in our obscurity. It is there (to the bottom) that Rembrandt leads us. Taking the red staircase, down to the bottom of ourselves, under the earth's crust,
This world is full of night and of golden stuff. The stuff of night is a clay. A mud. It is still moving, imperceptibly.
No landscape and no 'furniture' either. Instead of furniture, 'shelving,' 'shelves' of color. Bands, brush strokes. What do you see, there?
A man said to me, here's a cupboard. With linens piled up.
Another man, this one a painter: an architectural background, a pilaster.
A commentator said to me: the curtain has been drawn aside.
We have such a need of cupboards, of curtains, such a need to furnish.

The interior world is full of night and of golden stuff, of the stuff of night. Spools of nights.

Curtains? The curtains have been drawn aside? The stuff, the linens, the dark golds, the white golds, border on, play in major and minor, the body's blond gold.

The entire room is flesh. Sex.

The 'curtains' have raised themselves like eyelids, uncovering the clear pupil: the luminous body of Bathsheba.

I notice: 'the sensation of curtains drawn aside.' As if our naïveté were thinking: this, this light in the cup of flesh, only exists hidden, pre-served. It's *intimacy*. We can never see it, except by indiscretion.

(See the incredible Holy Family at the Curtain: it's about magic: how to make us feel the intimacy of intimacy, the *intimitude*?[2] We are graced with being shown what is hidden behind the curtain: same gesture as for gazing at a baby in its cradle: we lean over, pull the sheet aside, the veil, the curtain, taking care not to tear it from its intimacy. Bathsheba in the cradle, sleeps before us, very near, very far from us.)

It's about the discrete sensation of 'revelation.'

We see a mixture of slowness and agitation. The moment 'just after' – not yet. It does not yet have a name.

9. With what is she painted?

Van Gogh said that Delacroix said that Veronese painted white blond naked women with a color which, by itself, greatly resembles street mud.

Van Gogh wants to paint with the earth. To mould.

With what mud is Bathsheba painted? With what earth?

With the flesh's butter. With ghee. That rosy blond butter.

Libations.

Bathsheba nude.

I see Rembrandt painting the veil (that doesn't hide a thing) on her groin.

Rembrandt grazing Bathsheba's groin with a veil.

The veil, a nothing that creates the nudity.

Without this transparent nothing we would forget she is nude.

Bathsheba is in person. In a dressing gown. In body.

It is the body that is the face.

10. She does not look at us. She is of those who do not look at us. I mean to say: those women, Bathsheba, Mary, Hendrickje, don't look at us, don't stop living, (that is to say dreaming, that is to say leaving) in order to look at us.

They withdraw, they take their leave slowly, a thought carries them toward the unknown, far away. We hear – barely – the call from afar –

And we, looking at them, we see thought taking its leave. We see thought. It is a portrait of thought, according to Rembrandt. Thought is not the weighty thinker seated. It passes, inside, distracted, traveling, it is the foreigner, the stranger.

He paints the foreigner, the stranger in me, in you.

The times when under the letter's sway –

we suddenly become the stranger, the foreigner in ourselves. We separate ourselves from ourselves. We lose ourselves. From sight also.

He catches, paints, the point of departure. The hour, when destiny slips from our eyes.

Everything seems domestic. And yet such a strangeness wells up in our eyes, like tears. It's that she is already gone, she who is called Bathsheba. But the body remains. That much more body, that much more flesh, that much heavier here, now that she-Bathsheba is elsewhere.

The face is traveling: a great silence reigns in the painting.

'What are you thinking about?' we wonder.

11. A nude woman thinking. 'Thoughtful body.'

On the one hand the thoughtfulness accentuates the nudity: naked nudity. Nudity un-thought. Un-attended to, un-kept. Given.

(What does a naked woman think about – her rapport to her body, always the slight attention, like a veil, the glance or the gaze. Whenever I'm naked, I don't look at myself, I cast a glance my way (– the glance of the other, of you/me at me) – But no, Bathsheba does not look at her body. She is not before herself. She is not here. She is gone, behind her eyelids.)

On the other hand, the person who thinks in front of us, abandons us. A very slight betrayal rouses us: we miss her a little, she who is (only a little bit here) absent.

Distracted, she is abstracted from us.

'He doesn't paint great Historical subjects (said a contemporary). He paints thoughts . . .' (Roger de Piles, 1699, Paris).

(He paints thoughtfulness. This absence in the body. This leave-taking by the soul that leaves the body deserted like a living tomb. We think: we're parting.

Figure 1.2 Fragment of a drawing by Rembrandt. London, Victoria & Albert Museum.

12. The older woman further down at the bottom is a remainder. She comes back to us from this drawing (see Figure 1.2).

Bathsheba is also then this other woman.

The woman with the cap is: Bathsheba's strange foreignness, her exoticism, Asia.

Nude with a cap! extravagance: something aberrant in the coifed nudity.

And the coif: oriental . . .

This nude cut in two: the body is Bathsheba's
                            the coif is the older woman's . . . The cap! is at work.

The 'servant's' gaze moves off toward the future in the East.

Bathsheba's gaze withdraws toward the occidental future.

The two gazes descend slowly, toward the bottom.

Cross each other, don't see each other. Are on two parallel planes.

The two women withdraw from the scene thoughtfully.

The 'servant' wipes Bathsheba's feet distractedly. She is elsewhere. They are elsewhere. In soul they are elsewhere. The body, left, weighs more heavily.

What is the 'servant' thinking about? These two women are day-dreaming of the end of the year. At the end of the year, a path will have been lost,

The end of the year . . .

At first glance, at tenth glance, this is the face that at first I see. I should say: this demi-face. We call this: profile. In fact it is a side, a half, a demi-star. The other side belongs to the night. I will never know then but half of Bathsheba, the illuminated part.

13. Something unreadable catches my eyes. Maybe this, I tell myself, after a long time: it is something that glides from head to toe. A motion-less movement, a transformation. Now I see it, it is time, and even: it is time's writing, it is age. From the young head, the body goes forward, aging imperceptibly. Ah! so that's what was gripping my heart. This young woman is in the process of aging. The future is spreading through her limbs. Her breasts are still childlike, already her pelvis, her thighs, her legs are in the hands of age.

What? I mustn't say this? But this is nonetheless what Rembrandt paints: the passion (the suffering) of Bathsheba, starts here, in the body, between the knees,

where floats . . . the letter.

14. The Violence of the Letter.

At first I didn't see it. The letter.

Little by little the letter captures the gazes.

At first I looked at the body.

This body that lets itself fall into itself.
That weighs. Weighing. For? Against?

I looked at the body's dough. The flesh furnishes. Without muscles. (See the muscled thighs of the *Woman Bathing*.)

A despondency, a prostration. Of an animal that knows itself promised. To the sacrifice.
'The body lowers its head.'
(It seems there has been a *pentimento*[3] of the head.)
(Whereas all the women rise, in one way or another. Even the modest ones, even Hendrickje. They have muscles or a cap.)
Bathsheba is drooping. Slightly.
Chin drooping.
An indolence has seized her.
Dejection? Resignation?

How she holds the letter: Weariness. She might drop it.

15. (N.B. the victory of the letter: the slow rise to the surface, the insistence.)
So there is a letter.
There is always a letter.
The letter, what violence! How it seeks us out, how it aims at us!
Us.
Especially women.
And more often than joy, it is some death it brings to us.
I don't know why I hadn't seen it. And you?
What's a letter, next to a big body full of buttered light? a crumpled paper, next to these unctuous linens?
Suddenly I am letterstruck. And I see only it.[4] This letter! no, it's a hole in the body of the painting, the rent, the tear in the night. If I see the letter, I no longer see Bathsheba. And now that I have my eyes on the letter, I see that it's the letter that spills this shadow on to Bathsheba's left leg. This letter is in opposition. To the veil. To the linen.
To the reading. It is a letter from the back. It turns its back to us. When I wanted to read it: forever forbidden. To paint a letter seen from the back! The Door is closed. It is David, an old tale whispers to me.
David is the outsider. The outside. The arranger.[5] Invisible.
'David and Bathsheba,' that's it: it is Bathsheba to the letter . . . The letter resounds throughout the entire painting.
Form

This painting is divided more or less into two triangles.
Shadow of gold and (carnal) light of flesh.
In the center, the stroke of the letter.

16. The letter has just been read.
The two women are under the letter's sway.
The letter has taken their breath away. Has dispatched them over there into the closed time, before the closed doors to the future.
Here in the painting, in the tent, they have already past, the present already past falls in heavy folds toward the bottom.

How white the letter is in the middle of the painting. Of a shadowy rosy whiteness. The letter is within the scale, so it is a part of Bathsheba's colors.
Letter one neither holds on to nor drops. Holds the entire painting under the indecipherable charm of its breath.

And how red the stain is at the corner of the letter.
Like a signature. The mark on the shoulder. A touch of purple on the white. Sign or signature. Piece of red seal? A bit of wax. So is it realistic? No, it is red. It is an element. Incarnadine.

Portrait of Sadness: presentiment of mourning.
Bathsheba's sadness:
She becomes sad under the insistence of our gaze.
The mouth made for smiling, the mouth doesn't droop.
The sadness is in the brow: the brow slightly rises like thought slightly rises as it attempts to think farther.

17. I've just seen, in the collection: *The Lacemaker*, *The Astronomer* by Vermeer. The *Erasmus* by Holbein.
The Lacemaker is a *sublime still life*. I remained in contemplation before the light and shadow of the lacemaker's fingers. The sculptured aspect of the light. *The Lacemaker* is a Cézanne by its ridges. *The Lacemaker* is perfect. In its every detail. It is a treasure chest full of precious colors. It isn't lacking in anything. We feel a great satisfaction. Like before the perfection of a doll's house: everything is there, down to the smallest cooking pot. And into the bargain there are those yellows. Everything is in order in the house.
Erasmus hasn't changed. It's really him, today as three centuries ago, the same dry, thin-lipped man. Erasmus's appearance hasn't changed in three centuries. It is a photograph. There is no interior. Holbein is the

master of the genial splendor of realism. I imagine the surprise of his contemporaries. Such a resemblance!

(It seems that certain buyers would complain about the lack of resemblance in Rembrandt's portraits. What must resemblance resemble?)

18. Why do I place Rembrandt above, elsewhere, apart? Since forever?
No realism: what he paints is a woman hidden under the appearance of Bathsheba. He paints the precise passing instant, the instant that is the door to eternity. In the instant is the eternity.

In Rembrandt truly no realism. To what degree it is the soul he paints, the soul in flesh and in light, can be seen by the indifference he manifests for the 'realistic description' of the body. The position is impossible. I tried. But this is of no importance. It is the soul that presses the thighs together.

He paints a woman struck by a letter, carried outside of herself and whom he calls – we call – Bathsheba.

He paints the bruised heart of Bathsheba. He paints the slight and uncertain intensity.

Rembrandt paints the secret: the trace of what escapes us: he always paints what escapes us: what has just happened, what is going to happen, and which traverses us suddenly, pierces us, turns us upside down, escapes – beyond the painting, beyond thought, and leaves us there panting, suspended, grazed, he paints the body that remains, maybe the skin, maybe the cadaver.

The painting is the place of passage.

19. And in order to paint this, one must be dead.
He paints like a dead man. Like a poet. Like a dead man.
See why Van Gogh places Rembrandt apart, elsewhere:
'Rembrandt remains faithful to nature, even when, there too and still, he goes to the heights, the highest heights, infinite heights, but just the same, Rembrandt could still do otherwise when he didn't feel the need to remain faithful, in the literal sense of the word, like in the portrait, when he could be poet, that is to say creator.'

'That is what he is in the *Jewish Bride.*'

'– What an immensely profound, noble sentiment. One must die several times in order to paint like this, now this is a remark one could apply to him.'

'Rembrandt penetrates so far into the mystery that he says things no language can express. It is just of us to say of Rembrandt: the Magician . . . This is not an easy craft.'[6]

The craft of death isn't easy. What does that mean?

For example this: it isn't with the appetite of desire that Rembrandt paints Bathsheba. It is with attentive love for the creature, for the miracle of existing. The profound amazement, joyous without splendor, almost pious before this invention: the human being. Nothing royal. Nothing extraordinary. The sober splendor of the ordinary. What is marvelous: the ordinary metamorphosis: these people are subject to alteration, to time. Time is at work. And not just time. Everything that endlessly paints us from the inside. All the blows and messages that knock at the door to the heart, and paint from the inside the troubled nervous agitation we call soul. (The soul, our capacity to suffer, said Tsvetaeva.)

That which wells up in Bathsheba, that which the letter has poured into her body, into her organs, into her brain, and which is working on her body, her face, her brow, from the inside.

She's listening to this: this transformation in herself. Which is still new, mobile, momentary. She doesn't know who, shortly, she'll be.

Traversed.

Traversed, St Matthew too? Transfixed. Cocked. All ears.

He paints us listening to ourselves change.

On the one hand he paints.
The heavy
Silence
of Bathsheba

On the other he paints *the Voice that causes writing.*

– The Voice – How to paint the Voice?

– We don't see the voice.

Rembrandt paints the voice we do not see.

   paints what we do not see.

   see?

   paints what speaks inside . . .

      the word   The Angel

20. I see *St Matthew and the Angel*

What I love is: the proximity of the invisible.

And the hand on the shoulder. The voice's hand. Because the mystery of the voice is this: it is that it touches us. And also this angel so close, so flesh – who is but a head and a hand: (The body . . . we imagine it.) The angel, I mean to say the voice, the body is: 'on tiptoe.' It is the tension. Toward the ear we're aiming for.

I approach: the truth is that the angel is a part of St Matthew. This man has an enormous square build. He radiates force, ruggedness, the wind. He passes from the road and the forest to the writing table. His cheeks are struck by the air. Colored by intemperate weather. One would think an earthly sailor, a woodcutter, a giant tamed by tenderness. A heavy handsome man touched by grace. The angel is his grace. Rembrandt paints to the letter: that which was metaphor is made flesh. The voice comes from very far, very near. With all his weight, with his whole forehead, his whole mane, the man listens. The voice (of the angel) passes through his throat.

Rembrandt paints this mysterious thing that mobilizes the body: the state of creation. Writing, thinking, is being in a state of waiting for what is yet to come, but proclaims itself – Proclamation and imminence – a force stronger than myself comes up behind me. And – I guess – painting is the same way, with the angel at your shoulder and eyes that listen and do not see.

This is also the attitude of the *Philosopher Meditating*.[7] The philosopher is 'listening.' He is nothing but an ear. All is audition. Slightly turned away from the light, from the book – and from the bust. Hence pointed toward the mouth – obscure ear . . .

What is 'a philosopher meditating'?

A somber conch.

Meditation takes place at the bottom of the staircase.

21. We, we have lost our heads a bit?

For we are on the road to our most violent, most foreign fellow-creature.

The Ox. The Hermit. The Turned Upside Down. The Acrobat. The Paralyzed. The Ancient Choir. The Truth. You, as I see you when I see you as you really are: and to do this I have to draw the curtains aside, to slaughter you, to open you up – (with my gaze only). And then, naturally, it is me that I see, it is us, nude, it is our nuditude,[8] magnificent, our power bound, our shining blindness.

Why do we adore *The Slaughtered Ox*? Because without our knowing it or wanting it, it is our anonymous humanity. We are not Christ, never, Christ . . . no I will not speak of this.

We are this creature, which even turned upside down and decapitated and hung beneath the earth – when it is seen with those eyes that don't reject the below, that don't prefer the above –

maintains its majesty.

Behold the portrait of our mortality. The being hung (by its shins), turned upside down, twice decapitated.

Figure 1.3 Rembrandt, *The Slaughtered Ox*, 1655. Paris, Musée du Louvre.

What we become under the ax and the slicer.

There is a butcher shop on our life's path. As children we would pass trembling before the butcher's window. Later on we want to forget death. We cut the dead one up into pieces and we call it meat.

22. And the Curtain? Or the frame?

To see the ox we must enter into the painting. The ox is framed. The frame is in the interior of the painting.

The painting has two doors. One in front. One in back. Let's enter. We enter by the front door. We're standing in the cellar. The ox is a lamp, an enormous hanging lamp. It is the aster of this night. It irradiates.

The ox is beautiful.

The ox shines in the darkness. Where? Back of a shop? Cellar? Tomb? The ox is a gigantic ingot of flesh.

The ox is bound. The ox is nude.

Who are we contemplating? Samson's truth, or Rembrandt's. The blind, the freed, the powerful slaughtered. The gazed upon. Who by their magnificent helplessness fill us with wonder.

the Vanquished sparkles. (Vanquished but Strong)

Nothing less 'realistic.' To paint this. With what admiration. What love.

The ox is hurled to the bottom. And there are no angels. The huge body is sideways. Everything adds to the impression that someone has left it all alone.

All of a sudden I see: it's about our captivity.

23. The ox is dazzling. The ox is pregnant with light.

To the extent that we don't see the woman's head – advancing prudently, in a halo of weak light.

The light seems to be the luminous shadow projected by the flesh.

In 'reality' it is doubtless coming from behind the door.

The woman pokes her head in through the doorway, to see? Furtiveness. As if she were looking at what mustn't be looked at.

Clandestine glance: curiosity wonders: is it there? Who's there? What's hidden there?

To one side the powerful body, the incarnation of slaughtered power, hung by its feet. Why is the ox hung 'head down' (the absence of a head down there)?

On the other the small head without a body, the question.

But we don't see her. The shining of the ox attracts my entire gaze. Attracts us. We are attracted by the open ox as by the illuminated carriage opening of a palace.

The light calls. We advance. Let's enter.

Here all is gold and purple.

We are in the breast.

24. Before me spreads the agitated space with its somber thicknesses of fatty haunted gold, so it seems, in the purple distances of the canvas, of flayed scarlet stairs in the geologic matter, the ground sheer like a deep hanging, past upon past, my mines, my reserve difficult to access, but overflowing if I arrive, with thoughts, with passions, with kin, before me my personal foreign land: everything in the nearby over there is mine, everything is strangely foreign to me: everything that, in its night dough, I discern for the first time, I recognize. The world, before me, so great, is inside, it is the immense limitless life hidden behind restricted life.

Do you see the steps? To the right, some somber steps tell us we are down below, in the cellar. Somber descending steps.

But here we climb up. These steps here, the interior gold and purple steps lead us toward the heights, toward the heart of the temple.

What are we present at? At a mystery. At a solemn representation.

This is not the crucifixion.

This is the Passion according to Rembrandt. Mourning and Transfiguration of the Ox.

It is there in the cellar, that I divine:
What does he seek to paint of Bathsheba?
Her solitude of slaughtered ox.
Bathsheba or the slaughtered ox.

P.S. Reading the big catalogues, I look for *The Slaughtered Ox*. For example in Gerson's beautiful volume on Rembrandt.[9] I flip through the index. The author has classified the work according to rubrics; Portraits: Self-portraits, Portraits of Men, Portraits of Women, Portraits of Children; Groups . . . (I'm looking for the Ox), Landscapes . . . Finally I find it: it is in Interiors, keeping company with the *Philosopher Meditating*.

Translator's notes

1 Vincent Van Gogh, *Lettres à son frère Théo* (Paris: Grasset, 1937), p. 181.

2 Neologism formed by Cixous from neologisms like *négritude* etc.

3 From the Italian. This painterly term means an alteration, an artistic second thought, which can sometimes still be discerned in the finished work. In French, the word for this is *repentir*, which also means 'repentance,' thus producing a double meaning I found impossible to render in English: of the depiction of the head as having been slightly altered during the act of painting, and of the head's drooping position as indicating a feeling of repentance on the part of Bathsheba. For a further discussion of the notion of *repentir* in painting, see Hélène Cixous, 'Without end, no, State of drawingness, no, rather: The Executioner's taking off,' this volume, pp. 20–31.

4 In French, the following passage plays with the 'femininity' of the letter (*la lettre*) in a complicated intertwining of feminine pronouns that refer at times to the letter, at others to Bathsheba. Unfortunately, this proximity and even confusion between the two is lost in English.

5 In French: *David est l'hors. Le hors. L'ordonnateur.* This complex sentence, impossible to render precisely in English, plays with the French word for 'outside.' The word for 'arranger' can also be heard as *l'hors donnateur* (the giver of the outside), thus referring back to what comes before, and so on.

6 Vincent Van Gogh, *Lettres à son frère Théo* (Paris: Grasset, 1937), p. 123.

7 In order for the rest of the passage to make sense, I have translated the title of this painting by Rembrandt directly from the French. In English, this same painting is called *Scholar in a Room with Winding Stair*.

8 See n. 2.

9 Horst Gerson, *Rembrandt's Paintings*, trans. H. Norden, ed. G. Schwantz (London: Weidenfeld & Nicolson, 1968).

2 Without end, no, State of drawingness, no, rather: The Executioner's taking off

Translated by Catherine A.F. MacGillivray

'I want the beforehand of a book.' I just wrote this sentence, but before this sentence, I wrote a hundred others, which I've suppressed, because the moment for cutting short had arrived. It's not me, it's necessity which has cut the text we were on the way to writing. Because the text and I, we would continue on our way.

'I've learned to tear up nothing of what I write,' Clarice Lispector tells me. But then comes the time for separation. The time for publication.

I would like so much this unknown untorn page. Everything we read: remains.

I want the forest before the book, the abundance of leaves before the pages, I love the creation as much as the created, no, more. I love the Kafka of the Journals, the executioner-victim, I love the process a thousand times more than the Trial process (no, a hundred times more). I want the tornados in the atelier.

And what I love best are Dostoevsky's notebooks, the crazy and tumultuous forge, where Love and Hate embrace, rolling around on the ground in convulsions which thwart all calculation and all hope: no one knows who will be born of this possessed belly, who will win, who will survive.

I want the world of pulses, before destiny, I want the prenatal and anonymous night. I want (the arrival) to see arriving.

Acts of birth, potency, and impotency mingled are what I'm passionate about. The to-be-in-the-process of writing or drawing. (*Mais pourquoi avons-nous perdu le gérondif en français? Le vrai temps de ce texte est le gérondif.*)

There is no end to writing or drawing. Being born doesn't end. Drawing is a being born. Drawing is born.

'Sans Arrêt, non, Etat de Dessination, non, plutôt: Le Décollage du Bourreau' was first published in *Repentirs* (Réunion des musées nationaux, 1991): 55–64; this translation first appeared in *New Literary History* 24, 1, 1993 (Winter): 90–103.

– When do we draw?

– When we were little. Before the violent divorce between Good and Evil. All was mingled then, and no mistakes. Only desire, trial, and error. Trial, that is to say, error. Error: progression.

As soon as we draw (as soon as, following the pen, we advance into the unknown, hearts beating, mad with desire) we are little, we do not know, we start out avidly, we're going to lose ourselves.

Drawing, writing, what expeditions, what wanderings, and at the end, no end, we won't finish, rather time will put an end to it.

(N.B. I'm saying writing-or-drawing, because these are often twin adventures, which depart to seek in the dark, which do not find, do not find, and as a result of not finding and not understanding, (draw) help the secret beneath their steps to shoot forth.)

I write this accompanied by seeking drawings.

It is the dead of night. I sense I am going to write. You, whom I accompany, you sense you are going to draw. Your night is waiting.

The figure which announces itself, which is going to make its appearance, the poet-of-drawings doesn't see it. The model only appears to be outside. In truth it is invisible, but present, it lives inside the poet-of-drawings. You who pray with the pen, you feel it, hear it, dictate. Even if there is a landscape, a person, there outside – no, it's from inside the body that the drawing-of-the-poet rises to the light of day. First it exists at the torment state in the chest, under the waist. See it now as it precipitates itself in spasms, in waves, the length of the arm, passing the hand, passing the pen. Eyes open wide in the night, staring wide-eyed with hope, the one who draws follows the movement. S/he obeys. Ecstasy: technique. Because not seeing doesn't impede the pen from noting. To the contrary.

I write before myself by apprehension, with noncomprehension, the night vibrates, I see with my ears, I advance into the bosom of the world, hands in front, capturing the music with my palms,

until something breathes under the pen's beak.

(I've just written these lines eyelids closed as usual, because the day and its huge light keeps us from seeing what is germinating.)

Now we turn on the lights, and lean over to see the work born. Then, surprise before what, passing through us, was drawn; and if it is *I* who drew this unknown child then who are I?

The drawing is without a stop. I mean to say the true drawing, the living one – because there are dead ones, drawn-deads. Look and you shall see.

Barely traced – the true drawing escapes. Rends the limit. Snorts. Like the world, which is only a perennial movement, the drawing goes along, befuddled and staggering, with a natural drunkenness.

All that exists is naturally drunk: the boat, the Egyptian pyramids, the executioner's coldness, the iron. Who said that? If it's not Rembrandt or Rimbaud, it's one Montaigne or the other.

To think there are those who seek the finished. Those who seek to portray cleanly, the most properly!

But some portray passing. The truth. The passing (of the) truth. This is what gives to their drawing that panting and unstable allure.

Look at the child barely seated on his mother's knees: on the one hand the little arms are in the drawing, in the circle, but on the other hand the legs sketch the escapade. This little one doesn't stay put.

You will recognize the true drawing, the live one: it's still running. Look at the legs. I'll come back to that.

For the moment, I am, following, the error, without fear but with respect. To what extent we need error which is the promise of truth, to what extent we can't do without the silvery burst of error, which is the sign, all those who go by pen don't cease to marvel at this in a similar way, from century to century.

Felix culpa, St Augustine calls it, and then *portal of discovery*, says Joyce, *submissão ao processo*, says Clarice Lispector, the writing process is made up of errors . . . And before that, 'naïve and essential submission,' said our wandering grandfather Montaigne; and we're all in agreement, how to draw other than by groping in the night, 'inquiring and ignorant.'

Necessary error, school mistress, faltering essential companion, we love her, because she is the only way we have on this earth to feel the truth, which is always a little farther, exists, a little farther away.

And repentance? No repentance. We who draw are innocent. Our mistakes are our leaps in the night. Error is not lie: it is approximation. Sign that we are on track.

And: to not become gloomy from not 'attaining.' We don't lose anything by erring, to the contrary.

The unhappy thing would be to believe we had found.

As long as we are seeking we are innocent. We are in naïve submission. In prenatality.

I advance error by error, with erring steps, by the force of error. It's suffering, but it's joy.

I seek the truth, I encounter error. How do I recognize error? It is obvious, like truth. Who tells me? My body. Truth gives us pleasure. It makes us burst out laughing, trembling. Blushing. It's hot. It's like this: I grope. I try the word 'hesitation.' I taste it. No pleasure. No taste. I cross out. I try: 'correction.' I taste. No. I taste ten words. Finally I fall on the word: 'essay.' Before even trying I already sense a pretaste . . . I taste. And, that's it! Its taste is strong and fine and rich in memories of pleasure.

Truth strikes us. Opens our heart. Our lips. Error makes us sense the absence of taste. Drops us like a dead person, apathetic tongue, dry eyes. Error really can't fool us.

We've just drawn an executioner. Just a little while ago he was amassing in our entrails, in our lungs, we felt his storm rumbling. Now we look at him standing on the paper, and we don't feel anything. In us the storm is always alive, on paper, no. I submit myself to the invisible truth of my vision, I obey the strange and foreign voice in my body.

– A little farther! Go on! Start again! Forward!
– To the right? Shall I draw to the right?
– Try . . .
– I'm trying.
– I'm still trying.

See why I guard against effacing my first steps. I need to lean on, to start again from my error.

In order to be able to draw a crime, Dostoevsky began again a hundred times. It was such a subtle crime, which escaped him, so profound. He felt it. Missed it. Approached it. The other escaped. The essays accumulated. The scene was turning, the pen, trying, a door – a victim – Here? – That's not it – was distancing itself, shall I knock? and if that wasn't it, the drawing wouldn't take, its heart wouldn't beat, the knife was rising, the victim was falling – Is that it? – Not yet,

then is it in the stairway? – take note, D. told himself, but that wasn't it, was there someone behind the door? N.B., D. noted, N.B., N.B., annotating his notes. These notebooks were a joyous carnage. N.B. – You have to have found the key by midnight. With the result that wanting to discover the invisible heart of his crime before midnight, he managed to play four books at the same time and one against the other – one barring the other, one killing the other, one chasing the other, one haunting the other denying – four books from only one hand, on the same page we go straight to the confession. Three words later we leave running.

These notebooks so many failures! Before the midnight scissors what fecundity.

What do we want to draw?

What are we trying to grasp between the lines, in between the strokes, in the net that we're weaving, that we throw, and the dagger blows?

Not the person, but the precious in that person, not the Virgin, not the child, but what is between them in this very moment, linking them – a secret, that which mysteriously renders those two unforgettable. I sense: it's not divinity, it's whim. That little grain of meanness which *makes* the little boy. Do you see?

Figure 2.1 Leonard da Vinci, *Vierge à l'Enfant*. Paris, Musée du Louvre.

It's not a question of drawing the contours, *but of what escapes the contour*, the secret movement, the breaking, the torment, the unexpected.

The drawing wants to draw what is invisible to the naked eye. It's very difficult. The effort to write is always beyond my strength. What you see here, these lines, these strokes, are rungs on the ladder of writing, the steps which I have cut with my fingernails in my own wall, in order to hoist myself up above and beyond myself.

And drawing *'the living of life'* (what else is there to want to draw?) – is maddening; it's exactly what none *knows* how to draw, the quick of life. But it's not impossible.

It's something small, precise – I'm guessing – it must be red, it's, I'm guessing, the fire speck – or the blood speck – it's – I'm searching – the point which nails this drawing, this page, this verse, in our memory, the unforgettable stroke – the needle planted in the heart of eternity – I'm searching – a minuscule fatality, a point which hurts my heart and hurts the world's heart, it's no bigger than the red spider which continues on while Stavroguine thinks about the crime, thinks about the crime, and doesn't repent . . .

(– I'm advancing, I'm approaching, be careful because if I see what it is, just as quickly I won't see anymore –)

the trace of the quick of life hidden beneath the rounded appearances of life, life which remains hidden because we wouldn't bear seeing it as it is, in all the brilliance of horror that it is, it is without pity, like the drawing must be.

This morning in the museum, I was passing in front of the drawings, in the slight alarm of the reading which doesn't know from where the blow will come, and I was looking, distracted, at these morsels of worry, these stuttered avowals of nothing, nothing clearly delivered.

It was then that the blow came from whom I wasn't expecting it at all. What is this moment called when we suddenly recognize what we have never seen? And which gives us a joy like a wound? This is the woman who did that to me: the Woman Ironing.

This Woman Ironing hurts us. Because the drawing catches 'the secret' in its (contrary) enmeshed threads. 'The thing,' that sharp thing, 'life.' We thought we were drawing a Woman Ironing. But it's worse. This Woman Ironing is a tragedy. A needle blow right in the middle of eternity's chest. But in order to pull the needle out, to strike the blow, one had to scribble furiously. We struggled. Against what or whom?

Against the *idea* of Woman Ironing. The drawing carries traces of blows, of bruises and even of blood. She's tumefied.

By dint of passing and ironing over the body of the woman ironing, what ended up appearing – is – one would say a crime. From the body broken and streaked with strokes comes the body hidden in the body of the woman ironing, or more precisely the soul's head, and, neck exposed, she bellows.

I don't want to draw the idea, I don't want to write being, I want what

Figure 2.2 Pablo Picasso, *Etude pour 'La Repasseuse.'* Paris, Musée Picasso.

happens in the Woman Ironing, I want the nerve, I want the Revelation of the broken Woman Ironing. And I want to write what passes between us and the Woman Ironing, the electric current. The emotion. Because as a result of drawing her with my eyes, I felt: *it's death* that is passing through the Woman Ironing, our mortality in person. I want to draw our mortality, this quiver.

The emotion is born *at the angle* of one state with another state. At the passing, so brusque. Accident. Instant of alteration that takes us by surprise. And the body which expresses itself before the word. First the cry, then the words.

When it's not entirely clear, what is being felt or being thought in the body – of Christ, of the woman ironing – that's the moment we seek to

Figure 2.3 Rembrandt, *Décollation de Saint Jean Baptiste*. Paris, Musée du Louvre.

draw. Are we going to die? Kill? The hand rises, the head, the pen falls once more.

The drawing feels death passing.

We believe we're drawing (going to) the Beheading of St John the Baptist. But it's worse. At the moment of Beheading, suddenly, there's been a change of heart. Or rather of life. Something unpredictable has happened between the two characters *during* the drawing. We were bending over the saint in horror, and at the moment we contemplated his body with curiosity, that is to say the two parts of his body, suddenly so contrary

our entire attention was diverted and carried away in the opposite direction by the executioner. Because, at the moment the drawing wanted to draw the body's pain and the head's mourning, there was a sudden rise of life in the executioner, which the drawing was unable to resist. The executioner's joy burst out. This couldn't have occurred *before* the drawing executed the saint. Because the saint had to have been properly beheaded in order for the executioner to have suddenly been transfigured, and become one, on the spot, body with saber. At the instant we were describing the saint's collapse, (and at the sight of the decapitated body trying to get up, pushing with its arms), the executioner straightened up like a spring, I mean the pen, and with a grand full stroke signed the executioner's strong and sudden jubilation.

We want to write the torment, and we write the joy. At the same time. At each moment I am another myself. The one in and on the other.

What was the first stroke of the pen? And before the first line there were many others. In truth the first line is the survivor of the mêlée: everything starts in the middle.

One must jump into the middle of the sheet of paper, fell the quill, as soon as the race begins, or else it's battle.

And now I see what the Woman Ironing, the Executioner, the Saint, the little boy, have in common: it's Violence. It's about combat.

Drawings of combat, these drawings which, fatally, touch me, wounded though they are, and therefore similar to us.

Drawings par excellence: because every drawing (is) combat(s) itself. Drawing is the emblem of all our hidden, intestine combats. There we see the soul's entrails.

What is the page of a book? What remains of a sheet of paper becomes a field of battle on which we, writing, drawing, have killed each other ourselves. A flagstone of paper under which a carnage effaces itself. In writing, all is disputed, and sacrificed. As soon as Kafka took his pen in his right hand, his left hand jumped on it (on his right) and the combat raged. This made for such drafts that, in the inability to give reason to the one hand or the other, Kafka dreamed of dragging into the fire, with himself, the innumerable traces of his hostilities. And if he didn't do it himself that's just because he tried to repent. We try to repent, but we never repent. One doesn't repent. One doesn't manage. One makes essays.

When Rembrandt wanted to draw *The Beheading of St John the Baptist* there was an explosion, and the two men, the executioner and the victim, fought one another for the paper with ferocity, Rembrandt, the executioner, the victim, moaned with long cutting wails. What was drawing itself between himself *is the decapitation exploding in the body of the executioner*. The pen has captured the transfer, the brutal and rapid explosion in the process of instantaneously transforming the two adversaries. Everything, drawn from the point of view of the executor. The drawing was called: *The Executioner's Taking Off*, but subsequently this name was crossed out and replaced . . . N.B. And precisely in this scene where Rembrandt became an executioner, *no repentance*. I mean to say: no Christian repentance. (The executioner is searching for his accomplishment, and in a few strokes, becomes the incarnation of the cutting blade.)

Because our soul has no firm footing.
Agitation reigns in these drawings. This is perhaps why painters draw? Because drawing is the right to tumult, to frenzy. The right to: no. The drawing cries out. But painting, even frenetic, even Van Gogh, paints all the same after the tempest. It takes a little time. But the drawing is: essay: before. 'Work in which the author treats his or her matter without pretending to say the last word . . .' We don't have the last word: truth always has the word before, and we run out of breath at its heels. In the essay entitled 'Of Repentance' Montaigne recounts how he always in fact guarded against all (Christian) repentance, while at the same time giving himself up to the Essay, the only form of writing faithful to the truth, the desirable unseizable. '*If my mind could gain a firm footing, I would not make essays, I would make decisions*,' but it is always 'in apprenticeship and on trial.' Our soul never has its footing on this earth. Graze the paper with the soul's foot, and immediately the foot slips. It's always this same story of the foot and the ground, one and the other in motion, the one missing the other. How then to draw a firm footing, when our soul is merely a staggering? Our drawings, our books and us, we all go along at the same pace, with an uncertain foot. This is why it is the legs above all which, in our drawings, are the most agitated.

To come back to what escapes: we want to draw the instant. That instant which strikes between two instants, that instant which flies into bits under its own blow, which has neither length, nor duration, only its own shattering brilliance, the shock of the passage from night to light. Here, the instant is the height which this executioner's arm takes (a single double arm), grand high gesture, extremely fine and rapid line of extreme actuality. The instant is a drama without a stage.

I wanted to call this text: 'For the Instant,' or 'At the Instant,' but I changed my mind.

The instant, see how it's just fallen, between St John: the body is still living, but already the head is dead. It's this instant: the cut-off between life and death.

This is what we draw, tripping, because, instead of throbbing, we trace. We want to throw ourselves ahead and we go backwards. Do you see these footprints? We are advancing backwards.

How to draw speed?

Thinking about 'repentance' is extremely tiring. It's as though I were trying to think about the skin of thought with the skin of thought. One must think faster than oneself.

Observing it from very very close up very very fast, thought doesn't go straight ahead, as we think, but in a frenetic movement, invisible to the naked-eye-of-thought, it goes straight ahead of itself like lightning and almost simultaneously returns backwards on its own streak to step on it and erase it and almost simultaneously shoots forward like a rocket – if only I could draw *one* thought! – if I could photograph it – then we would see that thought is not a sentence at all, but, after several explosions, a fallout in words,

or else take the photograph of a dream!

I want to draw the present, say da Vinci? Picasso, Rembrandt, the fools for truth. How to make the portrait of lightning? At what speed draw speed? We have all cried out stop! to the instant. We who are the immoderate, through our slowness rapidity passes, through our narrow head the lightning of a thought passes.

The truth is approaching.

Arrives the Vision that neither we, nor even the saint, can predict. Be careful! It's coming . . .! Salvation! What agony! We fall like a dead body.

We don't have salvation: it is dealt us like a blow, we faint. We awake with a start, quick a pencil, and take down the ultimate glimmer of illumination, however much we say: 'what's the difference, we've seen our vision already,' we never resign ourselves.

At a gallop, the snail! We scribble while crawling in the wake of God.

We live more quickly than ourselves, the pen doesn't follow. To paint the present which is passing us by, we stop the present.

One cannot after all write a book with only one stroke, of only one page, and yet we should.

But we are born for lateness.

Time, the body, are our slow vehicles, our chariots without wheels.

Look, I've just this instant 'seen' a book – now I'm going to need two years and two hundred pages in order to recount it with my hands, with my staggering feet, and my breath harnessed to my chest, and from forward to backward and inversely.

This is why we desire so often to die, when we write, in order to see everything in a flash, and at least once shatter the spine of time with only one pencil stroke. And with only one word draw God . . .

N.B. There is not one single sentence in this text which I didn't write twenty times – As soon as I said the word 'Repentance,' it jumped on to my page, it spread everywhere, however much I denied it. One says this word and that's it.

N.B. N.B. Because after all that which they call Repentance is no one other than the demon of writing.

N.B. And now, what to call this essay?

– 'Without End' – No. – 'The Executioner's Taking Off' – No. Rather: Oh no, enough already, it's time! No more repenting! Not another word!

Ringing in the
feminine hour

3　In October 1991 . . .

Translated by Keith Cohen

In October 1991 . . . When I chose the title for this lecture, it was 1990. That meant that the future lecture was without title. That I didn't know what would be essential. It meant: I don't know what will be the shape of the world, or of me, in October 1991, or if I'll still have a shape. It meant: blindness, non-clairvoyance, unpredictability. And then, too: *will I be* in October '91? Who knows? I like being in the present; am interested in what's in process: of passing by, of happening. The instant – the eternity of the instant.

I come not to you this evening with *tomorrows* [*demains*]; with two hands [*deux mains*], of course, but with *nows*.

I like being in the present. You're going to say: then keep running! That's exactly what I try to do. And besides I have a particular affection for the present because it's the time of the theatre. That's something I discovered working in the theatre: the singularity of this genre that invents, invents for us, incessantly, a time without time.

The present is also always a just-after. But for us, October – for us in the past – was back-to-school, the tenth month which was the first month, the beginning and the end of an epoch. It was the first day, a threat, and a maturation.

So, in October '91 and just after, what was there, what's left? What makes this October and what gets away? What has passed away?

To give a fast answer, with a scene that remains for me that of writing: one of my lives, for example, is also: the USSR. It appeared, through the different readings that have been offered of what I've managed to write – of what *Cixous*, as they say, has managed to write – that I am – that is, *she* is – often, perhaps mainly, concerned with the loss of her paradoxes. This one, for example: I cannot save from perdition that

'En octobre 1991 . . .' was first published in *Du féminin* (Le Griffon d'argile and Presses Universitaires de Grenoble, 1992): 115–37.

which I've already lost. Obviously, I'm not going to try to save the USSR.

But on the other hand, my path through perdition has been traversed, or crossed, by the catastrophes and cataclysms of our century. And I was thinking, around October or thereabouts, of the witnesses; of the fact that we are the distant, foreign, insufficient witnesses of non-witnesses. We are the strange privileged, non-privileged witnesses of the non-witnesses. It seemed to me that we have a duty to act as reverberators by writing the history of this century's pain and sorrow. This history produces a set of signs, metaphors, one of which seemed to me fairly familiar – as it is to everyone – I know it was primordial for me, subjectively: it's the metaphor of the *wall*. In us. The wall in us, outside us. And followed by the question: what if we took away our wall? History of walls, history of annihilations: that's what we shall have had to deal with in that October '91.

I use the word *we* – it's true, I'm always having problems with pronouns. When I say the word *we* I'm aware of the double value it has. In one sense, it's violent, I admit: I say we as if I were you and you were me. But it's also a form of humility.

The disappearance of the USSR. I do not plan on giving a political presentation. I'm always back at the theatre, our theatre. Theatre about us, subjected to the winds of History. Here: outside of France. And a few of the remarks I shall make are precisely because of travel. I'm going to report on one effect, out of a thousand, of the disappearance of the USSR, such as it can be observed in France – a characteristic item of our period, inscribed across the French scene. A kind of flash effect of events on our ideology, on our discourse, on our desire: for example, in France, an effect on something that belongs to our recent memory and which is the downfall of what they called 'PC.'

At the outset there were newspaper articles which I would call ill-intentioned or written in bad faith – as always: thus, the usual – articles on 'PC' – but the American phenomenon! That is – and this won't be news to you – on the notion of 'Political Correctness.' Typically, in French public opinion, a vast confusion was created, a hodgepodge of PC [French Communist Party] and 'PC': what the PC was in any case was infamous, because it was the PC. Inscription, therefore, of a phobia in France. France manufactures and sells phobias and phobogenic products. You have to be in Paris to smell the daily odor of the hunt, this desire to kill, this desire to set up for decapitations. Odor of newspaper. But in October, it was the French PC *and* the American 'Politically Correct' that were rejected, both of them, placed on the Index!

Why am I recalling these incidents? Because it's true that when I write in fugue style, when I write on the lam, I am of course always pursued and caught by echoes of the great scene. Right now, for example, because of the intensity of contradictory struggles, it's a question of identity, of nationalisms; it's the sad phobia of non-identity that has arisen in Berlin for instance, and in general the phobia of difference. Each time I say to myself: luckily there is a voice, that voice of poetry-philosophy, to think with or, in any case, to sing with; to inscribe, to play on, to strum the contradictions and the world as tragedy.

In this regard, I shall speak of the theme of betrayal. You must have seen, as I did, those scenes cropped from the stage of history and politics and apparently already mise-en-scène for the theatre: I'm thinking in particular of the face of Gorbachev, a Shakespearean face. Suddenly, we saw a diminished, humbled Gorbachev reintroducing tragedy across the political airwaves. There is no way that I'm going to cry over Gorbachev. On the other hand, I watched with enormous interest the stripping, the despoiling, the uncrowning of the Statesman. All the more so in that Statesmen fiercely resist, I must say, being uncrowned. I have never seen any Statesman, in France during our epoch, submit, without resistance, to such a stripping or uncrowning. The last tragic 'act' that we saw was de Gaulle's back. But the unmasking, the ripping away of the persona and the projecting, the hurdling toward a denuding of the human – that's something we've never seen.

What was seen was an uncontrollable suffering, regardless of its cause or quality. And it's true that a Statesman does not show that, does not suffer. I shall speak therefore about betrayal, our betrayal; the betrayal that we always indulge in. About neglect. About the infantalizing situation produced by neglect. For as soon as we're betrayed, we are little children. I shall speak of persecution: of the subject that becomes object, a thing that falls between the cracks. About the abrupt, shattering, terrible, magnificent confession of blindness. The confession that Gorbachev made of blindness. Of having been blind. Of being blind. We saw him being blind. Blindness seen is the stuff of theatre.

What else did I think about that summer, heading toward October, on the point of turning into October? *About point of view.* About the expression 'point of view.' An expression that I wouldn't be able to make as much as I want of in a language other than French. For thanks to our language – such are the gifts we get from our languages – *'point de vue'* is the same as *point of view* in English, but also: 'point of non-view.' The place where there is no [*point*] view [*vue*]. The point of view always carries with it: no view.

The point of view: a story, for example, that I borrow from *The Imitator* by Thomas Bernhard. A story about a beautiful view, about belvedere. It involves two university professors who climb Mount Grosslockner; and Thomas Bernhard tells us that these two characters have a bond of friendship; that they have reached the point where there's a telescope; and that, inevitably, once they've gotten there, and despite all their professorial resistance to the idea of believing what they've always been told, that they would find themselves before a landscape of extraordinary beauty, each of them wonders who will be the first to grab the telescope. With that, a new circle of point of view opens: it is very complicated to figure out which one, decently and without bringing on feelings of guilt, has a right to the telescope. Thus our two academics debate, and at the end of their discussion they finally reach an agreement. It's the elder – and, Thomas Bernhard says, the wiser, the more foresightful one – who is the first to look through the telescope. And he is filled with wonder. Then it's the other one's turn, so the colleague takes the telescope, looks, lets out a loud cry and falls down dead. After which, there's only one left to wonder just what it is in the point of view to cause so significant a difference. How was it that . . .? But since there's only one left, no one will ever know. Because you need two for point of view to function.

That's why I always liked Plutarch when I was little. He's the one who taught me that when you tell a story, you always have to say: 'according to such and such version,' 'according to this version,' 'according to that version.' That's just what the newspapers don't do, naturally. Nor do we.

The most important point of view for all of us is, I believe, in this example: only Brutus can kill us. Only the person who can't kill us can kill us. Ah, but that's Caesar's point of view. Brutus's point of view is, of course, that only Caesar can kill him. That is, only the pre-killed Brutus, only Brutus seeing Caesar's knife coming at him, can kill first. The question being precisely who is going to kill first. Depending on point of view.

What did I think about that summer? About love being full of non-love. About the quantity of non-love in love. And especially about the conflation of the executioner and the victim.

(*Nota Bene.* This is a self-reproach: I want to say right off that I'm not talking about the executioner and the victim of the major scene, before which I feel humbled: not about the Holocaust. I'm sticking to the domestic scene.)

How, in private, the executioner – you or I – feels he's the victim of the victim. How the victim is the executioner of the executioner. Which makes our relations of amorous persecution very difficult. I was thinking about the fault of the victim. I was thinking about the tragic truth that the victim is guilty of being victim. About the danger incurred by being the cause of a feeling of executioner, of guilt, in you, in the other.

But pay attention: I am now taking the point of view of the victim. Later, I'll change.

We are all guilty innocents. We are guilty of being innocent. That is, guilty of innocence. Or of guilt. That is, innocent guilty ones. That's what makes so dense and difficult the mystery of . . .: there I don't know any more if I can use the word 'innocence' and the word 'guilt' separately. So, let us speak instead about the mystery of forgiveness. Forgiving is imperative. Except for one thing: it is extremely difficult to forgive. I don't even know if forgiving exists. I don't know if there is such a thing as forgiving. In general, our practice of forgiving is a revenge. To forgive . . . If I forgive, I signify that there's a fault. To forgive is to offend.

What's to be done to forgive, to be forgiven? We need forgiveness. Every day. Every day we need forgiveness. Every day we need to be forgiven and to forgive. We who are guilty of all the faults in the world. What's to be done when instead of forgiveness there is, in general, repression or avoidance? I don't know. It seems to me that we'd have to find a forgiveness beyond forgiving. A forgiveness that is neutral, absolute, unexpressed. *Advance forgiveness*. Forgiveness afterwards is already much more difficult to express. So, advance forgiveness, yes.

And accordingly, since I've been moving about these intense states, these difficult situations: what's to be done so that love – our principal activity, even if we don't believe it – *loves*? I've gotten to the point of saying to myself that only love without trust, love that can do without trust, is *love*. Love without trust is greater than love with trust. To love is to love without trust. And accordingly: the greatest proof of love is not to tell the greatest proof of love.

Often we say to ourselves: how short life will have been. What I have been saying to myself: how short death will have been. That's also a point of view. The point of view of time is always the most subjective point of view.

Now that's a text, I think, that will never manage to get written: the text that accounts for the expansion and contraction of time. Things that we know all about perfectly. The fact that suddenly one day lasts a year; or that suddenly – a frightful thing – time stops. How could that be written? I don't know. I've had the experience, but I still don't know how it could be translated.

I was thinking about the challenge that life and death lay down to writing. For writing moves at the pace of the hand. And life and death go by in a flash. We catch fire, surprised. Writing is far behind. How are the fiery moments to be grasped? How can that fire be caught in our hands? Besides, we had better catch the fire in our hands quickly. Because if we catch the fire in our hands quickly enough, we won't get burned. Fire grasped with the speed of fire: that's how it must be done. To write.

What made me laugh this summer? Ah, I had a good laugh. I have trouble laughing, especially at plays, but in this case I really had a good laugh. It was Stendhal who told me a wonderful story. From the age of thirteen to the age of fifty-three, without the slightest variation, with the greatest faithfulness, he had two passions. A passion for Shakespeare and a passion for spinach. You'll laugh, too, as I did. You laugh because it's true. Strange to say, it's what I love that makes me laugh. Gives me satisfaction, makes me rejoice. I, too, from thirteen to fifty-three have loved Shakespeare and spinach. I am not Stendhal. I have loved Shakespeare, that's true. What made me laugh in what Stendhal said: the beauty of his text, of course, and its truthfulness. 'My sole reading pleasure was Shakespeare, a passion that has lasted as long as my passion for spinach and its health benefits, and that is just as strong, at the very least, at fifty-three as at thirteen.' He says it three or four times. It seemed to me to be a marvelous definition of writing. That writing is made of Shakespeare and spinach. That Shakespeare is to writing what spinach is to good health: that the great is small, depending on your point of view. That seeing the small great and seeing the great small are true, and that's what makes us laugh. It's a transmutation of values, in true life, concretely. And provided that the great and the small blend together, as in Shakespeare, everything ordinary is endowed with a supernatural quality.

When I say that the great and the small blend together, that's where of course there is difference. There is *some* difference. In the mixing together of the great and the small: the gardeners with Richard II; the porter with Macbeth; and the exchange or collision of good with evil.

I therefore followed Stendhal joyfully into those areas of self-reproach: in the sense, precisely, of *pentimento*, of repentance in drawing and painting. Not in his novels but in his *Journals* and in his *Memories of Egotism*; in *The Life of Henry Brulard*, which seems to me to be the youngest text, the most eternally young text that I have ever encountered.

What has Stendhal brought us? Brought us definitively? The point of view – for example – of the person who does not see the battle. Not just in *The Charterhouse of Parma*. Just to savor it, here's one little gem: how Stendhal saw the Revolution in Grenoble. He's at his window; he hears a charge, rifle shots, soldiers, and he sees an old woman running in the street at top speed waving her slippers and yelling: I revort! [*je me révorte*] I revort! And I, at Stendhal's window, said to myself: who in the world could summarize the French Revolution better than Stendhal and his old woman with her slippers? I revort!

And still from the same writer – who basically had a taste for the good and evil of writing – a story about taste, the sensation of the taste of the meat of evil. Here again, something that he saw, and which he says he was very close to: after the execution of a condemned man, he saw the drops of blood running along the knife before they fell. 'And that,' he says, 'horrified me so much that for I don't know how long I couldn't eat boiled beef.'

And what made me weep? What made me weep, and think a lot, was the *Nibelungen*. I reread the *Nibelungen* and I experienced extremely powerful emotions. For me, it's one of the most powerful texts in the world because of its narrative process. It's the story of a betrayal. It's a single book, though there are several books in the *Nibelungen*. The first book is the book of joy, of conquests. It ends with marriages, and everybody is very happy. That's the moment, obviously, when everybody is about to be very unhappy. In the second book – the one that stays with us in general, that hurts us the most, that leaves a scar on our memory – we are told the story of Siegfried, treacherously assassinated. In the third book, we go through a very long period of time that allows for the development of the revenge of Kriemhild, Siegfried's wife. She lives only for that, to dry the tears of her pain by some sort of getting even. The text tells us, moreover, that Kriemhild has wept continuously for thirteen years. Perhaps at one point in my life I might have said: thirteen years of continuous weeping can't possibly happen. Now I know that one can weep continuously for thirteen years.

The *Nibelungen* is a text that weeps, and that makes one weep like no other text. It's the narrative that's to blame. The narrative that knows everything in advance, and that forewarns us incessantly. It's a text that gives us notice. We attend the marriage, and the narrative tells us, while we're attending the marriage: 'and at the end of this joyful ceremony we will be unhappy as never before.' And we attend the marriage, torn between the joy that we desire to feel and the fearful despair that has been promised and that will come to pass. We? We readers. And we do not know very well who we are. Because as a result of being forewarned, we are in a process of split identification. We die, we do not die. We know that he is going to die, that she is going to die, and we are finally powerless accomplices in this series of tragedies.

And also, in the *Nibelungen*, 'everyone departed, no one came back.' In saying that, I am citing Akhmatova. All the Russian poets departed, no one came back. It's out of the ordinary. The *Iliad*: everyone departed, a few came back. The *Nibelungen*: everyone departed, not a one came back. And they are numberless, we know them all, each one in turn is going to spill his blood, while we shed tears, and they do too. A shedding of tears like that we can't even imagine. Who would have believed that we had so many tears?

However, the tears are not alone. As we trot along – always from the point of view of mourning, that prior mourning that follows us everywhere, precedes us, envelops us – as we follow this course, saying to ourselves that we are going to weep – and we weep for them, these men who alive are already dead, these men riding along dead-alive – during this time flowers grow, the prairie is lovely, it's spring, soon blood is going to flow. I don't know if it's the flowers that make the blood beautiful or the blood that makes the flowers beautiful, but one can't be without the other. As in the *Song of Roland*. As soon as there are flowers, there's blood.

The *Nibelungen* is not the first book to have all these tears and blood flow. The oldest, the one that's the most familiar to us, is the Book of Job, whose motto – so to speak – is that all that we fear comes to pass. There is nothing more terrible. And I wonder why I read the *Nibelungen*, why I drink that blood. Why I shed those tears and why I need to go into mourning. You and I. Why do we read books that make us weep? Undoubtedly because we never have, in reality, enough to lament. We need to gamble with fire, with blood, with mourning, not because we are gamblers, but because we need to almost die. We need to mourn for ourselves. And yet to stay alive. That's what a text like the *Nibelungen* is good for. Everyone mourns, and everyone is mourned for. Everyone drinks up, and everyone is drunk up.

But it so happens also that I have a relation to texts that make me neither laugh nor weep. And yet that give me joy. There aren't many of them.

In homage, just the same, I'll say that the only text that has this effect on me – doesn't make me laugh or weep or tremble yet gives me joy – is that of Clarice Lispector. But that's a mystery. I can only tell about it quickly. She is beyond good and evil. How? Because she writes posthumously. She writes afterwards. After dying. In effect, one has at that moment a feeling of intense joy, which hurts but which remains silent. Now that's a work that is without pity and without mourning. It's the only one.

Let us leave the book and return to the bedroom, to the bed, to ourselves. And to point of view. And to our personal tragedy. Something that I've always found beautiful and terrible and untransposable: the degree to which the characters of tragedy are *laughable* – that is, to us – when they are without an audience.

As I was about to evoke my October '91, I remembered: I must say something as a *woman*. One day, when I'm two hundred and fifty years old, I won't have to do it any more. And I'll be relieved. Because it's the greatest, most fabulous, most marvelous trap of our epoch.

I'm not going to do theory here, or try to disentangle things that I've often tried to write. Let's just say that, as a woman, if I am a woman – and I believe that I can say I'm a woman only because, from time to time, I have experiences that belong to that universe – the idea comes to me that perhaps the two great intimate and strange experiences of life that have to do with childbirth (I purposely use an uninterpretable word), would be: childbirth itself and then: dischildbirth [*désenfantement*]. It just so happens that we can be dischilded. It's the experience of mourning. I believe that in mourning, no matter who the person is we've lost, our grandfather, our old mentor, our friend, we always lose the child.

And the love of women? An uneasy, disturbing subject. I will say right off: we don't know much. What experience has whispered to me is this. The degree to which we have not yet very well thought out – we have lived it but not thought it, inscribed it – the difference within women, or inside a woman. The fact, for example, that there exists a woman who is not a woman and yet who is woman. The difficulty of thinking, for example, that Clytemnestra, according to the Greek tragedies, has a virile strength; that she is described as having a virile force in the act of assassinating Agamemnon. If I take literally the unconscious of my great Tragic Greek, I am forced to wonder who, in Clytemnestra, kills Agamemnon. For Clytemnestra is going to be condemned as a woman, whereas it's as a man that she executed Agamemnon . . . Now, these are our daily experiences: vacillation, difficulty, lack of definition. Where, in fact, we might perceive, inside, on the interior, behind appearances, this sudden murky appearance of identity. But it is true that the social scene and all our investments, our speculations, forbid us from really looking.

At times, woman and mother go together. In my case, I tend to think that way. I tend to maternalize woman. To feel that a woman is all the more woman as she is mother. But the question can be asked. I prefer to speak of myself, because it's less dangerous than generalizing: if I'm mistaken, I'm mistaken only about myself.

I'm very often caught in the act of being the mother of a son. For example, when I saw Gorbachev, I felt pity for someone for whom I have no pity. And I felt that it was this bizarre person in me, 'mother of a son,' who was moved to pity. The worst – this is a ticklish confession – I have to say that I even felt pity for someone whom I hold in unspeakable horror: the judge Clarence Thomas. I think that this threatened many women as mothers-of-all-men. It must be said that this is fine, but that it's dangerous.

I am also mother of a daughter. That's an extremely complicated, but particularly pleasant and rich situation. A situation that we work perhaps the least on, because, in fact, we are always being called on to be mothers-of-sons. It's in that type of relation that can be found, in certain cases, the greatest hatred but also the greatest love. A love that could be sublime friendship.

I was heading toward October '91 when I said to myself, suddenly: but after this, there will be October '92; so there, for once, totally perishable words.

Everything passes away, as said our mentor-to-all, our grandfather, Montaigne. In writing, I have the feeling – Mireille Calle has spoken about me obviously better than I ever could – I have the feeling that I always write from the perspective of what passes away. Which is problematic, as she has shown. I perceive writing also in a differential: I am not a painter, I am not a musician. For it seems to me that painters and musicians paint, write, amidst the deluge, that which does not pass away. That their effort, even when inscribing what is passing, is to grasp that which does not pass away. I beg the pardon of painters and musicians if what I've said is foolishness. It seems to me that there is something *permanent* aimed at. For us writers, on the contrary, what's important is the process. The tempest, the rough draft. 'I'm straying.' (That's not from me, it's from Stendhal.) That's love – that is, what passes away. It's the difference that passes away, it's what escapes us.

This is why I've always had a passion for a particular kind of book: *books that get away*. Understand this by letting language resonate: books that get away, that escape on every page the fate of books. That can't be closed, that leave us behind, that can't be finished. There are some that are of an extreme violence toward us. For example, those of Thomas Bernhard, which close the door on our faces, kick us out. That say to us 'now that's enough.' These are of a slightly artificial sort.

There are innumerable texts – which for me are the most beautiful – that don't know how to end. Just as in life. Texts that don't end or that are forced to end. *The Idiot* by Dostoevsky. One puts an ending on it, one muzzles it – meanwhile the book goes on, in other directions, other ways.

We pass away. We all want to forget that we pass away. Yet – yet we are more real when we admit that all we ever do is try. The dinosaurs lived for three hundred million years and then, all of a sudden, they disappeared. We are all future dinosaurs. We live for three hundred million years, and then, all of a sudden, we entirely disappear. Entirely. That's how we pass away.

We can think that three hundred million years is soon, or not think it. It's a thought that I find very necessary, very beautiful, precisely because we do not live that knowledge. We would certainly be more often inclined to laugh, certainly more humble, if we knew that in three hundred million years, no matter what, we will have disappeared.

Who is able, who knows how, to be humble? I tend to think – but it's a thought that I form with caution – that certain women might be close to humility, to the extent that they have had the experience of 'going back to zero.' That passage that goes from zero to zero, from the infant to death.

I don't know. I have trouble talking about 'gender,' as they say. Clarice Lispector says sometimes, remembering vividly that one must never forget: what about turtles? I haven't thought about turtles for at least ten years! I don't mean to compare men to turtles, yet I have to cry: what about men? Obviously, they are unforgettable. But the problem, for us who are supposed to be women, is: how to talk about them? I shouldn't talk about them. I shouldn't talk about men. I can write, can love. But that's another affair.

I shouldn't speak about power either, that is, about assassination. I should speak neither about what I am not nor about that of which I am not a part. And at the same time I should like to speak about these things because I'm afraid of being taken for a 'feminist.' I do not say that 'women' are 'better.' Simply that they do not have 'the' *Power*. Why? (1) 'They' (men) are there so that they won't have it. (2) But when they do have *It*, so often there pops up a drifting away of their sufficiently masculine desire, a moment of distraction, of hunger for love, and The Power gets away from them . . .

A few words on the mother. I sometimes think that, 'fundamentally,' in a human being, what makes the difference, *his* or *her* difference, is the mother. Who the mother was, how she left her mark. At times I tell myself that we ought to set down the invisible meridian not between men and women, but between vengeance and patience, between the insatiable and the nourisher.

I am inclined to use 'mother' as a metaphor, yet at the same time it is not a metaphor. This is the secret and decisive figure that one feels living and writing in those who write. One might say, for example, that men and women who had a good mother are not big steak-eaters, are not big eaters. Those who have the mother in them meet the other with circumspection. Or else with circumfession [*circonfession*]. The mother is a quality.

Careful: I've just said something that is entirely debatable. I'm acting as though the mother were good. I believe that, absolutely: a good mother is a good thing. But that's my point of view. And the question of point of view comes implacably into play in querying this kind of utterance. A good mother can be seen with an evil eye. She can be very bad for being good. Et cetera.

I'm going to recount a memory from October. A mother's memory. My first memory of my first October is of having cried, cried, cried for my mother when I went to school. At that time, it was during the war – the way they refer to back then, 'during-the-war'; and there was no school. So, the school in my hometown was a little room in an apartment where one lady was the schoolteacher for heaps of Jewish children of every age. So that when I managed to get to school – which happened very rarely – I was in a very pretty little 'class' because there was a first row, a second row, and so on down the room, from the first row where there were those who were already learning conjugations, to the back of the room where there were those who were learning to write in cursive. That was me. But I rarely came to school. And at the same time I learned everything because while I was doing my strokes and curlecues, I would hear: 'qualifying adjective.'

Upon arriving in front of this sort of school, I cried. I couldn't stop crying. The whole world was nothing but my tears. The first day I have no other memory except that: having cried infinitely and having been entirely transformed into this flood of tears. The second day, upon arriving, there we go, it starts all over again! . . .

So I got into the habit of saying, just before going in: 'Ma'am, I'm going to cry.' And she would say to me: 'OK! So cry. You'll come in when you've finished crying.' Sometimes in the end I went in. And I would hear 'qualifying adjective,' and I was in heaven. I finished crying and I would go in. Other times, I wouldn't finish crying. I cried for my mother. At times I could get over my mother, at times not. And it didn't depend on me. It was beyond all control. It was an all-powerful force that was unleashed like a magic ray as soon as I got to school.

That's the way I spent my whole first year of school. I believed that it was a fate, a dart that had come from outside, a sort of arrow that had gotten me. That it wasn't me who cried, that it was the unhappiness that cried in me. The second year: no tears. I concluded that my sorrow had doubtless a regular rhythm, and that I would cry every other year. Therefore, I told myself, next year I shall cry.

The next October came, I expected tears. And nothing. I wonder sometimes if that magic isn't still at work in me.

Regarding my mother, who just turned eighty-one yesterday – I can't talk about her, but I can say one thing: I have always called her my mother, and once when I saw her: she was a young girl. I was already thirty. And it's through writing that I figured out all at once that my father was a bird and my mother a young girl. I said to myself: thus, all my life I've failed to understand to what extent I was overdetermined by the fact that my mother was a young girl, even younger than I. And a few dozen years later, I said to myself: I've been mistaken my whole life. My mother has always been a young boy. I could talk to you about her, but in a certain manner I'm terrified because she is so young. As for writing about my mother, I've done it with extreme succinctness. What I've done, in fact, amounts to nothing. It seems to me that we can't write about our mother. I'm sure about it. It's one of the limits of writing.

Thus, my first memory brings together the imagined death of my mother and school. And since then, I have never ceased crying, going to school, learning, crying, exchanging. Pouring out and taking in. Never ceased forgetting, getting over the loss of my mother's body. Or on the contrary: not getting over it. Inventing it. Picturing to myself the horror of that loss. All the while asking myself who's crying.

Curiously, I know that it's not my mother whom I lost; it's my father who died and whom I didn't weep for, my father whom I loved. I obviously mourned him, in other ways, but I shed no tears. There is a frightful happiness in tears, in certain tears, which is connected to the theatre, to representation, to the fact that there are witnesses. One weeps in front of witnesses, in company. In a certain way, one is happy. One doesn't realize it because of the suffering. But it brings happiness just the same. Unhappiness is having no one to weep with. No one to remember with, no one to tell. But I'm digressing.

How did I 'write' this? I took notes. I thought: I'm going to draw the portrait of October as it comes and goes. It was on a notepad, on perforated sheets. This isn't a journal woven with daily threads. October appeared in puffs of air, in fragments, in sorrows, and I think that's the way one writes: discontinuously. Then, in a way, one cheats: one reassembles, pastes together, puts it all in order. The order doesn't come solely from outside, of course. What is order? It's a form hidden in disorder.

In truth, I wrote this, or noted this down, while sitting in my bed, at the end of summer, around October; at the school of mourning I wrote this, in my bed. Which never happens to me. Except in the case of dreams. That is, I write in the dream and I write down my dreams while asleep. But writing during the day – never. And in this case, yes. It was just before October. It was already October. And I took notes very quickly as summer was coming to an end, life, death, coming to an end.

There is this question of the speed with which things happen around the edges of your heart – and that's my concern. To escape a predator, a lion, the deer runs faster than itself. It runs with a force greater than it has. That's a zoological fact: it produces surplus energy. It goes beyond its forces to survive. And it survives the predator, but it doesn't survive the effort. The lion has been left behind, but the deer dies. It survives, and dies from it.

I believe that in order to escape death, we go through death. Obviously, this is untenable. I was in the process of writing in my bed, worn out from an errand. And what came to me, what remained with me, was a speed, a lightness that I haven't been able to hold on to.

In October '91, where am I going? Who's moving, who's speaking, who's about to go, about to speak to you, who's passing away? Who's still living and who answers in my name? I do not know. If there weren't my name, my notorious, unpronounceable name, to which I've finally resigned myself – if there weren't my name to go ahead of me and to replace me, and to be me in my absence, and to fill my gaps – and if there weren't a you/roof [*toi(t)*] when I'm not there, and if there weren't my shadow, it would be quite a catastrophe. It is possible – I fear – that there are such times as these: meanwhile, in place of me, an interval, it so happens . . .

I would have liked to inscribe a state, probably impossible to write down – a state, an instance of discontinuity, break in continuity, interruption – to get through it you have to beat your heart. Invent something to get by death.

I am not confiding secrets. Nor even less making confessions. But, in a certain manner, I am giving my address, where I can be reached, where my boat and my plane are, latitude and longitude. I am drawing my attention, your attention, to our fundamental duplicity – simple, naïve – we who act and think and move forward relying on continuity. Positing continuity. As though we were: (1) all immortal; (2) all dead. When I think of the university programs that we set up! We are asked to promise, one year, two years in advance, to be present, that is, alive, at such and such a place. And we do it. What's more: we are asked, we even ask ourselves, to say right now what we will think in two years. We expect ourselves to be prophets or to be dead; to think already, to be at once past and future. It's a crazed vision of human time. But we do it. We all feign immortality.

Sometimes, when I go off to write, friends ask '*about what?*' What is the subject? I never know, of course. It is known, nevertheless, I know that it is known. I mean: *id knows*. Otherwise, I wouldn't go off to write. It's a mystery: where it is that id takes, where id grows, where id gathers like rainwater. Luckily. I count on it. *Id must know.* Not me.

You see, I'm a woman of the period of time – and time, too, is in the process of passing – in which we didn't know if, when pregnant, we were going to have a girl or a boy – not till the last minute. I want the last minute. I don't want to know before the last minute. Even if *id* knows. The problem: when is the last minute? The last minute is in the other world. It's afterwards.

Stendhal goes off into the other world, he tells us: 'As for me, when I go to the other world, I'll go, if possible, to see Montesquieu. And I'll say to him: so, what do you think? Did I write well or not? He shrugs. Well, if he does that to me . . .' That's the scene between Stendhal and Montesquieu. It's beautiful; it's courageous.

It's no accident that I feel close to those who have written on the edge, in transit, just after or just before. Especially written very quickly. And dying. What about me, am I going to die? Why not, I think. Because if it's not me, it's my other; if it's not my other, it's me. One of us is going to die. I could say that that's fine, yet at the same time I lament it. I live it nostalgically.

If it's not me, it's you, who are me, I say to myself. How you're going to miss me! I mean: how I'm going to miss you. That is: how you miss me. That is: how we miss each other. I'm declining mourning and nostalgia.

And now, after so many considerations, I'm going to be born. That's not a sentence by Hélène Cixous, it's a sentence by Stendhal. Quick, let's live, let's think about it.

When I've finished something – when I stop, or when it stops – I wonder: what have I forgotten? Naturally, I've always forgotten something. (It's true, the end is like that: a labor of memory and forgetting.) This at least: pay attention when reading texts. Aside from those very rare ones, such as *The Life of Henry Brulard* – and even in that case I wouldn't swear to it – in which the main characters of the texts, all those who are visible, are not the main characters of a life.

4 Hiss of the axe

Translated by Keith Cohen

Love begins with *a bench*. I recognize it: that's the one where Pushkin throws over Tatiana. The one before which Marina, a hundred years later, stops, struck by waiting. Under the influence of that story.

But in truth the story began with running through the garden. The approach of a horse can be heard. It all comes from extremely far away. The one who fled before coming is Onegin. Someone that author (Pushkin) doesn't like very much, knowing how he is. Tatiana flees into the garden, she runs, she flies, not daring to turn around, not daring to see that he's not following her, him whom she awaits she is fleeing from, the arbor, the footbridge, the meadow, the pathway, the little wood, breaking the lilac branches, the stream, the flowers, and out of breath she collapses onto the bench. One can flee no farther. Here hope is brought to a stop. Fear. The bench, the stream. On the other side sorrow begins.

What I love: the running, what Marina loves: the bench. Each of us reads in our own book. The author: hesitates. In Marina's book: a bench.

A bench. On the bench Tatiana. Enter Onegin. He doesn't sit down. It's all over already. She's the one who stands up. To make amends? They both remain standing. Standing: Separation? Both. But he's the only one who speaks. He speaks for a long time. All the time. She doesn't say a word. Between them speaking doesn't yield a word.

Time has entered into it, the long time, estrangement: with huge shovelfuls it digs away between the two of them deeper and deeper: 'I was not made for happiness, to my soul it is unknown. Marriage would kill us. Loving you up close would very quickly become a routine for me, and love would cease. If I were to love, it would be from afar, once in awhile, separately.'

Marina reads. That's love, says the story, a bench, and between *her* on

'Respiration de la hache' was first published in *Contretemps* 1 (1995): 104–111.

the bench and *him* who enters: *he* and *she* in the halo of the isolating italics.

. . . But before the bench, the running. And before the running, the letter. Tatiana's letter. She writes for a long time: 'This has been decreed from on high: it's heaven's will. I am *yours* . . .' She says '*tu*' to *him*, she says '*tu*' to the one who will come, who is going to come, who comes, to the stranger who is *him*, yes it is *him*, and there she is hearing him come from the end of time, she strings her bow and says: '*Tu*.' '*Tu*,' the violent 'Tu,' with which I address God, because I do not know Him, because there can be no distance between us, the 'Tu' by means of which I order Him into existence, and *He* is *him*.

She says to *him*: '*Tu!*' And in her first letter to *him*, Marina says 'Tu' to Rilke, '*Du*'; she writes her first letter to him, and she suddenly says '*Du*' to him, in German, in *his* language, which to her is a foreign language, the language with which she comes toward him, foreign-like, flying, getting into view: Rainer Maria Rilke! She calls him and rejects him (she loves him).

'Why did I not come to you? Because you are what is dearest in the world to me. As simple as that.'

Tatiana's letter is always in front of us: 'I am yours. It's heaven's will.' It's one letter too many. Her coming: too much, from too high, from too far away, and departed too soon, much too soon.

That's Love, says the Story, it involves the letter that's gone out too soon. It involves the timing of the letter. The time it goes out, the time it gets there. The arrow flies out of one life, and aims at another. It involves the juxtaposition of two stories, it involves the two of us, one seated, the other standing, between us God knows how many time zones. The letter goes out, it can't help but go out. This is decreed from on high. It's the will of heaven. Which isn't familiar with our time-frames. *She* is not the one who wrote it. The inspiration is that stranger. It came from *him*, it struck her, in the breast. 'The soul was awaiting . . . someone. The waiting came to an end, her eyes opened, she said: it is he. Ah, now the days the nights and the scorching solitude of sleep – he will fill all of it . . .'

It is the Author of the letter who writes this story, our story. The Letter goes everywhere, too fast, too soon, too late, the stranger who says 'Tu' to us and hurts our feelings. That's love: the letter that never gets there at our time, that gets there at some foreign hour. It's a question of the time change.

It (the letter) races, it flies, it flees, it wants, it passes, the meadow, the mountain, the river, it searches every country for the person who will know how to translate it without robbing it of its life.

One day she finds Pushkin, the child of the Abyssinian, the white man of black blood, the joyful poet born for the pain of absence in presence, born for difficulty, and the grace of difficulty, to dance into exile and to sing the marvelous liberty of that which doesn't have a right time. In his life, nothing comes at the right time. And each day of his springtimes he plays all the instruments.

One day she finds Shakespeare the Egyptian, the queen's fool. Oh him – with one mishap he loses and wins three continents.

It starts with a ship. Cleopatra is lying down inside it. But already it is not she, she is already more than queen, more than life, she throws every description out of whack.

Behind him, Fulvia, Rome, a crown, an alliance, and yet another, a world, and before him coming down the river a fate befitting Antony. He calls but his voice gives out, it fades away, leaving a hole in nature. Antony falls. He's no longer Antony. He is in her, he is hers. And she goes down into him, all the way to the bed he was born in. So it's over?

Then it starts up. The unlivable, which endures. Love threatens them with perfection. Side by side, they might be able to forget death and die.

'I take leave of you, Madam.'

'A word . . . We are separating, then, you and I. No, that's not it. Lord, we love each other, you and I . . . No, that's not it either. You know all this, as I do . . .'

'Let us go away. Our separation will bring about a strange thing: though remaining here, you will be going with me, and I who am leaving, will nevertheless remain by your side.'

What? Between love and separation, no separation? Between absence and presence, no difference?

And is that love? What does it matter, love, a word.

It's necessary to feel, necessary to enjoy, necessary to be struck.

So let us separate. Let us separate beyond separation. Or else, let us love beyond loving. Go further.

But the letter has gone out. It is thrust between them. War breaks out between passion and love. In order to draw slumbering gentleness out to the point of fierceness. Living is not enough, it is necessary to set fire, climb the flames. Desire is their synonym. They shall sleep no more.

And all that is decreed from on high. We are playthings, we know, we run in the direction that is contrary to our heart, because the force is beyond our control. We obey the Foreign Woman – and we don't even know her name – her who stands ready to separate us.

We make strange, mixed-up declarations to each other. Joy is such pain. She calls it: 'my pain,' and it's the most beautiful name. And that pain, ah, that pain we shall never give it up. Go, go away! She cries, I want to lament over you. I want you to give me my tears.

He really does go away. She really laments. Twenty times a day she believes she's going to die. The pain is real.

By force they reject each other, deny each other. The force that guides them from farthest point to farthest point away from each other, like the blind gone mad, goes all the way around the world. And from one instant to another reunites them. They embrace. At that moment the letter falls. Peace, faith are snatched away from them, spared them.

To what extreme must they go to love each other beyond loving? Oceans won't suffice to separate them, she hears his horse carrying away the loved one, across the Italian plain, down to the clopping of its hoofs in the sand, she can still hear it, it's not enough to keep them apart, more than a world would be needed to appease such a great urge to fling themselves at each other, on horseback, hopping, or in a dream.

From what echoing distances does Antony ceaselessly draw near her, going so far as to marry Octavia, the deep, gentle, heart-breaking Octavia, going so far as to love Octavia, going so far as to walk by the light of his words.

From the farthest, most ancient, most god-forsaken, most Roman of lands, he goes to her, the Stranger, her who is lacking – giving in to her sincerely, a little more a little less sincerely than we think, going so far as to have a child with Octavia, so far as to accept from Octavia the unexpected daughter.

The most remote, the most separated, the most held back, the most tied down, married, sworn, pledged, he goes to her, toward Egypt where he is forbidden to go, more and more forbidden, toward which he goes, in spite of everything, in spite of himself.

If we could see. If we could read the Letter. If, seated on high, amidst the authors of our destinies, we could read the book of our life. Which is written. Already written, finished. But we shall never know our story. We are only characters in it. And to think that there will be readers of our book. They will open it. And they'll make fun of the murkiness of our night. Says the author –

We, for so many years, see them, trying to find themselves, get lost, a hundred times on the point of finding themselves, seeing themselves, looking at themselves, recognizing themselves; finally tearing away the lovely, thin veil that blurs their vision, the guardian of truth, and thus living for years, on the edge, quivering with desire, that is, fear, that is, desire.

By means of what infinite trickery does the Queen ceaselessly draw near him, disguising refusal as need, disguising pride as humility, disguising jealousy as adoration, revolt as submission, distance as closeness, triumphant self-assurance as timorous hope, never daring to believe, to take, to keep.

We see them for years missing one another. In proportion to their strength, their armies, their fleets. Near-misses mingled with betrothals.

It's the ship that goes too fast. She was already going down the river when it reached the bank. She is always a little more than there, one oarstroke away from him, one page away, an arm's length, a meter. Carried away by fatal anticipation. Will you follow me? She beseeches. And she would give up her life to follow him. But it is not granted to him to follow. It is not written in the book. Will she try to follow him, on sea, into the decisive battle – there she is in flight . . . Or is it rather him? But it matters not which one leads and which one is led toward the Egyptian tomb, their cradle.

They still have a long death to die, a whole hour punctuated with errors to be drawn toward one another, the music is that of the last mishaps, anger a low-pitched cello, the viola fades – one hears in its place a clarinet trio – then comes back in; by the end of this hour will they find the identical moment, will they draw their last breaths for the first time together, when there is nothing left any more in the world to distract them, no kingdoms, no men, no wives, no letter, no news, no honor, no desire, not even they themselves, will they see at the last second the smile of truth?

Up till the end of the book we keep hoping. We cannot believe that they will say farewell before the curtain falls. We think that, with a furious hand, somehow or other, in a final outburst, she will tear away the night, or he will. Daylight will come in time. At the last minute. It's with this hope that we can bear to read. Perhaps to live. We're not going to die bereft, so close. Without having seen, heard, said.

'Will you have loved me?' she asks, as she dies, at the last minute, and she keeps asking herself. Because in the end we die without ever knowing. Was that – the running, the two slightly staggered voyages, the trembling encounters, the contrary gazes, one life going Westward another going Eastward – was that love?

That was the story. We who read the book know – we've actually always known – that nothing could keep them apart, nothing will have kept them apart. The tiny heart that beats from beat to beat. It's the letter that gets there too late. Just the letter, just words. When Onegin finally receives it, ten years have gone by, Tatiana is on the other side. She loves him, but there's no more time.

It always involves a story: the names can be changed, as well as the address. Enter the Duchesse de Langeais. And an instant too early

Armand de Montriveau. Or else an instant too late. The flight begins, and we don't know who is pursuing whom, in which direction, east, west, or whether we're going toward Africa, our heroic mother, or rather away from Africa, whether toward the flesh of Egypt, the eternal meat, or towards the Catholic fasting, towards prohibition, towards starvation accompanied by the music of angels. The sea comes into play. It ebbs, it flows, we miss the tide. And death snatches the bread from our mouth. What am I saying? No. We're the ones who refused the bread, the spices, the food.

And the letter? Yes, there's always a letter. She had dashed off a letter to him. Alas, it's the one that never gets there: for in that letter there is time. There is the hour. The limit. She gave him a time. Believing naturally that she was giving him everything. But we can't get there on time. That doesn't exist. You who love us must give us everything. Not even time: everything, nothing, yes. The mother's waiting, she who gave us everything, all the departures. Who gave us what we wanted to have: absence, presence, return, more, never, I don't know. This is the only way, in the infinite space that watches us impatiently and lets us give it up, that we shall return.

But she, a childless woman, a woman starved for a vociferous African mother, she gave him the time. At times one commits suicide when one wants so much to live.

And the title that Balzac did not give to his narrative is: *Do not touch the axe*. Because in the end he no longer knew who the axe was. We begin by telling a story to deliver a blow, but in the end, while we've been writing, the axe has turned. It's not our fault, or hers, or his. There's the axe. The hour. She was too young. He was too young. The story begins before us.

We are always too young when it begins. Our eyes are still glazed, deep blue. Imperious babies at the breast, we claim until we're forty, then fifty, then longer still, that love should come at the right time. That's our hope, our innocence and our source of torment – we the claimants.

The time change is from birth, it's the human discrepancy, we don't want to know it. Fortunately for us who are mortal, we don't know it. Otherwise, we would never love.

A story that we despise and love to read. Could it be that we love to read the stories that we despise?

To what extent we need death – that's something that can't be spoken of. How we call on it with our terrified prayers, how we beseech it not to come, with what horror we adore it – no, that can't be spoken of. We aren't happy unless it's lying across our path. And how to speak of the fierceness that we call love. And the number of times we fling ourselves upon the adversary we love, we fight and are defeated together. We live backwards, it's a tendency that can't be spoken of.

It's secret. It's so secret that it can't even be spoken of in French.

This story, I exclaimed, I have heard enough. It's a mistake, a lovely nastiness. Each time the letter fails to get there, Tristan turns around to the wall and I weep. I don't want that. The hour – the wall – the axe. Yes, we like to weep. Or rather, we like to be able to weep. But only in books. Not in real life. The books that tell this story had better not become in the end the authors of our life. In reality we do not like death, we like only its shadow, its footstep in the garden, the hiss of the axe above our bed.

We like to play at dying: there's our unknown crime. The one that can't be spoken of.

What's unfortunate is that authors need to commit this crime: I'm now beginning to draw near truth. Careful, because when it bursts forth, it will vanish on the spot.

I proceed: Shakespeare cannot help but write of love in light of the axe; cannot help but write the letter that comes *too* early, too late, and never at the right time, because: he writes with writing. He writes, and writing eludes him, it flees from him, he pursues it, the delay spreads throughout everything like poison, writing is itself the spirit of the mishap. While Cleopatra and Antony are in an embrace, plunged in the now of the flesh, a single mouth, their two souls mingled, there's not much to say. It (writing) just waits for their separation: that's its domain.

I accuse writing of being the author——of

——I've lost truth, as I feared. And so I had found it.

It's getting dark under my land. I'm a bit lost. What I wanted to say, I've perhaps said. If only I could go back over my pages and reread myself. But in such darkness I can only write, keep on going forward, till the end. I am now in the dark part of truth.

5 What is it o'clock? or The door (we never enter)

Translated by Catherine A.F. MacGillivray

The first time I saw Jacques Derrida (it must have been in 1962) he was walking fast and sure along a mountain's crest, from left to right, I was at Arcachon, I was reading (it must have been *Force et signification*), from where I was I could see him clearly advancing black on the clear sky, feet on a tightrope, the crest was terribly sharp, he was walking along the peak, from far away I saw it, his hike along the line between mountain and sky which were melting into each other, he had to travel a path no wider than a pencil stroke.

He wasn't running, fast, he was *making* his way, *all* the way along the crests. Going from left to right, according to the (incarnate) pace of writing. Landscape without any border other than, at each instant, displacing him from his pace. Before him, nothing but the great standing air. I had never seen someone from our century write like this, on the world's cutting edge, the air had the air of a transparent door, so entirely open one had to search for the stiles – later I would call this tableau:

– Circumcision of the world –
'*Alone*, very alone on a line – a line of poetry,' as it says on page 107 of *Schibboleth*,[1]

Drawing the inner margin of the universe, thus the universe, nobody in person, the ultimate surveyor of ultimity.

'To see oneself always placed *at the head*, if one may say so,' this is how we recognize him, placed at the head, on the crest, at the peak. Alone without solitude not yet followed or pursued, alone (I tell myself) like a Jew amongst Jews, and amongst Jews and non-Jews, alone like a 'J'[2] trying to slip his crazy *signifiance* out of the game of fatal definitions,

'Quelle heure est-il ou La porte (celle qu'on ne passe pas)' was first published, in a slightly different version, in *Le passage des frontières* (Galilée, 1994): 83–98.

spinning his path beyond the points (of departure), and, for this, attempting to be de-born, without denying the being born that aims beyond the border, the bound.

Alone, not less alone than a poem

not less strong on air than a ship that travels the sea, which opens and closes, without slicing it.

What was separated by his step was the on high and the most high (the up above).

First vision, which acted then, for me, without my knowledge, like the revelation of a door. There is a door. In the world, there are doors.

Happily there isn't only the world. Beyond the world is the Other side. One can pass over, it's open or it opens. Happily one can go there. Where? There.

(How? We need a door.)

Who invented doors? I dedicate what follows to the inventors of doors, and of nexts, to the angels, to the peoples of Apocalypses, to the secret angels, to secrets –

> Next I had a vision. Behold, a door had opened in the sky, and the first voice that had spoken to me, like a trumpet, said to me: come up here, that I may show you what must come next.
>
> (4:1)

said the angel of the *Apocalypse*, apostrophizing to his John like his voice apostrophizes to J.D. in *Circonfession*.[3]

No revelation without a door. But which door? A non-door, a door that stands aside so as to let pass: (The door is not a shibboleth). A smile perhaps, or the sensation of a smile. A door so as to better open. Smile.

'The door opens' – one never knows who opens it, from which side he or she enters or leaves.

The door opens.

Enter   –   the Hour.

The Hour is my story's main character.

'The door opens,' says the language that doesn't say 'someone opens the door.' Is it mother, is it cat, is it wolf, is it you?

The door opens, says the poem – that knows that all doors are magic spirits, and all poems are doors, and, in the same way Time opens and closes, according to its strange magic, Time, which is the very matter of our soul, our very substance, strange and dreaded.

What time is it? That is the question.[4]

In the wee hours, when I'm no longer sleeping but still dreaming and I'm in the midst of waking, it comes, the question, to spur me on, and in the same way in the middle of the day, it comes to rouse me. What time is it, do you know what time it is? As soon as I wonder what time it is, I'm lost.

What time is it, I mean to say where am I, I mean to say where have I gone – I don't know anymore, in this instant when I call out to myself, where I'm passing or where I'm going.

When do we wonder this? So often. We grope our way along in time, worried, distracted. And blindly we forefeel.

What time is it? is the best-known fateful question, the one we repeat ten times an hour with automaton lips, and time doesn't pass, the one we listen to with the tips of our ears, the gravest question in its familiar appearances, the question that admits our anxiety without our knowledge, the most wily, the least recognizable, the one that announces. Something is going to happen. And we don't know if it isn't already, the thing, the hour, already on the way to happening, already there, a little to the left, we find ourselves on a terrestrial platform, held back, there to the left in the sky, this isn't the moon, it's the all-white face of a handless clock, and we too we have an all-white, uncertain face.

I've always loved *Julius Caesar*, the one from the Shakespeare play, this play bathed in the light of a handless clock.

First I loved the love, by which Julius Caesar and Brutus were mortally bound. Two beings who loved each other equally, as much as mother, as much as child, elected son chosen father, two beings bound by the same possibility of giving each other death, each one life for the other, therefore mortality.

Caesar can fear blows from no one, if not from Brutus. This is why Caesar is fearless. This is why Caesar is mortal. Brutus can fear betrayal from no one, if not from Caesar, the one he loves so much. This is why he doesn't fear Caesar, this is why he fears him: if there is betrayal, it can only come from the one who can't betray. Caesar alone is to be feared, if there were something to fear. If the hour to fear were to arrive.

It was then, while I was loving them, Caesar and Brutus, that I discovered, trembling: so there is a time to fear. It was the story of a dangerous hour. If the hour doesn't come this year, Caesar and Brutus will live to the age of ninety-two.

O this sentence disguised as cliché, 'what time is it?' – see how it sounds ceaselessly as soon as the play begins, each goes around asking the other what time it is (What is it o'clock?[5]) As though one knew! What are they all up to, even the smallest roles, the walk-ons, looking at their watches all the time? How does Shakespeare tell what time is it? In a hundred ways: What is it o'clock.[6]

Brutus: What, Lucius, ho!
    I cannot by the progress of the stars
    Give guess how near to day. Lucius, I say!
    I would it were my fault to sleep so soundly.
    When, Lucius, when? Awake, I say! What, Lucius!

. . .

Brutus: Get you to bed again, it is not day.
    Is not to-morrow, boy, the Ides of March?
Lucius: I know not, sir.
Brutus: Look in the calendar, and bring me word.
Lucius: I will, sir.

. . .

Lucius: Sir, March is wasted fifteen days.
                (Knock within.)
Brutus: 'Tis good. Go to the gate; somebody knocks.

. . .

Decius: Here lies the east: doth not the day break here?
Casca: No.
Cinna: O, pardon, sir, it doth; and yon gray lines
    That fret the clouds are messengers of day.
Casca: You shall confess that you are both deceived.
    Here, as I point my sword, the sun arises;
    Which is a great way growing on the south,
    Weighing the youthful season of the year.
    Some two months hence, up higher toward the north
    He first presents his fire; and then the high east
    Stands, as the Capitol, directly here.

. . .

                (Clock strikes.)
Brutus: Peace! count the clock.
Cassius: The clock hath stricken three.
Trebonius: 'Tis time to part.

. . .

Cassius: Nay, we will all of us be there to fetch him.
Brutus: By the eighth hour: is that the uttermost?
Cinna: Be that the uttermost, and fail not then.
                            (II, 1)

Publius: Good morrow, Caesar.
Caesar: Welcome Publius.
    What Brutus, are you stirr'd so early too?
    Good morrow, Casca. Caius Ligarius,

Caesar was ne'er so much your enemy
As that same ague which hath made you lean.
What is't o'clock.
Brutus: Caesar, 'tis stricken eight.
Caesar: I thank you for your pains and courtesy.

(II, 2)

Enter the SOOTHSAYER
Portia: Come hither, fellow: which way have you been?
Soothsayer: At mine own house, good lady.
Portia: What is't o'clock?
Soothsayer: About the ninth hour, lady.
Portia: Is Caesar yet gone to the Capitol?

(2.4)

Caesar: The Ides of March are come.
Soothsayer: Ay, Caesar, but not gone.
Artemidorus: Hail, Caesar! read this schedule[7]

(3.1)

The sulfurous odor of imminence goes to our heads.

It smells like time, as is always the case in a love story. As soon as we enter a 'love story,' what is imperceptible, colorless and odorless in ordinary life becomes extraordinarily insistent. The time-of-life substance begins to beat endlessly, reminding us of the High Fear of Love. Time is the Other's odor. The clock rises. The door opens, enter the outdoors. We fall outside ourselves. The clock strikes. Fire. We fall. In love. Headfirst. Arms open, torso open. The stranger enters our body, nervous, opens the avid mouths in the heart, in the belly, the mouths fill up with famine, it burns it bites in the breast, painful signs, nameless, very powerful phenomena,

finally all this inconvenient, invincible pain, this aggression, this displeasure that twists its great vital nerve, this martyrdom without malady, this voracity for meat, with hesitation we call it love. The odor of fire, the taste of blood, life enriched by wounds, enhanced by murders – love.

The day breaks[8]: the day breaks, with the night, with the day.

The hour is unknown. The hour that I don't recognize when I don't recognize myself – this hour troubles me. The hour is near. We don't know if it is coming upon us or if we're going towards it, and with what step.

The hour is foreign. Will it resemble us? Us who? We fear it, we hope for it. This precise hour we're thinking of.

It takes its time. It can take a long time, this *arrivance*. Afterwards, nothing more will be as before.

The hour is always not-yet and imminent. Waiting for it we are in a Night. The interval is dark. In this night we prick up our ears. We roam outside ourselves, before us Brutus worries about the time – hold me, give me your hand, Lucius, give me my name – the not-yet is on the verge of tears, it resembles so much already the nevermore. And if Brutus clings to Lucius like to the last light of the known day, it is because he is not in his time, but in the other, the terrible time, the hour that is going to make of Brutus a stranger. We're afraid of this hour.

– Time, are you there? – I'm putting my socks on, time grumbles. – Another minute, and I ask again, trembling: Time, are you there? – I'm putting my shoes on.

The hour frightens me. I'm afraid it may be the last one. The hour I call upon is always the last one, the last hour of this time, or perhaps the first hour of the next world.

'The sisterless hour.' The time towards which we are turned, obscure in the obscurity, is always sisterless.

I'm afraid of it, yes, and yet I hold myself in its power, I hold myself at the ready to flee in full flight from it, I make light of it, yes, and yet it keeps me in ecstasy . . . With delight we ask the wolf if he's there, if he's done, now it's time for the trousers, now it's time for the shoes, and now, we shout, what time is it Mr Wolf? It's time to eat you!

That's what we were waiting for! Now we must flee on both feet or be devoured. It's comedy – or it's tragedy.

We wouldn't miss this hour before the mouth and the teeth for anything.

But then, when it's time, at the last minute we run away and we lose it – at least when we were little. We did nothing else but: prepare to escape. What is poignant in the case of *Julius Caesar* is that when it's time, no one runs away. We go all the way to the altar, to the butcher's, we can't help ourselves, we go all the way to where we don't want to go, it's irresistible. Pushed by desire and terror mixed.

The hour we ask of the wolf is the only one that impassions us. Because it makes of our body an earth convulsed. One must almost die in order to take pleasure in being made of flesh, we've always known this. What time is it? Time to be eaten. Passion.

Ah if we could go over to die, taste, be tasted, and then return to this side. Ah if we could go all the way to the instant when what disgusts us intoxicates us,

The dream would be to be there, at that hour, this is the poet's dream – and getting there has always been the poem's hope. And the poem or poet is the hope for this meeting with ourselves at the hour of our most intimate foreignness, at our last minute. And then? – Then.

Ah if we could go out, and, once outside, turning around, see with our own eyes the face of our own door.

Have once on ourselves the other's point of view. Taste our taste.

Ah if we could catch ourselves at it.

Travel around ourselves perhaps.

To see, our limit, to have seen, with other eyes, other eyes. Be present at the marriage of nothingness and nascentness, of our life and our death.

Sometimes, trying to circumscribe ourselves, we graze our door. This occurs in certain circumstances, usually around a birthday, for it's then that the mother returns to us, and with her comes the aid of an other regard, the only one that 'remembers' us since our first second.

Or else around a fateful event, the death of a parent or a child, the disappearance of someone close to us by blood, who awakens in us the always forgotten source (blood). Alive I die piece by piece, I die several deaths before my own death, I know it but this is what I've forgotten. For this is the mystery of my body that stretches out beyond my body, my body at the mercy of your body.

*

Give your name, your age, your address, the judge enjoins. I say my name. *My* age? How to say? We aren't an age, and it isn't us. We're never of age for the judge. That one we never manage to be. Something makes it precede us, like a mobile border. 'You know I was, I am, I just turned sixty?' a friend tells me who can't believe it at all and neither can I. We announce it to each other, we denounce it, I took, I caught, we're hit, defamed, marked, amazed. We would never have believed, and we don't believe. If it wasn't for our mother, the one we love. My mother, the dawn of the anniversary of her giving birth to me, asking me, when was it, do you remember?

fifty years ago? More. Is it possible, I can't believe it, my mother says, taking me as a witness.

Alles ist näher, als
es ist, Alles ist weniger
And it's true: seeing my mother . . .
Jahre.
Jahre. Jahre.[9] Years. That's all. Years. It doesn't add up. Only years. It *makes* time, without taking any off.

No, we are not these little scraps, tiny finished scraps of an infinite

Time. We are not the fingernail clippings of God. We are books, we are
wholes, we are ourselves the subject of our books,
  Celan is right to ask *when when*.

> *Wann,*
> *wann blühen, wann*
> *wann blühen . . . ja sie, die September-*
> *rosen?*[10]

> When do they flower, when
>   yes they, the Septembers
>   the Seven ambers
> Roses, when when

The September Roses – when – at what time will it be time, my time?
  'Our age,' 'if it counts,' is for our mother, it's our mother who is it, it's
she who keeps count. We, we are always interiorly our secret age, our
strong-age, our preferred age, we are five years old, ten years old, the age
when we were for the first time the historians or the authors of our own
lives, when we left a trace, when we were for the first time marked,
struck, imprinted, we bled and signed, memory started, when we man-
ifested ourselves as chief or queen of our own state, when we took up our
own power, or else we are twenty years old or thirty-five, and on the
point of surprising the universe.
  The other age, the one which our mother authenticates, remains forever foreign to us, and yet, bound to the mother, it is sacred to us.
  Sometimes we write a book so as to name an age, the one that comes
to us from our mother, sometimes to celebrate the natal event and the
author of the event, the mother. We keep count, humbly: *Circonfession*: 59
periods, the book due to the mother. This is where you've led me, you,
mysterious and innocent accomplice, co-author and co-mother of my
mystery, see where I now stand, what I owe you, how much, with what
love you have wounded me once and for all times, wounded and dated.
Apparently, we are in 1992 after J.C., but Circonfession comes to pass in
59 after the birth of J.D., since it writes itself *from the invisible inside*
(second period)
  writes itself, setting off for the outside, writes itself all alone, masculine or feminine, with J.D. aboard, flowing from the first notch,
  extracting from the inside of his life small volumes of blood that he,
the forever-child, still looks at with the same surprise, today still a child
before the blood feels the same surprise, the child remains, the blood
remains, time passes without the blood changing, without the child

passing, the limitless child (Period 2), without the child knowing what blood is, this inside that exits, and which, one says, has a voice, the same voice for you and for me, the voice of blood.

He himself wasn't there at his own circumcision, but afterwards what jealous curiosity for his own inside! At the beginning of this whole book, to begin, there will have been this moment of separation within me, the instant of opening what must remain closed, and then, the dazzling effusion of blood, frightening, sudden appearance of what can only be interior – at the beginning of every book, there is this: the 'unexpected discovery': I see my blood gush forth, I see the inside come out, and that there is an inside. With my own eyes I see the stranger who lives inside me, the inside who doesn't obey me, and who has my numbers and my keys, I saw my blood, my unconscious, my kinship. I see my invisible. I see the age, the blood, the one that is and isn't there; through a tear, I see my marrow my secret; and if I quiver it's because I feel what I do not know: behold my death which I will never see. *Our* death, ours, the instant of our life which we cannot appropriate. Our death which strips us of our death. We have the experience we have not to have, of not having. The thing that will come from us to us so as to escape us. Like blood. Once the wound closes up we speak of it no longer, but we never forget it.

*

'Ah! in three months I will be fifty years old. Can this really be?' exclaims Stendhal, another limitless child, to whom the raw unbelievable happens, the same unbelievable –

> That morning, October 16, 1832, I was at San Pietro in Montorio, on Mount Janicule, in Rome; it was a magnificently sunny day. A slight, barely felt sirocco wind caused a few small white clouds to float above mount Albano . . . I was happy to be alive. I was able to distinguish perfectly Frascati and Castel Gandolfo four leagues from here . . . I see perfectly the white wall that marks the last repairs, those made by the Prince Franco Borghese . . .
>
> What a magnificent view! It is here then that Raphael's *Transfiguration* was admired for two and a half centuries . . . Thus for two hundred and fifty years this masterpiece was here: two hundred and fifty years![11]

and all of a sudden a cry: 'Ah! the hour breaks, over there, in three months I will be fifty years old.'

. . . Ah! in three months I will be fifty years old; can this really be? 1783, 93, 1803: I count it up on my fingers . . . and 1833: fifty. Can this really be? Fifty! I'm going to be fifty, and I was singing Getry's air:

When one is fifty.

This unexpected discovery didn't irritate me at all, hadn't I just daydreamed of Hannibal and the Romans? Greater ones than I after all are dead . . .[12]

When one is fifty – in fact the song says sixty. I'm going to be 'sixty.' Is this the name of an illness? of a medal? I've become a 'sexagenarian!' a friend laughs. What a nickname! What an adventure! Can this be? Perhaps: but not true. This then is what can happen to us, a signifier, full of sound and laughter, signifying nothing. If not: '*auch einer.*' He too, me too. I too have it, the mark – the virus – the circumcision continues . . .

Indeed! Then, under the shock of incredulity, one tries out circonfession: attempt to make oneself spit out the most secret blood so as to try to see with one's own eyes the interior color – of what? – of one's own spirit, the personal juice of life, inner proof of the existence of self,

an attempt to capture the mortal matter that irrigates the immortal soul, so as to *see* the principle; Ah! what a shock, at the sight of this red inhabitant who keeps our secret numbers. The hematology Apprentices that we are exclaim: And me, am I the result of this blood and the sum of these decades? Is my life in me, before me, behind me, ahead of me, longer than me? Who's in charge here? I want it to be me! Me who? We would all like just once to have hands so as to take ourselves entirely in these hands, and arms to embrace ourselves from the first day unto the last.

And Stendhal, who starts to write 'Life-of-Henry-Brulard-written-by-himself' because of this 'unexpected discovery.' And better yet, shedding his own trousers in a gust of wind, pouncing on himself, and catching himself in full foreignness, ah! I've got myself, and I'm going to write my *Life* myself. Here's to the two of us, Life! He throws to this life, his own, the one who gallops, trips, throws him, he can't stand that, the one he mounts and who doesn't obey him, he's crazy about her, like about a mare. The stubborn one, the one who overruns and unseats him, he called her *Life*[13] – as though he had felt her fleeing since forever, and escaping *à l'anglaise* from her French master.

And J.D., going to see, climbing back along the vein so as to circumvent himself, going so far as to travel around Derrida fifty-nine times, for we know ever since the Bible that in the long run, the walls surrender. The dream would be to be there, at the first hour, so as to be able to answer, to witness one's own birth, to arrive at the place where she was, Esther, my mother, *Wo Esther war soll ich gehen* – my mother the proof, my mother who circulates within me, my mother who is in me as I was in her, what a strange, red, contained link, that doesn't reassemble itself, doesn't stop, that passes, escapes, pursues its course across generations, carrying our colors well beyond ourselves. Here, in the invisible inside, I no longer know if I'm the subject of the verb in the past tense, in the present, or if today is already the day before yesterday whereas erstwhile is a part of the future

In truth, I saw and I see, simultaneously, as Stendhal has written. I am I was she is me still already she begins to (not) be (born), I follow her she doesn't follow me, she precedes me.

The most surprising is not that I, I will die, it is that I was born, that I am not you, and that I am me. I would like very much to know that me.

> I seated myself upon the steps of San Pietro and there I daydreamed an hour or two on this idea. I'm going to turn fifty, it is high time I get to know myself. What have I been? what am I? In truth I would be hard-pressed to say.[14]

What nostalgia! What jealousy! All the world will have made his acquaintance except me? I would love to love him. What an idea! An idea that comes to us when it leans its elbows on the edge of me and sticks its neck out, sticks its head outside of time so as to perceive me. I would love to confess myself, and the circonfessor is me. This is circonfession, confession is inside, it comes to pass between myself and myself, circonfession is passing one's head outside of the silk tent, passing one's own skin, passing one's own death so as to catch one's own life by the hair by the mane. Where are these surprising books written, books that surprise themselves? In order to surprise themselves, they must go to the interterritorial places, in the spaces that run along me and prolong me.

The fifty-nine periods and periphrases of Circonfession are 'written in a sort of inner margin, between the book by Geoffrey Bennington and a work in progress'.[15] Where to write the words that traverse us as we pass across our body's bridge, attracted by an event that we sense and repel, the barbed thoughts that transpierce us as we dash like madwomen towards the hated, venerable event, where that which we cannot speak of to anyone is written, this secret without audible sound, that precedes us, of which we are both the keeper and the celebration?

Where? Between two books, between a book and a work, in a sort of inner margin, between my belly's skin and my trouser's waistband

In the end I only descended from the Janicule when the light evening mist came to warn me that soon I would be seized by the sudden, terribly disagreeable and unhealthful cold that in this country immediately follows sunset. I hastened to return to the Conti *palazzo* (Piazza *Minerva*), I was exhausted. I was wearing white English trousers made of [twill]; I wrote on the waistband inside: *October 16, 1832, I'm going to be fifty,* thus abbreviated so as not to be understood: *I mgo ingt obe 5* [*J. vaisa voirla 5*].[16]

Written straight away, at the extremity, between day and night, just before death,

'abbreviated, so as not to be understood,'

not understood by whom? by the person who is going to read the message written on the trousers' waistband. I mgo ingt obe 5: It mustn't be said! Let no one know! It's the secret.

Secret proclaimed aloud, but in the presumably posthumous book.

But then secret for whom? Secret hidden from whom? Even from me. I mean: from him. I mean from me. Secret announced, but not revealed. Instantaneous. Written so as not to be read. But so as to have been written. Who will know? Abbreviated: urgent inscription: one must make haste, because I mgo ingt obe 5 from one minute to the next. And the first thing that comes to hand is the trouser.

'I was exhausted – I was wearing trousers' – the team is wild, it gallops.

'I was exhausted – I was wearing trousers, I wrote' – I call that writing raw.

My waistband murmurs this message to my belly's skin in disguised language. Utterance much closer to the insane truth than the other with its air of correctness, the non-abbreviated one. What is going to happen to J. – who is not H. or I – is incomprehensible in truth.

The scene comes to pass between (me) these two (he); he who writes and he-who-reads. The scene comes to pass in the foreign interior. The foreignness comes to pass between me and me. Between the skin and the trouser. To write a book in code, very foreign to myself, is the height of writing. And more precisely: to write oneself a book. Because writing doesn't address itself first to the outside reader, it starts with me. I write; I write myself, it writes itself. The trouser is the scene of writing in its native clandestinity. Few writers are magic enough, childlike enough, raw enough to make this gesture and transcribe it raw.

Montaigne paints the passage with tamed, matte, mounted words.

Stendhal will have been as one body with writing against the horseman that he was.

The book escapes itself. Like this age, his own, that of Henry Brulard, *unexpected!* this fiftieth year that comes upon him. But all the same it is his. How to keep and unleash at the same time? Have what we have not? Let's try to bring back to the inside of the trouser the 'unexpected discovery.' The waistband is going to keep the secret.

Without knowing it we have passed into another world. Here reigns a slightly mad causality. All obeys, in this decisive moment, chance and fancy. We hear them, these divinities, cause the story to lisp, with a zurreptitious zibboleth, the story of a musical, capricious genesis. Listen:

'I hastened to return to the Conti palazzo piazza Minerva. I was exhausted I was wearing white English trousers made of twill; I wrote on the waistband inside: I mgo ingt obe 5.' Here is the seed of a book that will always be a few necks ahead of its own horseman.

How old was Stendhal, I mean Henry Brulard, how old did he dare to still or already be when he wrote I mgo ingt obe 5 in five sort of words? The age when it's magic that is the law. Let's say five, six years old?

And everything will have been the fruit of this elusive hour!

*

As soon as it's a question of thinking about a date, of carving out a notch in the flow of blood, of bridling the wind, we are crazy,

> A date is crazy, that's the truth.
> And we are crazy about dates.

And how crazy one can get when one is alone with one's trousers! Crazy, that is to say free.

> A date is crazy: it is never what it is, what it says it is, always more or less than what it is. . . . It is not dependent on being, on some sense of being, this is the condition under which its crazy incantation becomes music. It *remains* without being, by dint of music, remains for the song, *Singbarer Rest*, it is the *incipit* or the title of a poem that *begins* by saying the rest. It begins with the rest – that is not and that is not being – by letting a wordless (*lautlos*) song be heard, a song perhaps inaudible or inarticulate, a song nonetheless whose circumference and melody, whose sketch, whose outline of melody (*Umrisse*) stem undoubtedly from the cutting, sharpened, concise, but also rounded, circumventing form of a sickle, of a writing . . .[17]

A date tells of our human madness. To think we date God! What freedom!

We plant flags in blood,

Nonetheless there are turns, whirlwinds forming a series of curves in our lives, and we who have a tongue give ourselves names that remain to what does not remain.

In the country of writing, the great, I mean the courageous, all write the passage, this is the most difficult, it is the most painful to do, this gesture, it requires an extraordinary strength of the body of the soul, and in the end, one loses everything at it except honor – but those who write the passage, from Aeschylus to Clarice Lispector or to Derrida, passing by Montaigne and Stendhal, know in advance that they are moving towards their perdition, magnificent. And into the bargain they are begrudged their confession, and this too they know in advance, moving towards the zones where truth's luster turns, sparkling

(Knowing, as the Portuguese says, that God writes straight with crooked lines.)

*

Quel jour sommes-nous?

*

And for our greatest mourning, there are days that don't come to us, for nothing in the world would we want to miss them, these are great, singular, ceremonious days, those we want to witness in person, with our whole person, but whatever we do, we don't manage to find ourselves there, it is precisely these that make us feel the rigor of our limits.

In the 'momentous'[18] moments, we are surpassed.

In the moment of my father's death, I wasn't there, I wasn't up to it, the world was falling apart above my head, an icy fire devoured space; as for me – I was below everything, no bigger than a pebble.

This is our misfortune: in the case of apocalypse – when we are invited to rise above ourselves, so as to see the worst, as though to see the best – almost always we faint away. Mourning shows us the door, we are dislodged from our interior habitation, an absence moves into our place.

For once I don't entirely agree with Montaigne:

> Now Homer shows us well enough how much surprise gives in addition, when he makes Ulysses cry for the death of his dog and not cry any tears for his mother; the first accident, slight though it was,

swept him away, all the more so because he was unexpectedly assailed by it; he withstood the second, more impetuous one, because he was prepared for it.[19]

(*no*: it's because we are just big enough to cry for our dog, but never big enough to cry for our mother.)

However prepared we are, we are *never prepared*.

We don't believe in death. We never stop thinking about death. Grief and mourning begin long before the event, begin on the first day of love,

for years we fear, but we don't believe, fear doesn't believe, certitude stays outside the door, outside the skin, I'm too afraid of losing you and of your losing me to let believing enter my heart. Outside, I know, but fundamentally I don't believe, everything we think we don't think, that's because we're alive, we inhabit the country of the living; that which is beyond, outside – we don't have the heart to believe. We can't believe in death in advance, it remains inadmissible. Our immortality is: not-believing-in-death. This doesn't stop us from trembling. Until the day when the long-expected worst occurs, by all our strengths so unexpected. And as we are never prepared enough, behold how we are caught unawares. What is worse, in truth, is not that this hour comes, but that we miss it – it's a unique chance, and almost always, it must be said, we botch it – but not always.

Tearless I cry for all these scenes, our dearest scenes, which come to pass outside of us, where we pass outside ourselves, which we can't share with ourselves, tearless I cry for the tearless scenes, the scenes so violently cruel they take our tears away and at a blow dry us out and deprive us of beverage and libation. I know them and we know them, the lightning ones, who transport us with a single phrase, with a sentence, to the other side of the word. It's like this: with the announcement of Portia's death to Brutus, or of Lady Macbeth's to Macbeth, enters, monumental, Silence. My voice is cut short in my throat because she is no more, the person to whom I was addressing it.

No one can live this moment. One can only die it.

At the approach, at the evocation of the scene of my loss of you, no matter from how far away, when a thought adventures in that direction, everything is extinguished, I 'die' to me, I go away. Rather die than undergo your death. Your death I could not live.

None has ever lived in the present the death of a loved one. The death of a dear parent at first eliminates us. At the time not a tear for my father, not a tear for your mother.

Nonetheless god knows we have rivers of tears to shed. Where have they then gone? Elsewhere, far away, into the future, to the neighbor's.

They will return later, indirect, displaced. For the friend we will weep the tears that were first extracted before the body of the beloved. The great griefs come to us disguised, long after, as ghosts, when we believe them far removed, it is then they come, slip, unrecognizable, anguishing, in incomprehensible forms, changed into vertigo, into chest pains,

What's wrong with me, we torment ourselves? I have my mother, I have my love, I have my daughter biting me to death.

Three months after his death the brother explodes in the sister's body. The brother become sobs. The sister loses the body-brother, loses the brother's bones, long after the foreign scene of the burial. (First the earth. Later the waters that I lose.)

The terrible hour that I cannot live is the hour of your death. The hour that cannot come to pass, not with me, that comes to pass beside me,

No, to me this hour cannot come (I cannot suffer it.) The only absolutely 'impassable' border, the one that doesn't pass is this separation that takes place inside, the outside-of-me in me, the uprooted heart in the heart, in the outside interior of me. There is an outside in me.

Where do they come to pass, these unlivable hours, when do they come to pass, these hours that happen in the foreign me, in the my region where I couldn't stand being me?

How to pass over the border that I cannot cross in reality, how to go where I cannot go?

Luckily there is the Night.

What is outside of us during the day takes place in us during the night.

In dreams I have witnessed my own suppression.

I was 'at home,' in a very busy place, on the morning I was told my mother had died during the night, at home getting up she had fallen, I was immobilized, everything in me became immobilized, this didn't reach, this didn't reach me, I didn't move, I didn't go there, I didn't think, I remained inert, I didn't feel, the thing was happening beyond, over there, and beyond in the very depths of me, where, like someone who is afraid of feeling a lot of pain doesn't move at all, I didn't move a thought, I didn't move my soul, I petrified myself, I knew what was waiting for me, I wasn't living this time, I didn't live it, I was with a couple who had a big black dog, the dog began to lick me, I wanted to push it away, but they told me it didn't bite at all: I let it happen. The enormous black creature wrapped itself around me, and licked me, my neck, my ears, gently, I let it do it. Under the creature's tongue, I 'thought' without thought about my mother, I was in a trance, it was a question of burying her tomorrow, I didn't think about it, I could perhaps have rushed and seen her again, but I didn't, this wasn't, I wasn't, what for, things were happening, I remained, immobile without movement, the coffin was doubtless already closed, I could do nothing neither think, nor feel, feeling rumbled dully in the depths of me, what this would be tomorrow I couldn't think, I knew. There was a suitcase with my mother's things. I began. What came out first were her shoes. The infinite love that I felt for these large-sized shoes, these beloved, cherished shoes, I felt terrible chagrin at the idea they were way too big I couldn't wear them, I couldn't do myself any good by putting on my mother's shoes, by keeping her on my feet. I felt grief prepare to invade me, I was still inside me like an absent woman, like a madwoman, but it was getting closer, already with the shoes, it was my mother who was coming, should I run to see her? I was separated

Death: something terrible that doesn't come.

This is orphanhood: I miss your death. The blow falls next to me. I want to suffer and I don't manage. There I am surprised. An immense opaque transparent inconsistent wall rises between you dea(d)th and me on this side. This wall is (made of) separation: impalpable. It doesn't exist. Nothing stops me / something stops me from passing. It's the impossible. The impossible is matter purified of all materiality. Clarified butter. It's what does not exist. What does not exist manifests itself violently as the impassable.

I want to tame the impassable.

It isn't that I don't want to lose or lose myself; to the contrary, I know very well that losing teaches us to live

But I want to be there when I lose, I don't want to lose the loss.

But see how I discover that this too must be lost.

The worst part of grief is this grief that doesn't let itself be suffered, this absolute, infinite, indolorous suffering. This too I will have had to come up against, and consent to.

I will have had to pass through this non-incarnated non-place with just a sort of leaf of carbon paper for a soul,

in order to experience the tragic experience of expropriation that is our lot.

What! (one can't even suffer one's suffering) one can't even eat the bread of suffering, and drink one's own tears? Amongst the unexpected discoveries that await us, the most unexpected is this one, that reveals to us what we call mourning: the worst part of mourning is that we must mourn grief. (One can't even enjoy one's own suffering.) All is less, all is much less, and therefore much more, than what we had imagined. We don't manage to put the maternal shoes on our feet. We are deprived of our pains.

If this is how it is, it's because these events occur in our home's foreign land (where we have never gone), in the strange and foreign regions of the heart itself, *hinaus in die Fremde des Herzens*. There where there is no witness at all. We ourselves are not our own witnesses. We are without us. Without God. God not having followed us. We, being in the abandonment of God. The sign of these scenes: even God doesn't make it there, even I. This is tragedy according to Celan, according to Aeschylus, the tragedy of no one, tragedy according to Akhmatova.

Here we are absolutely alone, no one has ever been here, there is simply no one, we ourselves are not there, no one has preceded us, no one has taught us, it's the first time, suffering is always the first time, the loss of you, my own loss, it is the first time, and what renders it alarming is that 'I' am not there. I don't know how to be there, I don't manage. All the world's tragedies have warned us, uselessly. (It's even 'worse' . . .) They have never been but the *sung/singable Remnants of that which is without music and without words*.

But this is not a reason for renouncing our human heritage. It's even rather the most urgent reason for not renouncing. Our lost pains are our ultimate goods, our silence renders a sound beyond the ear.

The harpooners or the harpists of the ultimate hours are occupied with this challenge: to fish in the space between the lines beyond the heart for what must return to the heart, and to make it sound once more.

It is this hunger for flesh and for tears, our appetite for living, that, at the tip of forsaken fingers, makes a pencil grow.

*

It's very nearly the end. It's very nearly life.

Extend the hand, write, and it's all over with the end.

Writing is the movement to return to where we haven't been 'in person' but only in wounded flesh, in frightened animal, movement to go farther than far, and also, effort to *go too far*, to where I'm afraid to go,

but where, if you give me your hand, I'll endure going. I write, I extend my hand; without my knowing it, this is already a prayer, I extend my hand to you so that you will exist because you do exist, beyond my fingers, your fingers, without my knowing it this is already a response, already I draw to my side the site for you, with one hand I call the other hand,

it is in this modest, all-powerful way that I begin to save what is lost.

When I write I ask for your hand; with your hand I'll go too far and I won't be afraid anymore of not coming back. Without my knowing it, it is already *love*.

Love is giving one's hand. The hand is so powerful (one is not mistaken) one is clearly right to ask for it

In her little books of notes to herself, Clarice Lispector wrote one day – *in English:*

> I want somebody to hold my hand (in Brazilian: Papa the time I was hurt). I don't want to be a single body. I am out of the rest of me, the rest of me is my mother, it is another body.
>
> To have a single body surrounded by isolation, it makes such a limited body. I feel anxiety, I am afraid to be just one body. My fear and my anxiety is of being one body.[20]

I cannot live with a single body cut off from the rest.

I want ways of holding on to what surpasses me, of adding to myself a mother or other. (I know at least two for holding my hand and chasing away the limit that threatens my body.)

I am the finite that wants its infinite. Love infinites me.

Without you I am a pebble, and my skin closes narrowly over me. Without you, stub, stump. All I need is you in order to pass over into infinity. The fall of walls, the bursting of doors, the dissolution of the skin's wall, the dissipation of bars, this is what the loving-beloved brings us: my flesh plus the world's flesh, the world as flesh, a body finally on a scale with our soul. With the other for endless mother, melt the dikes that impede the carnal soul from rolling its waves to the far ends of the worlds.

The favor you do me in the act of love – this possibility for evasion, this chance to enjoy extravagance, without suffering from madness,

I call this freedom.

Who then can make for us cosmic flesh

The being who says: go ahead.

The being who accepts, in a way as disaffected, elementary-elemental, as the earth, the air, the sky accepts us, us, going, passing through their involuntary matter. Whoever is capable of an acceptance this vast can only be the equivalent of the maternal breast, not of an exterior mother, but of the one who doesn't lean over the cradle, who doesn't say 'I am your mother,' of the mother who doesn't congratulate herself. The mother who loves like she breathes, loves and doesn't know

it's the incarnation of a yes.

What would this elemental love do? To start, this person wouldn't say: do you know what time it is?

Not doing this, she would give all her time without even having to give it, by not putting it in danger, no cutting, she wouldn't touch the delicate immortality, with words that bite.

Everyone knows or has known the country without Fates, without thread, without watch hand, where passing time adds itself to time instead of deducting itself.

The country where one saves what passes and where you protect for me what surpasses me.

I'm not claiming that we are all gifted at dwelling there, but I affirm that it can exist, it is, since it depends entirely and only on two acquiescences.

Two at a time, of the same faith.

One – this was Tsvetaeva's wish: you are the fruit I am the knife.

No, not only one body for two
But for each one two bodies
Each one my body
Each one your body
Never less
Always two, always all
Not an only
But, per person, two
Each one for me, each one for you,
Each one asking for
The hand

But everything I say is only the echo of those magic phrases that pass through a page of *Schibboleth*, following the trace of a few words by Celan – wizard words, that deliver love's password in parentheses, in clandestinity. Love that is always clandestine.

To let the word pass through the barbwire border, through, this time, the grill of its language or grace. The passage of the other, towards the other – respect *for* the same, for a same that respects the other's alterity. Why did Celan choose the word *Passat*, this wind name, to say in *Sprachgitter* (in parentheses) 'We are strangers'?

(*Wär ich wie du. Wärst du wie ich.*
Standen wir nicht
unter einem Passat?
Wir sind Fremde.)

Strangers. The two of them strangers. Strangers one for the other? The two of them strangers for others still, third parties? The two of them – both of them, the one *like* the other, *unter* einem *Passat*.[21]

A single wind – *but* we are strangers *and* we are strangers. Lodged, lost in the frail cavity. A single wind for roof, for the two of us. And no one other than the two of us under the windy roof. This wind, haven't we invented it?

Under the same wind, stranger to the world except to us, we are strangers together of the same foreignness and yet each one in her own foreignness, but we were once under a single wind – whispering of love, in parentheses, apart – and in parentheses, between me and you, incertitude. But the two incertitudes are reunited by a single blowing foreignness. Strangers to the world, runaways, we are held in the fragile arms of foreignness, each one in the arms of the other's foreignness,

to be strangers together, and trembling in the wind, is the condition of love, the lovers' condition.

What there is of election is held in the arms of this parenthesis. Pact of the lost ones. The Wind carries off our words. In the gust one doesn't speak, the Wind says our truth.

Let's take a plane. Now each of us is at one end of the earth, each one on her continent. Let this be two 'observers.' Each one is linked to a referential that depends on her localization. Each one is working in a different referential.

Let's imagine an event: a telephone call.

For one it's daytime for the other it's night.

What time is it? the one asks. Where you are nine o'clock in the morning where I am five o'clock in the afternoon; and inversely,

See how with a single telephone call a fitting, intrinsic referential is established, that takes its coordinates in love.

Our observers' time now has two times. On one side it's Friday, on the other it's Thursday, and yet it is the same day. In separunion we are one day and the next, and we are also one round-trip day, life is double, it is continual, now is the time for you to get up for me to go to bed to go to sleep to wake you up daytime is at the same time night,

And it is always like this, under the Passat Wind. The hearts: two strangers who unite their foreignnesses, and then double day double night double pleasure, hearts that telephone each other, between the two a transparent distance, carefully kept, thanks to which the communication is never interrupted.

It's separation that weaves the intrinsic world. A fine, tender separation like a baby's skin like an amniotic membrane that lets the sound of blood pass through but impedes an exiling limit from forming its clots.

*

Now let's get back to our meeting point, at the hour of *rendons-nous*, render-yourself-I-render-myself.

Continents no longer separate our two observers.

Here the common country is going to open up, it is the unique continent, and it is interior. This continent is hollowed out in time, as are dreams. Love comes like this: to the interior. The *arrivance* of love is the genesis of the interior. Behold: the interior is. Everything that lives is in the interior. The interior is so vast that an exterior is infinitely distanced outside of space.

One step – love takes a step, and they are both, and at a single bound, inside the room-inside-the-room, they are hidden, lodged inside the cosmic hiding-place and no more outside, the outside is not, has no more place, if it is someplace, is at the devil's, is outside –

A suave concavity spreads out, the world is entirely hollow, we are equally hollow. One recognizes the scene by its disposition, always the same: wherever it takes place, in Egypt, in Verona, in Paris, in Manhattan, in a palace room, hotel room, in the open air under the moon, on a Pantheon square, in the middle of a crowd, or in the isolation of a nutshell, an intimacy rises up and takes the two characters in its arms.

This scene is always under a cape, under a cloth, under Passat. A foreignness separates the two from all humanity. Something that beats in their flesh, a blood perhaps, acts like a silent shibboleth. Neither seen nor known the two pass into their secret country. The door to the country is the first look. We enter one through the other. We are there. It's like having entered into the answer itself. The one that was waiting for us. And immediately the foreign seizes us, already it flows, all strange, in our veins.

What comes to us is the certitude of foreign nationality, an undeniable sensation, nationality doubly foreign, that sharpens our nerves, that awakens in our flesh accompanied by a tumult of messages and excitations – I could say a personality in us – but that's not it, it's really a nation's nationality for two – a nationality we share between the two of us alone, the two of us alone before the world, furtive behind the world's back,

nationality that in our turn we divide into two interior foreignnesses, you and me clearly different, and endowed each one with the strong foreignness of the other.

Once in this country, one doesn't stop there. It's the moment, it's the place to go, the one thanks to the other, at the depths of the instant, finally realizing the dream of all human beings, which is to take the present by the root and eat the root. We all who in truth live only for this hope, and in reality renounce it most of the time. We all who almost always make everything except love, and we are entirely invaded by exile and bordered by solitude. Now it's only in the act of love that one finally attains the present's speed, the intelligent, interior, slow speed, the non-measurable, precise, unknown speed, that transports us into the incalculable, deep, borderless, strangely marine instant – because in joy, as we know, we swim – and the instant is joy, more precisely felicity, congratulation, that is to say joy rejoicing, joy and joy of joy –

it's that, in joy, all is forgotten, except a slight sensation of glory, it's like a triumph, like knowing what the getting there on time has cost us in effort and fear, everything must be paid for, and we have paid very dearly, nothing is given except the chance, then everything needs to be wrenched with vital strength from death

it's because of the cruel price paid that, in joy, we can rejoice.

But to earn joy, one must first have broken with one's self, life so great is knocking from the inside with big blood blows against the too-small body, till it breaks, till the flesh, still camped around the bones, lets go. Fall. And if it wasn't for the abyss, the soft abyss of an unknown color, if it wasn't for the night of a deep color, in which we throw ourselves, joy would remain totally painful. But when in an agile fisticuffs the two strangers knock each other down, each one cleaving the other's unbearable kernel, and when they rush swirling into the tender night like a pocket of succulent water, the fire, the pain, are put out in the fountain of nourishing blood.

What are we doing here? An act of birth. Already living, we are born.

Finally, for once, we make it, on time! We're on time and the time is good. It lets itself be captured licked drunk slept, each pulsation vibrates for a thousand years. I don't know how to explain it scientifically, but the fact is that joy lasts limitlessly as long as it lasts.

We left language behind us a long time ago of course. From very far away words appear to us, minuscule flotilla, totally surpassed dust.

The language spoken here is silence, silence of two silences, silence sighing from the other side of the spoken word, silence to respectful silence, silence as superior word.

We are greater than ourselves here.

From instant fragment to instant fragment the greatness that surpasses us augments.

See how now the eyes too are surpassed, the gaze doesn't follow, doesn't bear seeing its own sacrifice. It's very difficult to see your face become so human, so originary. I can't look this face in the face without becoming frightened: that's because it is on its way to becoming sacred. I throw an oblique glance its way. All of a sudden I don't see your face: because it's become my face. Here we are the two of us lying under a single face. From now on there is no longer any image of appearance.

And till the hour's end we remain in the immense inside, eating one another feeding each other, eating nourishing one another without swallowing each other, absorbed in each other like the child in the mother. And at the end happy to separate so as to find one another again as strangers.

*

I sense I have gone very far in this reconstruction. That's done. I return to the side of words.

Now I'm going to make my (silent) declaration of love to a person I've loved since birth; double birth, ours, like the mother is born of the child's birth:

'Go away. I love your departures. I give you complete freedom. This is the condition for my being able to hope for your comings, hope, heart beating, hope spiced with fear, fear that is never without hope's *élan*, contraction and dilatation, this is the rhythm of my organism in love. And the freedom I give you takes nothing from you.

The first gesture that linked us was to have cut the umbilical cord. Each one for herself: you can go, I'll wait for you. I'm not waiting for you: you can come. I'm not (like) you. You're not like me. I don't mistake you for me. I don't think I know you. Leave, my love, you who's just left (me).' Say I.

It's not easy but it's the gift's promise.

Sometimes in the morning I look at my daughter, and with happy surprise I do not recognize her, my child even, I do not recognize her. The benediction is to be able to say to the beloved: we are going to turn thirty, forty, can this be, and I don't understand you! Thirty years, forty, foreignness shines with the same *éclat*. Faithfully from the first minute I haven't ceased not understanding you with amazement. Often, always, you come to me, unknown, moving, outside of me, still a little in me. I called you egg, a long time ago. It's the story of the hen who doesn't recognize her egg.

> Inside of her the hen doesn't recognize the egg, but outside of her she doesn't recognize it either. When the hen sees the egg, she thinks she's caring for an impossible thing. And, heart beating, heart beating so hard, she doesn't recognize it.[22]

With the child it's the same, the work of art is the same. The heart beats because this way of not recognizing is a way of recognizing, she recognizes it without recognizing it. She doesn't know she recognizes it, but the heart beats. My heart beats from not recognizing you, from recognizing: I don't recognize you, I sense that I don't recognize you. (To sense that I don't recognize makes my heart beat); what makes my heart beat is that something remains non-recognized, that I sense the unknown, that I keep it unknown. This is love. I will never know how I love you. I love you I don't even know it. You will never know how I love you.

I love you: I work at understanding you to the point of not understanding you, and there, standing in a wind, I don't understand you.

Not understanding is a way of holding myself in front and of letting come. Transverbal, transintellectual relationship, this loving the other in submission to the mystery. (It's accepting, not knowing, forefeeling, feeling with the heart.)

I'm speaking in favor of non-recognition, not of mistaken cognition. I'm speaking in favor of closeness, *without any familiarity*.

How good it is to not understand you. I don't understand you with an incomprehension so vast it surpasses all my great understanding of you.

But I pass through an incomprehension of you towards you, one that doesn't abandon you. It's a great activity of feeling and not translating. I say to you: world. What an emotion when the feeling that before me you begin is accorded me, before me spreads out your promised thought which I do not enter, which isn't forbidden me, which remains, which speaks towards me, which doesn't disappear, which is fruitful. O you of whom I'm thinking, in front of whom I think of you, from very near as from afar,

you caressed nearby as from afar, *without any familiarity*, contemplated belly to your earth like contemplated from the ground up, you pure manifestation of you, you moon, you other,

my togetherness with you I will never know, but it exists. My secret, unknown country – thus without limit.

The password? No password. But there is the sign that says natal, fatal, destinal country: heart beating.

If there were a word, it would be the most ordinary, immense word, synonym of infinity, distracted word, unnoticed, word that passes, so humbly, almost useless, a word that could just as well fall silent, it would be, yes, you have recognized it, yes, it would be yes, the raw word, the believable, the unbelievably vast, the open door to all that will come, a courageous word, open-handed, yes, I receive, I let go.

But in the region under the Passat, all the words without exception are easily worth a yes, they all say yes too. No too.

I tell you yes. I begin us with a Yes. Yes begins us.

*

All of us here who 'write,' we do not know what we do, we are crazy, foolish, we wander along invisible streams, we run backwards and forwards incessantly before metal-grating that doesn't exist, we seek, till the exhaustion of the contents of our heads, to pass, to pass what, to pass from a region of feeling to a region of what, of painting with words what moves us without words, we pass days or even months or years feeling our way, wandering abandoned along deserts without knowing where the door opens that gives access to the other side

all of us here, we want, more than anything in the world, transposition.

It is not with *a* word, *a* shibboleth, that we will manage to pass. Tongue in our mouths, we must change tongues, another tongue must come into our mouths, and into our bodies another body.

Why is it so difficult to write?

The most difficult 'border passage,' the most torturous, we cannot make it on purpose, not wittingly.

It's a dream. It doesn't obey us. It's a dream: it's a wind. The wind blows at its hour.

*

I realize I've returned to my native site. There where one morning (it's always at dawn, when we see the light of day once more), upon lifting my eyes, I see a stranger up above, native of the summits – not a professional – a wild man.

'What exalts me in my race, he senses, is that I don't know what I'm going to write in the next lines, he senses. Each new book leaves me completely surprised.' The most surprised of all.

As long as creation lasts, there is only this panting chase that pursues itself, in the virgin space between one book and another. The hunter is completely given over to the hunt. The hunt is entirely animal, naturally. It's a prayer on all fours, at a gallop. The prayer asks: may I catch the words that will know how to surround the mystery, without biting on and crushing it. And with the blind sureness of archers, it sends into the darkness arrows that plant themselves in the desired words, refined, sensitive, sensual words, exact escort for 'the thing' aimed for, unknown.

The blind man sneaking away up there is aiming for precisely this: he wants to escort the unseized thought, without limiting its free course. But there is no end to freedom,

Well? Well, one time,

Comes a voice that says: you there, who dreams, do you know what time it is?

Yes, yes, all right.

Well, the wild man of the agile feet puts his shoes on – and, once shod, we call him philosopher. The chase is now enchased. The door closes.

Happily, we already hear foreign footsteps approaching . . . day breaks, or else it's night, the hour – come – for writing.

Notes

1 Jacques Derrida, *Schibboleth: pour Paul Celan* (Paris: Galilée), 1986.
2 N.B. 'That's an *A e d*,' my mother used to say, '*auch Einer*,' to her sister in the streets of Germany, denouncing with a complicitous shibboleth someone whom they, between themselves, recognized as an *Also*. Another J. He also.
3 Jacques Derrida, 'Circonfession', in Geoffrey Bennington and Jacques Derrida, *Jacques Derrida* (Paris: Seuil, 1991).
4 In English in the French text. (Translator's note.)
5 In English in the French. (Translator's note.)
6 In English in the French. (Translator's note.)
7 In English in the French. (Translator's note.)
8 In English in the French. (Translator's note.)
9 Paul Celan, *Strette* (Paris: Mercure de France, 1971), p. 102.
10 Paul Celan, *La Rose de personne* (Paris: Le Nouveau Commerce, 1979), p. 122.
11 Stendhal, 'Vie de Henry Brulard', *Oeuvres intimes II* (Paris: Gallimard, 1982) pp. 529–31.
12 *Ibid.*
13 Throughout this passage, the word 'life' appears in English in the French text. (Translator's note.)
14 Stendhal, 'Vie . . .', p. 532.
15 Derrida, 'Circonfession', p. 5.
16 Stendhal, 'Vie . . .', p. 533.
17 Derrida, *Schibboleth . . .*, p. 68–9.
18 In English in the French. (Translator's note.)
19 Montaigne, *Essais, Oeuvres complètes* (Paris: Gallimard, 1962), pp. 1646–7, n. 4.
20 Clarice Lispector, unpublished notebooks, in English.
21 Derrida, *Schibboleth . . .* pp. 92–3.
22 Clarice Lispector, 'O Ovo et a Galinha', *Felicidade Clandestina* (Rio de Janeiro: Nova Fronteira, 1981), p. 53.

6   Love of the wolf

Translated by Keith Cohen

This is a bo(u)nd for a wolf.

On November 11, 1967, Clarice Lispector wrote in favor of fear: 'I am certain that in the Stone Age I was exactly mistreated by some man or other's love. A certain fright, which is secret, goes back to that time.'[1]

Some paleolithic man or other, a sort of ravishing monkey. Another woman, Marina Tsvetaeva for example, would say a wolf, and another a tiger.

The Stone Age, for Tsvetaeva, is the age of blood and passions, the age of the garden at the Convent of the Flagellants. First blood. Game of blood: the blood rushes up and down, one grows pale, one blushes, the blood rushes away, called back, disobedient.

The landscape of that age is one of anguish and nostalgia. The little girl is running. You can't tell if she's running away. Or if she's lost. If she's running after the tiger. Or if the tiger is running after her.

Following in Tsvetaeva's footsteps, this reading *is a bo(u)nd for a secret wolf.*

*

Tsvetaeva is 'descended' from Pushkin, according to her own version of her genealogy. She comes running from every direction out of the works of Pushkin.

The initial fright that inspires Tsvetaeva comes from Pushkin's fear.
And out of all of Pushkin, her first Pushkin was 'The Bohemians.'

'L'amour du loup' was first published in *La Métaphore (Revue)* 2 (1994), La Différence: 13–37.

I had never heard such names: Aleko, Zemfira or – the Old Man. As for old men, I knew only one: Ossip, in the Chapel of Taroussa, One-armed-Ossip – his arm was like an oxbow because he had killed his brother – with a cucumber. Because my grandfather, A.D. Meyn, was no old man: you don't talk to old men, they live in the street. I had never seen any Bohemians, but I had heard of a Bohemian woman – she nursed me.[2]

Her first Pushkin was on the shelf, it was fat, she would read it in the dark. Her Pushkin, her source, her strange origin. He would always come from outside, that stranger, the one who carries her away. There is a door. The door opens, in comes the Outside, even inside he remains the outside, the Outside in person, that which I do not know, who strikes me very hard and loves me, thinks Tsvetaeva, the woman who loves the devils who carry her away. They are always beings who remain in hiding, who attract and then flee, who flee while attracting, who attract while fleeing, who escape and who call – bizarre beings, cossacks, funny words, clicks of the tongue; they have common, ordinary and yet extraordinary names, terrible names that sound like nothing, *kid*, *the guide* – they pass, and in their footsteps comes the word that the little girl had read in books, those foreign lands –

> Here's a brand new word – love. When it burns in one's breast, there, right in the middle (who doesn't understand me?).[3]

The parenthesis divides the world between those who understand and those who don't. Love always sets up its parentheses in the middle of the sentence, pitches its tents of silence.

> . . . when you don't say anything to anybody, it's love. From the beginning it burned in my breast, but I didn't know its name – love. I said to myself: it's the same for everybody, always the same. No: that existed only among the Bohemians.[4]

One day, I don't know when, it was decided to call *love* a set of strange, indescribable physical phenomena, is it pain? – but from the moment that the name is given to that burning in one's breast, the violence of the strangeness is interrupted and the ancient horror, hidden behind the new word, begins to be forgotten. Let's go back to before language, that's what Tsvetaeva does, let's go back to that disturbing age, the age of myths and of folktales, the age of stone, of fire, of knives. Before language there is the fire that bites but doesn't kill, the evil that, like all pain, separates us, the dehiscence that opens in us closed organs, making us seem strange to ourselves – and all that begins with: 'when you don't say anything to anybody – that's it – it's love.' It begins with the kept secret, with the silent separation from the rest of the world. You love yourself [*on s'aime*]: you sow [*on sème*]. You throw the others off track. You go underground. You leave the world in broad daylight. You betray it. You're cheating. It's a crime. It's a kind of glory. Love abjures in order to adore. It burns in your breast and the world is burned.

Don't say anything to anybody – because it's forbidden? That would be the case of Romeo and Juliet. No – it *is* allowed, but you won't say anything to anybody anyway. One says nothing to anybody because one rises to the absolute; one begins speaking the language that no one else speaks – a language spoken only by two. By these two undivided individuals, a language [*langue*] that makes of two but one, especially when it's your tongue [*langue*] that I have in my mouth.

(N.B. Ah, I shall always regret in French the absence of those words that in other languages name the set of one made by *two* when it fuses two individuals who from then on are no longer two; I shall always regret *both*, *ambos*, *beide* . . . .)

Joyfully you become incomprehensible – two strangers together. You begin to adore a god that nobody else bows down to. A very powerful and very fragile god, very threatening and very threatened. Nobody else believes in you except me. This very-much-god must be well hidden in order to protect it from incredulity. My god is made of glass, poof! and it's broken. But so long as it's intact it gives the universe. Invisible transparent god made of glass [*verre*]. I meant to say of verse [*vers*].

But the amorous break also speaks of the danger of winning. The danger is when you create a world, designed as a whole and for a whole people, made up of two individuals. This world-of-two depends for its survival on a single other person. The world-of-two is immediately surrounded and threatened by death. Death closes in around it tightly. Love immortalizes me. Only that which gives me life can take it away from me. That which gives, gives to enjoy, that which gives to enjoy, gives to fear its loss. Give to lose. The gift and its opposite.

It is on the basis of love that one recalls mortality. We are mortal only in that high region of love. In ordinary life we are immortal, we think about death, but it doesn't gnaw at us, it is down there, for later, it is weak, forgettable. But as soon as I love, death is there, it camps out right in the middle of my body, in daylight, getting mixed up with my food, dispatching from the far-off future its prophetic presence, taking the bread out of my mouth. It's because I love the beloved more than I love myself, you are dearer to me than I am to myself, you are not me, you don't obey me, I was sure that I was myself immortal, otherwise I couldn't live, I live only on that assurance, but what about you? I do not order your immortality. I can no longer live without you. That need overwhelms us. That's why anguish bursts forth: because the need pushes us toward the realization – no matter what, yes, I must die.

In *The Kid* nothing – not need, not infinity – can stop it. That's what the prose of the text says at the opening:

> And this is again the story of an old mother who knew too much about future things[5]

> Go, go, little girl!
> Youth has but one time[6]

> Maroussia: Dance, mother,
>   Smashing into everything! . . .
> The mother: Your senses are eager
>   Your heart is blind.[7]

Knowledge from experience: the heart goes blind because the need is stronger than anything else. Your ego is blind, your id is eager. It will get to the point of smashing everything. When there is a danger from outside, you bolt, but when the danger comes from inside, how can you bolt? The danger from inside is that complicated thing, the love of the wolf, the complicity that attaches us to that which threatens us.

When the I-ego and the I-id are adversaries and friends, inseparably, like the wolf and the infant, flight becomes unthinkable. When hatred and resentment show their teeth, we flee – but when it's love, tortuous love, who shows us their teeth?

Don't say it to anybody, love is so delicate, it's mortally fragile. A passerby could pulverize that god made of glass. But if you don't say (it) to anybody, this departure, this madness, you're at the mercy of the god. Nobody will come to your rescue the day the god takes on the aura of devil.

'Don't say it to anybody,' it's the same refrain that runs through a splendid text by Ingeborg Bachmann, *Der Gute Gott von Manhattan*. Don't say it –

– to anybody. Not even to yourself? Not even to the other person? But who is the other person? For Tsvetaeva?

The one whom you keep secret even from your mother, the one you don't name, not even to him? The one you keep. The one you kee – Shhh! –

Without being wary of him. The one whom Tsvetaeva, in her poem,[8] is careful not to call anything but *The Kid*. The Kid [*Le Gars*], one word, one syllable – a brief sparkle, a single phoneme, the very one for whom the glory tolls between Genêt and Derrida. But in the off-stage commentaries it takes place differently. From afar, from outside, it names:

> I read a story by Afanassiev, 'The Vampire,' and I couldn't figure out why Maroussia who was afraid of the vampire insisted on denying what she had seen, all the while knowing that naming it meant salvation for her. Why instead of yes, no? Out of fear? . . . No, not fear. Maybe fear, but – what else? Fear – and what? [. . .] Maroussia loved the vampire . . . and that's why she lost, one after the other, her mother, her brother, her life.[9]

Why instead of yes, no? Out of fear. But the kid also says clearly to his lover: if you don't tell that I'm a vampire, your brother is going to die, then your mother is going to die, and then you're going to die. What Maroussia wishes to hold onto is love as fear, and fear as love. They are inseparable. This is one of the most obscure experiences that we can ever have. Some of us really like what scares us. Just to be scared. It's appalling. O my love, my terror. 'O my son, my terror,' says Akhmatova in one of her poems. There is no love except where there is fear. Love run by fear, escorted by fear.

We love the wolf. We love the love of the wolf. We love the fear of the wolf. We're afraid of the wolf: there is love in our fear. Fear is in love with the wolf. Fear loves. Or rather: we are afraid of the person we love. Love terrorizes us. Or else the person we love we call our wolf or our tiger, or our lamb in the manger. We are full of trembling and ready to wolf down.

Love is vertical. First you go up. There is a ladder. Maroussia climbs up. Once you're at the top, you see, you fall. You've seen what you've seen. Seeing the other knocks us over. Seeing the wolf. Fear makes us fall from the top to the bottom, taking us back to the age of blood, in infancy, as we crawl among the odors, the appetites, the food, the earthworms and the dead.

'I loved a wolf,' says the little heroine of a text by Selma Lagerlöf, 'Herr Arne's Treasure.' And in the end of course, it kills her, or else it's she who kills herself for it.

As soon as one speaks of loving, it is there.

Love begins with a cat. A lost, accidental, fuzzy baby appears. A kitten one might think. A kitten *par excellence*: the found beast, the abandoned creature meowing – as in Aeschylus's *Agamemnon*. It comes into our home one fine morning, a poignant, mysteriously poignant figure of the unplanned child, and without any need of biological mother, or of father for that matter.

This kitten given by nobody, a gracious creature, is loved without being asked its name.

> One day a man reared in his house
> A lion cub still suckling, and he weaned it.
> The beginning of its life was full of charm.
> A friend to children, a joy to the elderly,
> Fed in one's arms, like a baby,
> Its ardent eye kept watch on the hand,
> Its appetite for food making it cuddly.
> But the time came
> When it showed its hereditary character.
> And to recompense the ones who'd nourished it,
> Needing no invitation, it feasts
> On a flock of sheep it massacred.
> The house is flooded with blood,
> Endless sorrow for the people of that house.
> Vast, devastating hecatomb.
> Sent by a god, an acolyte of Misfortune
> Had come into the dwelling
> To have a hand in the breeding.[10]

Eternally cruel seduction of the Foundling, whose frequent figure haunts those texts tormented by the riddle. Who is this child born without pain but bearer of a pain that we cannot help but suffer, in whom we cannot help but recognize ourselves, whom our narcissism nurses, who, at first feeding on our need, begins to devour us? And who is named at one time Oedipus, at another Heathcliff, and at another Nicolo alias Colino?

A stiff, black, withdrawn, silent savage, all the more loved in that he turns upon love with an appalling look. How is it that we love him – him of all people? What have we found in this foundling who fascinates us?

As soon as we embrace, we salivate, one of us wants to eat, one of us is going to be swallowed up in little pieces, we all want to be eaten, in the beginning we were all formerly born-to-eat, wolfing it down, eating like a horse; we are starved, full of whetted appetites – but better not say it, or else we'll never dare to love. Or to be loved.

Love is always a little wol-f-ishy [*loup-che*] – a little peckish, it's not nice to say, but . . .

(How) can a wolf be loved? By instinct, says Tsvetaeva. In what way is the wolf lovable? It's not the race of wolves that we love, it's not the wolf. It's about *a* wolf, a certain wolf, a wolf-but, a wolf-surprise.

> *I said 'the wolf' – I name the Guide. I say 'the Guide,' I name Pougatchov: the Wolf which – just this once won't hurt – spared its lamb, carried it off in the deep forest to love it . . .*
>
> *I'd say I loved that Guide more than all my own, more than the strangers, more than my favorite dogs, more than all the balls that rolled down the cellar, more than all the lost penknives, more even than my mysterious red armoire – where he was kept secret, mystery incarnate.*
>
> *More than the Bohemians, because he was blacker – darker than the Bohemians. And if I could say loud and clear that Pushkin lived in the secret armoire, today it's scarcely with a whisper that I can affirm: not Pushkin . . . the Guide.*[11]

'I said "the wolf," I name the Guide . . . I loved that Guide more than all my own.' I love my ball because it rolls down the cellar, we experience love through the loss it inflicts upon us: whether the ball is in the cellar or in the house, the ball is the possibility of rolling down the cellar. A penknife you have you don't love, but the *lost* penknife, yes.

O ancient pleasures of hide-and-seek, the first game of all, the game inscribed in our flesh (kitten flesh, newborn flesh) for millennia before our being born.

O the mystery of the mystery-game,

that all of us, of all species, children, felines, dogs, celebrate.

Crying 'look for me I'm hidden I'm lost find me.' How good it feels to be lost, to be looked for, to be found, to tremble with all those fears together: fear of not being discovered, fear of being discovered, fear of not trembling with fear.

I can't find the word to name the essence of these frightful delights. Look for me, says the hidden thing. Let's say I find it: that's *losability*. Not a very pretty word, but this concept is life itself. We feel like we're alive only through the painful excitation of our seventh sense, the sense of loss.

There is a connection between love and *being lost*. In familiar metaphoric terms, when it's a question of passion, we get lost, we run wild with a panting metonymy, we are lost, all the more so by being helped by the personage posted there to produce objectively being lost: that's the case of Pougatchov, known as the Guide. The guide leads astray. Guide to getting lost. Guide to the secret.

Let's follow the Wolf – that is, The Kid – that is, the Guide – whose name in the end will be Pougatchov. Careful because if we follow him closely, 'the Guide' could lead us to the deepest, the most remote place, down to where the roots of good and evil are gripped together in a single root, down to that depth at which we are all mixed together, the guide and I, *Pushkin and Pougatchov*, where Tsvetaeva is Pushkin, where Pougatchov is Tsvetaeva. *The Guide*, therefore, the one whom Tsvetaeva loves, makes appearances and disappearances in these little autobiographical texts in prose, mirrors of Tsvetaeva's unconscious, in the figure – not of a person – but of a scintillating Signifier, magic word, beacon beam, allusion, *promise*, let's say 'thing.' A strange sudden appearance, comparable to the sudden primitive appearance effected, at first indecipherably, in the mother-text, Pushkin's.

It is in a whole lineage of Pushkin's amorous mysteries that Tsvetaeva inscribes the genealogy of her own imaginary. This always involves duels, dual relations that are so intense, so red-hot, so white-hot, that the dimension of sexual difference, in the dazzle, is actually forgotten.

Such as the Pushkin and Pougatchov couple. *Pushkin and Pougatchov* is a title that sings of the passionate relation that Pushkin – himself the literary mother of Tsvetaeva – had with an ambivalent personage, an impostor, a cossack. One of those messianic figures from Russian history, a popular cavalryman who has come from the steppes to try to take the tsar's place. Now Pushkin wrote two texts inspired by Pougatchov: on the one hand, a historical piece, written for the tsar, and entitled *The History of Pougatchov*; on the other hand, a fiction, the short novel *The Captain's Daughter*. As an occasional historian, Pushkin describes the cossack just as the archives reveal him, a vile, cowardly personage complete with all the vices. But in *The Captain's Daughter* a complex Pougatchov surfaces – cruel, destructive, yet at the same time capable of an unexpected love for the little young man Griniov. This sixteen-year-old hero, Pushkin's creation, arouses in Pougatchov a tenderness such that the wicked creature will remain loyal to the boy till the end of his days. Pougatchov appears first as a 'black thing' that draws near during a storm in which everyone is lost, trapped in a *murky whirlpool*, bereft of all landmarks, in which everything comes loose, shapes are seen disconnected from their origins, everything is swallowed up in a huge white whirlpool, nothing is recognizable any longer: it is in the midst of this turmoil that all of a sudden there appears – a *what* –

What is a what? It is not a shaft. It is not a wolf. It might be a kind of peasant who will guide those gone astray, the little young man and his coachman, toward an invisible inn. And that's the beginning of the love story between Pougatchov – because it's him – and the little

Griniov. The guide who rescues people from being lost will reappear, later in the tale, in an inversed form. In historical 'reality,' the guide leads astray all of Russia, and all those who follow him, and does not lead them toward salvation. The one who, in the completely white turmoil, is a tiny black, shiny point, will dissolve, become murky, incomprehensible, yet will remain *the thing*, this obscure, unanalyzable link between the young man and Pougatchov. At the very moment of the encounter, a tremendous thing, Pushkin recounts the dream that little Griniov has in this inn where he has been rescued by the guide – the one that leads up and down, toward death and toward life: in the dream the little Griniov goes home. His mother is anxiously waiting for him because his father is going to die. In the father's bedroom the young man draws near the bed of the person he so dearly loves. Then the father gets up suddenly and pounces on the little Griniov brandishing a hatchet. We are overwhelmed by fear. At that point what the little Griniov sees is the look, at once gleaming and incredibly tender, of the paternal assassin, who turns out to be Pougatchov in person, the 'guide' who loves him and whom he loves, the crazed, bloodthirsty one, the monster of love.

Tsvetaeva takes note of the history of the two narratives and points out that Pushkin wrote *The History of Pougatchov* BEFORE he wrote *The Captain's Daughter*.

In other words, the poet is aware of who Pougatchov was when he writes his fiction. He thus paints *his* Pougatchov in glowing colors – and his is perhaps the true one. We don't know. In any case, it's the one that Russia, the peasants, and the cossacks loved, loved to invent and invented to love, as one should be loved: without telling anyone except in dreams. And for her part, Tsvetaeva–Griniov–Pushkin:

> Oh that guide – I fell in love with him right away, from the moment when, in the dream, the usurping father, the black-bearded peasant found in the bed in place of Griniov's father, looked at me gleefully. And when the peasant brandished his hatchet, when he started waving it around in every direction, I knew in advance that we – Griniov and I – had nothing to fear, and if I was entirely overwhelmed by fear, it was a dream fear, the fortunate fear of being inconsequential through and through – fortunate for me not to have fear to go through inconsequentially. (Thus in dreams we slow down – on purpose to scoff at the assassin, knowing that at the last second we'll grow wings.) And when the peasant – the monster – started to call to me tenderly, saying: 'Have no fear! . . . come let me give you my blessing! . . .' – there I was already blessed by his

blessing! . . . there I was before him, pushing toward him with all my little girl might – Griniov. – 'Now go ahead, now, go ahead! Love him!' I'm ready to burst into bitter tears because Griniov does- n't understand (Griniov is in general the tight-fisted type) that the other loves him, that he'll massacre everybody else, but that him he'll love – as if the wolf suddenly held out his paw, and this paw . . . you refused.[12]

Yes, love of the wolf is indistinguishable from love of fear. When we were little, how we loved to be scared silly! That was an extremely pure fear. The child is capable of two things at once, first to believe absolutely in the danger, and then at the same time not to believe in it. That's the way he gets his pleasure. Later we hold on to no more than half of these beliefs – it's either/or, and farewell dear wolf: either we believe absolutely in the danger, or else we don't believe in it at all.

The secret of the fortunate fear is in the strange scene in which Griniov throws himself on his dying father who is in the grandmother-wolf's bed. Today the reason the children's version of the story of Little Red Riding Hood probably has no pay-off for us is that the split between grand- mother and wolf has taken place in advance of the story's narrative. On the one hand, there's the grandmother whom Little Red Riding Hood loves and is bringing food to (but then the grandmother has been eaten by the wolf), and on the other hand, there's the wolf. When we are told this story, when Little Red Riding Hood is in the bedroom with the grandmother in bed, we children who are listening are horrified by the grandmother in that bed, because we know it's the wolf. Now, this is not right in terms of the truth of love. The truth of love is both-at-once: from one perspective, as little red riding hoods, we jump into the wolf's mouth, we think it's our grandmother, but it's no longer grandmother pure, and we love grandmother all the more so because she's the wolf – for loving a candy granny is easy; but from the other perspective, it turns out this grandmother-wolf who eats everybody up makes an excep- tion and doesn't eat us: we are the grandmother-wolf's favorite, the wolf's chosen one. Now that's the escalating value of love. There is no greater love than the love the wolf feels for the lamb-it-doesn't-eat. The other side of the scene is the paradoxical, refined, magnificent love of the wolf.

It's not difficult for the ewe to love the lamb. But for the wolf? The wolf's love for the lamb is such a renunciation, it's a Christ-like love, it's the wolf's sacrifice – it's a love that could never be requited. This wolf that sacrifices its very definition for the lamb, this wolf that doesn't eat the lamb, is it a wolf? Is it still a wolf? Isn't it a delupinized wolf, a non-wolf, an invalidated wolf? If it were a false wolf, there'd be no interest. No, we've made no mistake, this wolf is a real wolf: right up to the last second it could eat us, the axe doesn't stop hissing past us, up to the last second, with the little child's faith, true faith, we believe in the wolf and we're afraid. Then the grandmother holds out a furry paw and we are bowled over by the solemn honor. Thus the wolf, double-wolf, more-than-grandmother, sacrifices itself herself to us. And we triumph without ever having gone to battle!

Grown-ups pretend, but children get a thrill. The wolf says to the child: I'm going to eat you up. Nothing tickles the child more. That's the mystery: why does the idea that you're going to eat me up fill me with such pleasure and such terror? It's to get this pleasure that you need the wolf. The wolf is the truth of love, its cruelty, its fangs, its claws, our aptitude for ferocity. Love is when you suddenly wake up as a cannibal, and not just any old cannibal, or else wake up destined for devourment.

But happiness is when a real wolf suddenly refrains from eating us. The lamb's burst of laughter comes when it's about to be devoured, and then, at the last second, is not eaten. Hallelujah comes to mind. To have almost been eaten yet not to have been eaten: that is the triumph of life. But you've got to have the two instants, just before the teeth and just after, you've got to hear the jaws coming down on nothing for there to be jubilation. Even the wolf is surprised.

I've just described the lamb's laughter. What about the wolf? Where is its joy? I'm getting to that.

In Aeschylus's *Eumenides* the Furies pursuing Orestes, their prey, spend years saying to him: I'm going to eat you. The victim believes it, knows that at one time or another it just could happen. The horror of the situation is that it drags on and on; and the person being pursued bolts, knowing he's just a piece of meat. But in that case, it's a question of satisfying anti-love, really shattering the boundary between flesh and meat.

For us, eating and being eaten belong to the terrible secret of love. We love *only* the person we can eat. The person we hate we 'can't swallow.' That one makes us vomit. Even our friends are inedible. If we were asked to dig into our friend's flesh we would be disgusted. The person we love we dream only of eating. That is, we slide down that razor's edge of ambivalence. The story of torment itself is a very beautiful one. Because loving is wanting and being able to eat up and yet to stop at the bound-ary. And there, at the tiniest beat between springing and stopping, in rushes fear. The spring is already in mid-air. The heart stops. The heart takes off again. Everything in love is oriented toward this absorption. At the same time real love is a don't-touch, yet still an almost-touching. *Tact itself: a phantom touching.* Eat me up, my love, or else I'm going to eat you up. Fear of eating, fear of the edible, fear on the part of the one of them who feels loved, desired, who wants to be loved, desired, who desires to be desired, who knows that there is no greater proof of love than the other's appetite, who is dying to be eaten up yet scared to death by the idea of being eaten up, who says or doesn't say, but who signifies: I beg you, eat me up. Want me down to the marrow. And yet manage it so as to keep me alive. But I often turn about or compromise, because I know that you won't eat me up, in the end, and I urge you: bite me. Sign my death with your teeth.

We love, we fall into the jaws of the fire. We can't escape it.

> Open arms
> Facing forward –
> Red blaze, white birch[13]

This is the portrait of Maroussia hit at point-blank range, a portrait in green, red and white. It's the fall of Maroussia, struck by a mouth shooting off, by a shirt going off, and hit, pierced by the kid's gunshots.

That's what love is: falling into the jaws of fire. It opens up. There it is:

> The door opens,
> – Hello, everybody!
> Cheers, have a good evening!
>
> Neither gleam,
> Nor flash –
> Kid in red shirt.
> Neither ember,
> Nor blaze –
> Fire-red shirt.
>
> Greetings all around,
> Purse on the table,
> Shiny money streaming down.14

It happens so fast, much faster than lightning, so much faster than lightning that I don't know how I can tell about it. The way she does it: forcing, with gusts of wind, shots, signifiers, axe-blows, with the tiniest metrical denominator imaginable, tri-syllabically (not even in threes – in fewer than two beats), skipping causes, the effect remains, paring away, leaving out, pruning, syncopating, equivocating.

The door opens, in comes – someone? no, in comes the word – in two words –

Hello, everybody!

The telegraphic utterance, the tonic accent strikes, sets the beat.

Neither gleam,
Nor flash –

In four words, a dazzling scene of bedazzlement.

'Neither gleam nor flash' means also yes-gleam, yes-flash, that's what Maroussia thought she saw, the dazzle of the dancer and the complicity of the narration – neither feminine nor masculine, lighting effect, neither gleam nor flash then it's *kid in red shirt*, kid no article, neither the nor a,

as soon as she can, she gets rid of the semantic function, which allows the substantive to pass from the level of discourse to the level of language.

It's therefore possible to do without the article.

The a is missing. *A* kid? *A* could designate the first appearance. Once upon a time there was a kid. No. It's: Kid without a. Thus no first appearance. Kid as though he had always been there, always or forever, kid like God. – Red kid – or were(wolf)kid? There's still the shirt to cover up the wolf. O the shirt, that's what's so fascinating to the glares and the gazes – that's all that can be seen in it, just its red. A round in three times, mine, yours, his, in three persons, mine yours his, the third figures the space, the third wins, whether I dance or you dance, it's nothing just a blank. But the kid dances on fire.

The kid fires. Three times.

Mouth, shirt, eyes —
Fire! Fire! Fire![15]

All that can be seen – all that can be heard – is fire
Into which falls, open arms, the woman who is now nothing more than fuel for the blaze.

Fire! It's the order to shoot. Who gave it?
The wolf. Wolf, who are you?
The kid says:

Fire – I am,
Hungry – I am,
Fire – I am,
Ashes – I shall be![16]

A disturbing lover who tells not his name but his impulse, his appetite, his choice of object, his food

– Her I shall choose
A fresh-faced one among the fresh[17]

Time watches
Over all the graves it digs.
At the edge of the ear:
– It is I, my sleeping one![18]

It's the angelic-demonic voice of the Kid. The person who remains nameless and whose voice one hears – that's the Kid. '*It is I*' proclaims in terms of absolute intimacy that *the person who does not give his name is right now inside the person who is listening: it is I.* I read also 'It is I, my sleeping one,' as if in apposition: my sleeping one is me.

Hot cry from the womb:
– It is I, my promised one![19]

– Wolf, who are you? – Kid.
The Kid says one time:

At the edge of the ear:
– It is I, my sleeping one! . . .
Hot cry from the womb:
– It is I, my promised one!

The only one who can say *that* is the kid – and the internalized kid, the voice from the womb. Who cries? Is it the womb that utters the cry, or does the cry come from the womb? It could be the kid transformed into fruit of the womb.

No first name. Just this word, this single syllable, *Kid* (or fire, or soot), just a phoneme, a stifled sigh. One hell of a signifier this kid [*gars*] – who, being just one *l* away, if I let it slip, could sound Derrida's knell [*glas*]. Nameless kid, abrupt, sharp-edged, clear-cut at times by enjambment with hag-/gard-, playing, aggravating, flirtatious, chilling, burning, gnawing the text everywhere, leading the dance that throws you off, drives you crazy. Not counting the double-play that arises from the difference between this kid [*gars*] which literally posts a warning and, when sounded aloud, as *ga*, suppresses it.[20]

He's irresistible – the kid, the wolf, the fire. And for good reason: fire catches *before* you've even had a chance to see it, you can't get away, it bursts into flames and you're already in it, in the wolf, in the circle, in the dance, in the red, or else you're drowned in the devil's gray river. She can no longer extricate herself from him. We are born-eaten.

*

But sometimes it's the wolf that falls into the jaws of the lamb. The wolf, out of love, falls backwards into the circle of fire. It goes around so fast, it just so happens that the lamb catches the wolf, the double. A marvelous occasion for Tsvetaeva to plunge into the wolf's heart and to contemplate herself in there, she along with us as well, as in the mirror of a subtle narcissism: a mixture of heart throbs and nostalgia for our own goodness.

What ties this wolf to this lamb, she figures, is the fact that it hasn't eaten it. Painful mystery of the gift that returns through reflection: what the wolf loves in the lamb is its own goodness. It's thanks to the lamb that the wolf accedes to the plane of love – the love that gives of itself without hope, without calculation, without response, *but* that nevertheless gives *of itself*, seeing itself give of itself. The wolf given to a lamb of the Griniov type who doesn't even notice the enormity of the gift – that's really love. There remains the infinite solitude of the wolf, invisible and unrecognized except by itself. What interest does Pougatchov have in not eating the lamb? The ascetic and dangerous interest of self-love. The lover loves the beloved, which is the occasion for generous love. But thereafter – thereafter there is the aftermath. Now the wolf can no longer break away from the lamb, for the lamb retains, for better or worse, traces of the gift. That which is given in love can never be taken back. It is me my entire self that I give with the gift of love. This is why the wolf can't stop loving the lamb, the chosen one. Repository of the wolf. All of the wolf. That's how love can ruin the lover.

And this is not the end of it. What else? One more riddle: 'The black thing that loves the frail whiteness.' Me loves non-me. Othello loves Desdemona. But Desdemona loves the black thing as well. The round goes on. The lamb loves its wolf. The wolf turns all white and starts quivering out of love of the lamb. The lamb loves the wolf's fragility, and the wolf loves the frail one's force. The wolf is now the lamb's lamb and the lamb has tamed the wolf. Love blackens the lamb.

   Wolf, whom do you love?

   If only I knew! . . .

   Love – that's: it. That's id. That idself [*ça même*]. And it/id loves me [*Ça m'aime*]. And the fable is called the Wolf is the Lamb.

Notes

1 Clarice Lispector, 'A favor do medo,' in *A Descoberta do mundo* (Rio de Janeiro: Noveira Fronteira, 1987), p. 42.

2 Marina Tsvetaeva, *Mon Pouchkine*, followed by *Pouchkine et Pougatchov*, trans. André Markowicz and Clémence Hiver (Paris, 1987), p. 26.

3 *Ibid.*, p. 27.

4 *Ibid.*

5 Marina Tsvetaeva, *Le Gars* (Paris: Des femmes, 1992), p. 129.

6 *Ibid.*, p. 26.

7 *Ibid.*, p. 33.

8 Written in 1922 after having read the folktale 'The Vampire' in Afanassiev's collection.

9 *Le Gars, op cit.*, pp. 16–17.

10 Aeschylus, *Agamemnon*, from translation by Ariane Mnouchkine (New York: Viking, 1975), p. 135.

11 *Mon Pouchkine, op cit.*, pp. 32–3.

12 *Pushkin et Pougatchov, op cit.*, pp. 78–9.

13 *Le Gars, op cit.*, p. 28.

14 *Ibid.*, p. 26–7.

15 *Ibid.*, p. 28.

16 *Ibid.*, p. 29.

17 *Ibid.*, p. 28.

18 *Ibid.*, p. 109.

19 *Ibid.*, p. 110.

20 The French word '*gars*,' or 'kid,' is pronounced without sounding either the 's' or the 'r,' hence '*ga*.' Consequently, the signifier *gars*, when pronounced sounding all its phonemes means 'beware,' a warning which, when the word is pronounced ordinarily, is suppressed. (Translator's note.)

7 'Mamãe, disse ele,' or Joyce's second hand

Translated by Eric Prenowitz

I shall begin with a pair of endings:

> 16 *April:* Away! Away!
>
> The spell of arms and voices: the white arms of roads, their promise of close embraces and the black arms of tall ships that stand against the moon, their tale of distant nations. They are held out to say: We are alone. Come. And the voices say with them: We are your kinsmen. And the air is thick with their company as they call to me, their kinsman, making ready to go, shaking the wings of their exultant and terrible youth.
>
> 26 *April:* Mother is putting my new secondhand clothes in order. She prays now, she says, that I may learn in my own life and away from home and friends what the heart is and what it feels. Amen. So be it. Welcome, O life! I go to encounter for the millionth time the reality of experience and to forge in the smithy of my soul the uncreated conscience of my race.
>
> 27 *April:* Old father, old artificer, stand me now and ever in good stead.[1]

He had finished being born a man. But scarcely had he assumed his birth when he assumed also this weight in the breast: scarcely had he assumed his glory when an unfathomable experience gave him his first future wrinkle. Ignorant, worried, scarcely had he assumed masculinity when a new avid hunger was born, a painful thing like a man who never cries. Was he feeling the first fear that something was impossible? The girl was a zero in that bus at the stop, and yet, as the man which he now was, the boy all of a sudden needed to bow

This translation was first published in *Poetics Today* 17, 3(1996): 339–66.

toward this nothing, on this girl. And not even to bow at least from equal to equal, not even to bow at least so as to concede . . . But sunk into his man's kingdom, he needed her. Why? to remind himself of a clause? so that she or another would not let him go too far and get lost? so that he should feel with a start, as he was feeling, that there was a possibility of error? He needed her with hunger so as not to forget that they were made of the same flesh, this poor flesh of which, in climbing into the bus like a monkey, she seemed to have made a fatal path. Hey! but in the end what is happening to me?, he alarmed himself.

Nothing. Nothing, one mustn't exaggerate, it was just an instant of weakness and hesitation, nothing more than that, there was no danger.

Just an instant of weakness and hesitation. But within this system of hard last judgement, which does not permit even a second of incredulity or else the ideal collapses, he looked dumbfounded at the long road – and everything was now ruined and dry as if he had his mouth full of dust. Now and finally alone, he was without defense at the mercy of the eager lie with which *the others* tried to teach him to be a man. But and the message?! the message shredded in the dust which the wind carried toward the grill of the gutter. Mama, he said.[2]

Mamãe, disse ele. *Mater ait*. This is the final utterance of the last sentence of Clarice Lispector's text *The Message*. It is also the first of the sentences whose trace I will be following, a trace which is familiar and yet foreign. We all have the impression of having already heard it, but otherwise, and in another language. Mater, ait. Mater? Lapsus? No. Lapwing. Or else we have already said it. Mamãe, disse ele. A little sentence like this, at the end of a text, such a sentence to end with, is rare. What is more, it is the sentence of a 'beginner.'

Who says 'mama'? It is the infant who says this. (The Brazilian emphasizes that it is the *masculine* infant.) But how old is the infant? Ours, I mean the son that the texts we are reading give us, or else the son that we are, is a 'young man' of sixteen (Clarice Lispector) or of eighteen (James Joyce). Here we have a wee little eighteen-year-old who says: mama. Later the child could be seventy – or eighty years old. Mama, he says, the sentence does not have an exclamation point. But the fact that there is no exclamation point does not mean that there is no exclamation. What living being can say mama without making the *call* resonate more or less clearly? Whoever says 'mama' calls for help.

But one can utter a mute cry, or call without noise, or without the call tearing the air. Moreover, Clarice Lispector's text tells us that the infant man calls the mother who is not there, has never been there, has never been named in the text entitled *The Message*. But who, at the last second, literally *comes out* of the son, summoned by the call, so as to return at least to his ears.

I note that the utterance is Mamãe, *disse* ele (he *said*). And not Mama, he *cried*. In the non-cry of the saying, in this calm torment, there is a greater force, more disturbing than the panic of a cry.

But I recall that the utterance we believe we know by heart is not exactly that one. According to the tradition, the call is addressed to the father. Which tradition? The grecolatinojudeochristian tradition. Joyce's tradition. Our own. Yet here the expression *the call of the father* has called forth its other. If I say the call of the father or the call of the mother, being familiar with the use of the genitive case and its secrets, I will receive the call and its double or the call divided and reversed, the call which is addressed to the father or to the mother (they are not the same calls), and the call that the mother, the father, addresses to the son. It suffices that I say *call* or *mama* for the *address*, the destination to be forcefully inscribed: in the call (whether paternal or maternal) the addressee is understood to be *the son*. I will keep *the son* as the term common to my texts. As does Clarice Lispector in *The Message* where the word *filho, son*, very often applies to both sexes, boy and girl (even though other distinct nouns exist to say boy and girl, *rapaz, moça* . . .). Does the call always speak of the son, or is it the son who makes the call? In the texts we are going to touch on it so happens that it is always the son. Perhaps this is also our human tradition. Everywhere in all cultures, it is the son who is the hero of the call, because it's he who departs, who is parted from, detached, separated, who carries out or undergoes the separation. And it is the son who *complains about it*. Who appeals it.

I will add now another scene, another citation. It has to do with *Pater ait*.

> Stephen looked on his hat, his stick, his boots.
> *Stephanos*, my crown. My sword. His boots are spoiling the shape of my feet. Buy a pair. Holes in my socks. Handkerchief too.
> — You make good use of the name, John Eglinton allowed. Your own name is strange enough. I suppose it explains your fantastical humour.
> Me, Magee and Mulligan.
> Fabulous artificer, the hawklike man. You flew. Whereto?

Newhaven–Dieppe, steerage passenger. Paris and back. Lapwing. Icarus. *Pater, ait.* Seabedabbled, fallen, weltering. Lapwing you are. Lapwing he.[3]

Which is the son who calls the father *in Latin*? Who enters, into the text, between Newhaven and Paris, through the door of quotation? This text, indeed all of *Ulysses*, is thick with a company of quotations. Citation is the voice of the other, and it highlights the double playing of the narrative authority. We constantly hear the footsteps of the other, the footsteps of others in language, others speaking in Stephen's language or in Ulysses', I mean the book's language.

I said *citation*: the last sentence of *The Message*, in paternal (or maternal) form, is without doubt one of the most cited sentences and perhaps the most cited sentence in the world. It reminds us that we have been caught up in citation ever since we said the first words mama or papa.

Joyce took care in *Ulysses* to call papa in Latin, that is, to thus make us hear a good many messages. Among them, the following: (1) that when I call the Father, I am Latin, I am Greek, I am Icarus (and quite a few others who will be evoked), and above all I am of the *past;* (2) that through Latin I am taken back to the ecclesiastical domains; (3) that it is too late, I am dying or I am already dead. Dead, drowned, my mouth under water, I call the father in vain, and no one hears me.

In a certain sense, and the author of the *Tristia* and the *Metamorphoses* knew this well, the call for help is always grief-stricken.

There is a picture I would have liked to have shown you, the Portrait of the Stillborn Artist: it is a painting you know, Brueghel's *Fall of Icarus*. To the right of the picture or in the picture, one sees Icarus's two little pink legs emerging, perhaps he is saying papa, but if so it is under water. This picture is one of the most magnificent stories there are. In a single glance it permits us to see all the fatalities, all the destinies, human destinations and life and death in a single instant. In the relationships between measures, between the big and the small, as seen by me, what is most important, what is the biggest, what is the smallest? As seen by me, the shepherd or the plowman, nothing is more important and bigger than my furrows, my ox. And what is tragedy for me as I plow my life? Moreover, what I am saying is a tautology, to live and to plow are the same, I am in the process of living, and to my right someone is in the process of dying, I am in the process of plowing toward my East, and someone is in the process of dying to my West, and how could I integrate, in my own dimensions, tragedy (and even if one speaks to me every day of Sarajevo, or Rwanda . . .). It's not that it isn't there, it is there, but those are its dimensions: we pass each other, some go toward the left, others go toward the right, we don't meet and yet we are in the same landscape.

Let us speak of Icarus, that is to say of Daedalus, that is to say of death and of the name. The name of the father and the name of the son. Let us speak of the survival of the name.

In speaking of this father, of this son, of their names, I will only be returning to the point of departure. To the point of departure which begins *A Portrait of the Artist as a Young Man*, the epigraph taken from Ovid: *Et ignotas animum dimittit in artes*, and to the final point of departure; but a departure engenders a departure, in these texts which are related to each other, recognize each other and cite each other by the complex motif, or concept, of departure. What does it mean to depart? What does one want, what does one wish to accomplish with a departure? Does one want to depart or does one want to arrive?

In going to Berlin, Kafka would say, does one want to go to Berlin or does one want to leave Prague? Where does the departure lead Stephen Dedalus? (We know a bit about this, leaving a Dublin is perhaps a way of arriving in a Dublin.)

Let us return to our characters on the front lines of departure. And to their names. Because all of this mythical and mystical adventure is closely linked to the question of the name one carries, of the importance carried by the proper name, of the force hidden in the name. Force of the name of D(a)edalus, beneficial and malefic force. And do not forget that the name has the power to *survive*, to *outlive* the person who carries it, and thus – above all in the case of the artist – to be given over to 'the space of the epitaph.' There is nothing more and less proper to a person than the name, and nothing which carries life and death more mysteriously. The cunning Daedalus, Daidalos, has succeeded in spreading his name to every city. And above all in French where we speak commonly of daedaluses (*dédales*), without knowing that Daedalus existed. And fallen into the ranks of the common noun, he connotes no more than losing one's way. Poor Daedalus. Daedalus has become the synonym of his work: the labyrinth and vice versa.

Father and son make one or two, or heads and tails, as soon as they appear in Ovid, as Joyce saw and repeated. Indeed, ever since there has been the question of a boy being 'born a man' we repeat the path and tragedy. Daedalus does not come without Icarus. Neither does he go without him. Each one is the uncontained part of the other.

On the one hand the father is Leonardo da Vinci, he invents flight, he is both mathematician and physicist, and he does not miss the mark. On the other hand there is the son, who is the unmastered part of what must be called curiosity. There is a curiosity which brings progress or technical success; and then there is excessive curiosity, which goes hand in glove with *hubris*, with pride, with the in-addition, non-reflection, with disobedience. But one could also spend dizzying hours analyzing the scene of the sacrifice of the son to the father's desire by reading the Latin song carefully; and detecting with anxiety the strangely murderous and non-oedipal projection of the old man on to the child. The first Daedalus is the anti-Stephen Dedalus by definition:

> Meanwhile Daedalus, tired of Crete and of his long exile, was filled with longing for his own country, but he was shut in by the sea.[4]

Daedalus is also *a learned artist*. He produces works which, like all works of art, contain in fact a seed of death. Ultimately, the only people able to move about in art without risk are those who are in effect strong citizens having some authority within the art. Daedalus is the master of dead-ends *and* of evasions. He is at the turning point, at the passageway. Author of works which lead to going astray, inventor of the labyrinth; and also inventor of the antidote, maker of wings which on the one hand give man a superhuman power; and which on the other attribute to him a supplementary *genos*, a supplementary genus. Is the man who flies still and only a man? When he is a bit bird? Thus *hybrid*.

Through Daedalus, who steers from one extreme to the other, we thus have access to the passage, to the *trans*, to the crossing of borders, to the de-limitation of genuses-genders-genres and species, to construction and to deconstruction, to metamorphosis. Through Dedalus I mean a Joyce.

With the call of his name, Daedalus leads monsters, mutants, chimeras. His story is an entanglement of prison and freedom. He had constructed the labyrinth under the orders of Minos, to lock up the Minotaur; this implies also that the monster, half bull half man, was to be preserved. The Minotaur is very much a monster, but after all Icarus and Daedalus are other monsters, other human anomalies. Daedalus revealed the secret of the labyrinth's exit to Ariadne to help her save Theseus, who had been sent to confront the Minotaur in the labyrinth no one can leave. All it takes is not letting go of the thread.

This is also a lesson in reading, when you are in the labyrinth of a text, and a text *is* a labyrinth, a text which was not a labyrinth would not be a text, a labyrinth has its coherence, the rooms communicate with one another, and as a rule one cannot escape, which is a good thing, one must enter the labyrinth of a text with a thread.

But, friend of the lovers, Daedalus was punished and locked up *without thread*. His line was cut, it's the same old story of the telephone. He was thus locked up without a thread but with his son Icarus, and as always he finds the easiest way to escape what's inescapable. When one has no thread and cannot go by land, one goes by air. This is what poets do. Thus he invents human wings, he assembles feathers with wax. He needs time, because to make a sufficient collection he has to wait for birds to drop their feathers. The technical moment plunges the poet into voluptuous pleasure. This is how Ovid watches Daedalus adjust the wings:

> [. . .] he set his mind to arts never explored before, and altered the laws of nature. He laid down a row of feathers, beginning with tiny ones, and gradually increasing their length, so that the edge seemed to slope upwards. In the same way, the pipe which shepherds used to play is built up from reeds, each slightly longer than the last. Then he fastened the feathers together in the middle with thread, and at the bottom with wax; when he had arranged them in this way, he bent them round into a gentle curve, to look like real birds' wings. [. . .] When Daedalus had put the finishing touches to his invention, he raised himself into the air, balancing his body on his two wings, and there he hovered, moving his feathers up and down.[5]

Secondhand feathers. 'Mother is putting my new secondhand clothes in order.'

Yes, it's true, it is the mother – Daedalus the mother – who prepares the clothes of departure. Which are structurally secondhand. Yes, it is mother who prepares the second hand. The hand of the artist which is always second. But what is a mother? And a father? – That is the enigma. Enigma through which Joyce is going to set the thinking on genealogy reeling. After all, one can also imagine a new secondhand mother or father; and one knows that the stability of the reference to the mother, in opposition to the instability or to the improbability of paternity of which Freud spoke, has foundered over this last decade since a mother has become potentially replaceable and fictitious, surrogate. I will add that from Freud to Joyce there is also a bit of second hand concerning the theme of improbable paternity.

But before Joycefreud, Ovid had already begun to challenge the stability of the names which 'govern' us.

I will cite and comment on the wombtext of *A Portrait of the Artist* as I need it for James Joyce and because it is so beautiful:

> [. . .] he came too close to the blazing sun, and it softened the sweet-smelling wax that bound his wings together. The wax melted. Icarus

moved his bare arms up and down, but without their feathers they had no purchase on the air. Even as his lips were crying his father's name, they were swallowed up in the deep blue waters which are called after him. The unhappy father, a father no longer, cried out: 'Icarus!' 'Icarus,' he called. 'Where are you? Where am I to look for you?' As he was still calling 'Icarus' he saw the feathers on the water, and cursed his art. He laid his son to rest in a tomb, and the land took its name from that of the boy who was buried there.[6]

This is a story of name giving, and how one passes from the name of the father to the name of the son. It is the son who gives the name (and not the father). Because he is dead. Thus the dead son can be a kind of name of the father. The name of (the) father *which is not pronounced here, oraque caerulea patrium clamantia nomen. Excipiuntur aqua*, on the one hand the name of the father is engulfed in the waters to which *he* gave his name, *quae nomen traxit ab illo*, which gets its name from him, but from which one? We know there is an Icarian Sea, but after all *ab illo* could be Daedalus or Icarus. Here in the bursting forth of the name, in the circulation of the name between water and air, the names of the father and the son, and the call of the names, in the amphibology and the precipitated dislocation of times and spaces, the attribution of paternity of the name of the sea is undecidable *in* the text.

'The unhappy father, a father no longer.' *At pater infelix, nec jam pater: Icare, dixit.* In Ovid, we have here a magnificent foreshortening of the question, *What is a father?* which runs through all of Joyce's texts: what is a father, what makes the father, what is a father who is no longer father, one would need to imagine, a father father, a pre-father, a father still father, a father more or no more father, a father already no longer father, or an already no longer father, a never again father. If we were not so lazy in language, we would weave more precise and more just family ties, following Ovid's example here (the unhappy father who was already no longer father) and we would not simply say father, or mother. We could also say father-son, or son-father, or mother-son or mother-daughter. We would be sensitive to the presence of several kinds of mothers in a mother. We would come to say to ourselves, like Artaud: 'I, Antonin Artaud, am my son, my father, my mother, and myself.'

But we say: my parents, my children. But what are parents and what are children? Are there not children who are parents, is there a parental essence? Does one become parent for eternity? Once parent, will one never again be child, etc.? Our thoughts are unfortunately finite, that is to say finishing, that is to say murderous.

It is an unsoned father, already half dead and a bit deconstructed, the father-who-is-no-longer-father who says: Icarus, Icarus where are you? where must I search for you? *Icare, dixit, ubi es?* thus *he said*, not he cried. *Icare, dicebat, pennas aspexit in undis*, Icarus, he said, he perceived feathers in the waters, so he damned his art. The stripped down quality of Ovid's text and of Icarus, *of whom only feathers remain,* is extraordinary. Ovid's writing is also the writing of tragedy. Tragedy is all the more tragic in that it is sober and elliptical. The peak of tragedy is the posthumous inscription, the impossible dialogue between the still living and the scarcely dead. Icarus, he said: he saw the feathers in the water. This is the answer. Performatively.

Icare, dixit, Icarus said he, son he said, is a phrase which I will connect with Joyce's *Pater ait*, father he says. Who knows, when Daedalus the father who is no longer father says 'Icarus,' who knows if he is not calling his father, who knows if when he says 'Icarus' the situation as it is depicted in Ovid is not such, in the depths of the soul, that Daedalus is calling his father. Would the father who is no longer father, and who sees himself stripped of his child, not always be calling the father? Which one? The father that he was and that he is no longer, and the father that every child is for the father. The parent who first flies in front of the child and constantly turns around to see if the child is following, this is the parent of the early years, but then the parent's destiny is that the child should fly in front and that the child should turn around constantly to see if the parent-become-child is following.

From one fall to the other – from Icarus to Stephen, the call has changed its addressee, as we have known since *Ulysses*.

> Fabulous artificer, the hawklike man. You flew. Whereto? Newhaven–Dieppe, steerage passenger. Paris and back. Lapwing. Icarus. *Pater, ait*. Seabedabbled, fallen, weltering. Lapwing you are. Lapwing he.[7]

Rare example in literature, here Ovid's song comes back broken in two, departure in *A Portrait of the Artist* and – let us say *consequence* of the departure in *Ulysses*. Thus it is resurrection or ghostly reapparition. The drowned Icarus–Stephen reappears, a bit damp perhaps, in the library. He takes a place among the numerous ghosts that he himself calls to in this chapter. All are phantoms. Among those who are recalled and agitated we recognize father, son, brothers, uncles, the whole masculine species. But the mother?

The mother is the first-phantom, and perhaps the only real returning ghost. It is she who enters scene one:

Stephen, an elbow rested on the jagged granite, leaned his palm against his brow and gazed at the fraying edge of his shiny black coat-sleeve. Pain, that was not yet the pain of love, fretted his heart. Silently, in a dream she had come to him after her death, her wasted body within its loose brown graveclothes giving off an odour of wax and rosewood, her breath, that had bent upon him, mute, reproachful, a faint odour of wetted ashes. Across the threadbare cuffedge he saw the sea hailed as a great sweet mother by the wellfed voice beside him. The ring of bay and skyline held a dull green mass of liquid. A bowl of white china had stood beside her deathbed holding the green sluggish bile which she had torn up from her rotting liver by fits of loud groaning vomiting.

Buck Mulligan wiped again his razorblade.

– Ah, poor dogsbody, he said in a kind voice. I must give you a shirt and a few noserags. How are the secondhand breeks?[8]

*

In a dream, silently, she had come to him, her wasted body within its loose graveclothes giving off an odour of wax and rosewood, her breath bent over him with mute secret words, a faint odour of wetted ashes.

Her glazing eyes, staring out of death, to shake and bend my soul. On me alone. The ghostcandle to light her agony. Ghostly light on the tortured face. Her hoarse loud breath rattling in horror, while all prayed on their knees. Her eyes on me to strike me down.[9]

Let us return to 16 April, the date on which the departure is *declared*. As one declares war. Or as one launches an attack. (I note in passing that the use of dates gives the last pages of *A Portrait of the Artist* this air of urgency and of the concrete which makes the move to action felt.)

16 *April:* Away! Away!

It is the end and it is the beginning.

What could be stronger for a text than such an 'ending'?

It is the *Adieu.*

As is well known, Stephen's 'notes' of 26 April are from Joyce's 'first(?)-hand,' they involve a self-citation of epiphany 30, which he uses in *Stephen Hero* before reciting it a second time here, slightly altered.

As is perhaps less well known, they involve the reapparition of another adieu, that of a young man of eighteen who writes in French (he is *leaving* the Latin Quarter) – and who is named *Rimbaud*. I will recall it here:

Adieu

Autumn already! – But why yearn for an eternal sun, if we are committed to the discovery of divine light, – far from the people who die by the seasons.

Autumn. Our boat lifted up through the motionless mists turns toward the port of poverty, the enormous city with its sky stained by fire and mud. Ah! the putrid rags, the rain-drenched bread, the drunkenness, the thousand loves that have crucified me! Will she not stop at all, then, this ghoul queen of millions of souls and of dead bodies *which will be judged!* I see myself again, my skin pitted by mud and pestilence, my hair and my armpits full of worms, and even bigger worms in my heart, lying among strangers without age, without feeling . . . I could have died there . . . Frightful recollection! I abhor poverty.

And I dread winter because it is the season of comfort!

– Sometimes I see in the sky endless beaches covered with joyful white nations. A great golden ship, above me, waves its multicolored pennants in the morning breezes. I have created all festivals, all triumphs, all dramas. I have tried to invent new flowers, new stars, new flesh, new tongues. I believed I acquired supernatural powers. Well! I must bury my imagination and my memories! A great glory as an artist and storyteller swept away!

I! I who called myself a seer or an angel, exempt from all morality, I am restored to the earth, with a duty to seek, and rugged reality to embrace! Peasant!

Am I deceived? would charity be the sister of death, for me?

Finally, I shall beg pardon for having nourished myself on falsehood. Then let's go.[10]

I will not take the time to comment on it because the other Icarus, the Irishman, is calling me. But I will quickly underline several similar themes here: whiteness, the call of the open sea, invention, the fall (here *in* the earth), the call for help, etc.

Everything in the last pages of the *Portrait* is inscribed under the sign of passage if not rupture – beginning with the first takeover by force, the narrative anacoluthon inaugurated on the date of 20 March, where suddenly the journal form irrupts into the book, the *I* irrupts into the story, and 'the artist' goes from the status of character to the status of narrator.

Away! Away! is in the same movement of detachment and of interruption.

Away! is the bursting out of voice. The narrator's own voice operates an interrupting irruption, interruption-irruption which will be re-edited explicitly in what follows by the apparition of the *Voices*.

But Away! Away! twice also expresses the duplicity of the exclamation: Convocation! Revocation!

Let us listen now to what the new I who has come out of this story writes to himself *in the present*.

> The spell of arms and voices: the white arms of roads, their promise of close embraces and the black arms of tall ships that stand against the moon, their tale of distant nations. They are held out to say: We are alone. Come. And the voices say with them: We are your kinsmen. And the air is thick with their company as they call to me, their kinsman, making ready to go, shaking the wings of their exultant and terrible youth.[11]

Strange epiphany, whose strangeness will be redoubled by the *entry* which follows. In a minute we will be able to see, though just barely, that these two apparently dissimilar moments are nonetheless linked: over there and right here, afar and anear, it is a question of family. But at first it is from the angle of a defamilialization that the theme is played out. Neither father nor mother. And with roads and voices for *Kin*. Such perfect defamilialization, omission, or effacement of the parents which is not even declared, but only indicated by the substitution of *kin*. As if the family were surpassed or replaced by an archaic *genos* and which insists on fraternal consanguinity. At least for that day.

Because a few days later, and one line lower, the family comes back, in a premonition of *Ulysses*. 'On ne part pas,' Rimbaud would say.

Into the space of the domestic household, the landscape of the paragraph gathers poetic regions, crosses between land and sea, and between unknown 'divinities' and exultant youths.

What or he who speaks here is already the stranger, who comes from the other world. And he is not the only one to speak. It's a concert. 'The spell of arms and voices' – syllepsis of a metaphor – takes *arms* and *voices* at once figuratively and literally. In the second segment ('the white arms of roads, their promise of close embraces and the black arms of tall ships') the body becomes lexicalized metaphor. The tropic passion grows. Thus the arms begin to speak, in a prosopopoeia with a pressing and it seems paradoxical message:

'We are alone – come.'

But how can one say *we* are alone when the *we* already expresses the more-than-one? If not – on the occasion of the paradox – to make heard the fact that those who speak are a company of 'Loners.' 'I am alone,' these are the poet's words, we recognize them. *Aber ich bin allein,*

Hölderlin's words. Every poet's words. (1) I am alone, you who are alone come with us, this will not break the solitude. (2) Whoever says: 'I am alone' breaks the solitude and affirms it by this act of speech.

The arms speak. Discourse of the arms. Discourse of the voices. As if the voices were kinds of arms. The arms have voices. But the voices also have voices. And all these prosopopoeias remind us that for whoever has poeticizing ears there is the call.

But all of this resonates in the labyrinth of the inner ear.

Voice. Whose voice? (You would think we were already with Circe.) Voices of the *kinsmen*. Kin,[12] *genos* – tells of the common origin of consanguinity. In sum, we hear the voice of the Blood. The blood brothers of the kinsman are . . . roads with white incestuous arms. It's that all things touch one another and interchange themselves, away in the distance. And this common blood which circulates in the masts and the arms is – *the voice*.

Of *kinsmen*. Voices of 'brothers' in race, of unknown species. You are of the race of voices and of ships, say these prophets without form. We are voice brothers.

'And the air is thick with their company as they call to me, their kinsman, making ready to go, shaking the wings of their exultant and terrible youth.' Here is a superbly oneiric, coalescent construction where the syntactic amphibology prevents us from identifying who with what; a little labyrinth, with *their kinsman making ready to go* packed into the main proposition. To such an extent that the one who has not yet taken flight is already beating wings, the others' wings or the other wings.

This whole paragraph (or this verse, or this stanza) is worked on by the transferential force: the departure is already here, it propagates itself by hypallage, transferring the qualities of one subject to another, hypallage from the exultant youth to the ships. And this is how the arms become wings.

Who? There is youth and distance. And, subtly, sexual difference. White arms black arms, love, virile friendship. And what is the sex of the voices? The winged sex.

Indeed we do not forget that we have already experienced a first heralding version of this scene, at the end of chapter four. In the course of this long apocalyptic episode which took place on the beach in view of Howth Castle, we had been witness to the symbolic death of Stephen the schoolboy, to the ecstasy at the hallucinatory vision of a 'hawklike man flying sunward above the sea',[13] and to the resurrection of the soul destined through art for immortality.

It is there that the new-born, alone ('He was alone. He was unheeded, happy and near to the wild heart of life') had glimpsed his other: 'A girl stood before him in midstream, alone and still, gazing out to sea'.[14] This is an encounter which is at once real and chaste and sublimated in Dantesque concord.

During this scene which ended in *rose* and apotheosis as he 'rose,' Stephen had gathered and superimposed the triumphant and threatening promises of all his imaginary relatives, because: 'all ages were as one to him'.[15] All ages. The medieval age, the classical age, the Danish age, the Dantesque age. And all that flies and flutters was also a single great magic wing for him: the ghost of Hamlet, the ghost of Daedalus, and 'the likeness of a strange and beautiful seabird'[16] of the 'crane-like girl.'

This immense mythical material finds an airy synthesis here – and where the girl element has evaporated. This artist will depart *alone*, masculine, leaving Mother behind. Our Joyce, who always fed his work with his life, having swallowed Nora as Zeus did his Metis.

(A word about the signifier *kinsmen* which stands out here: in epiphany 30 the word which appeared was *people*. With *kinsmen*, a word of Teutonic origin, Joyce relates his hero to races that are much more ancient, more barbarian and more legendary. The *Kin* rings in the gathering of the Siegfrieds, working back from Norway's Ibsen all the way to Iceland, blood brothers, brothers by adoption and sworn brothers of the Icelandic sagas.)

The 16th of April thus goes about its preparations for the voyage in the form of a literary exercise. An old-young style, in part biblical by the anaphora of *and*; in part Rimbaudian or Verlainian.

But on 26 April, the same preparations for the same voyage take place in a familiar, familial version, with the return of the motif *away* in the domesticated maternal mode. As above, so below.

'Mother is putting my new secondhand clothes in order.' We have returned to the house. *Oikos*. Family economy, realism, poverty. Yes. But at the same time there is the *play* of the writing, and the infinite richness of the themes. Mother does the work of Daedalus here. And from all sides the theme of transmission resonates. With the very beautiful English expression *secondhand*, the idea of the heritage is introduced in all its complexity; in this case what is to be inherited is not a paternal possession, but rather what has been *cast off*. We can recognize the figure of borrowing which gives emphasis to the bitter relationship with Stephen's false brothers, in particular Mulligan in *Ulysses*.

So here is our artist who will be clothed in these garments which have been abandoned, rejected, but not given, making of him a doubled lining and the reticent inhabitant of a costume. Such that he is destined to be the kinsman of phantoms, himself a ghost who haunts a borrowed form and who is haunted by his predecessor. A single costume for two: this engenders the violent opposite of that admirable friendship which Montaigne celebrated. A friendship in which the sharing and the indivision was shared out thus: a single soul for two bodies. But to inhabit someone else's costume is to enter into the nightmarish labyrinth of alienations and of the schema of expropriation. In the first place the *new secondhand clothes* concretely introduce an element of interpretation for the powerful exile drive that animates James Joyce and Stephen Dedalus. *I do not want to belong,* they repeat. I do not want my soul to be clothed in a borrowed appearance which will phantomize me.

The entire ambition of the young man is to deconstruct the ties of kinship and of appearance and to remake for himself a sublime kinship. (The Joyce who signed his very first texts with the name Stephen Dedalus – a name which had not been lent him, but which he had seized upon and adorned himself with.)

But if borrowing hurts and humiliates, it is also the figure of an entirely different relationship. Secondhand expresses also the art of borrowing, of collecting (feathers) and of *the graft* which brings forth that 'loveliness which has *not yet* come into the world' dreamt of by Stephen.

Let us follow along the wily text. *Et ignotas animum dimittit in artes.*

'She prays now, she says, that I may learn in my own life and away from home and friends what the heart is and what it feels. Amen. So be it. Welcome, O life!' But who writes this *in the present??* Who is taking notes while she prays? All of this in free indirect style, with this confusion of the narrative authority with the character, thus of the son with the mother. Who says Amen? Who says So be it? The one translates itself into the other. The mother's prayer 'that I may learn in my own life and away from home and friends what the heart is and what it feels' returns inverted in the son's grandiloquent declaration: 'I go to encounter for the millionth time the reality of experience and to forge in the smithy of my soul the uncreated conscience of my race.'

Go learn, I will be master.

The sentences are spiced with irony. Because this Stephen is slightly undermined by Icarus's megalomania.

Dedalus the son bloated with the father uses the romantic cliché: 'Welcome, O life! I go to encounter for the millionth time the reality of experience and to forge in the smithy of my soul the uncreated conscience of my race.'

Thus the discourse of the mother in him is covered over by the discourse of the smith father *that he is. In this sentence.* Father in this sentence. And in the next calling the father: 'Old father, old artificer, stand me now and ever in good stead.' So is he a father or not a father? Both, alternately, in slippage, by the metonymies of the unconscious.

Who is calling whom in these lines of adieu? Because calls abound. Calling on notes, calling for the gods, calling to life. The call of the mother . . . However, some of them are called to help, invoked, and not even named, if not by antonomasia. Who are these clandestine companions who flank the young man with their phantomatic presence? In the last sentence we hasten to think that the 'old artificer' is Daedalus. But my colleague at the Sorbonne thinks it is the word *stead* which prevails, being the last word of the book, and perhaps the proper name – of a sort of symbolic father.

But in the *smithy* we can hear the semantic ambivalence of the *forge* resonating. Our artist will, in effect, forge truth and conscience, but simultaneously he will *forge forgeries.* These will perhaps be noble, as were the forgeries of Thoth who haunted him a bit earlier, Thoth the inventor of the fake which is writing.

Thus one can also *forge* oneself as a fake father or a fake son, that is a fabricated father . . .

Is he the smith, this boy of eighteen, who will forge the conscience of his race? But the smith is Daedalus, it is not Icarus, it is the father, not the son. As for genealogies, as for filiations, it is difficult to say in this text that Stephen sees himself or presents himself as a son. His mother says to him: go learn what the heart is, and *I* respond: I am the creator, I the son am the father of the progenitors. So in the labyrinth (in the *dédale*), the son is the father. I am the son of my mother whose father I am, I am the son-father. And this does not prevent me, the son-father, from calling for the help of the ancient father.

There is not only the Daedalus–Icarus couple, which in addition mirrors itself, reverses itself, exchanges itself in this text, but someone else who slips in here and who is imperceptible, a heroic character who forges something very particular, someone named Siegfried. This Siegfried went about as a bird a few pages earlier, in the University of Dublin. 'They crossed the quadrangle together without speaking. The birdcall from Siegfried whistled softly followed them from the steps of the porch' (Joyce 1964 [1916]: 237). Siegfried takes an underground path in the text like the old Shakespearean mole. In the Wagnerian legend, Siegfried is the fixer of the broken sword of his father, Sigmund, and after millions of attempts and difficulties he manages to resolder, to reforge, his father's sword.

Certain texts are on the one hand labyrinths, on the other forges where one performs operations like Siegfried's: one melts, like wax, one makes alloys, one resolders and rewelds.[17] Siegfried's sword is also *secondhand?* It is new because it is refounded, and at the same time it is *secondhand*. A text is necessarily secondhand and second *ad infinitum*. It is made of numerous swords which have been broken, then founded, then reforged to remake a new sword, and this is the case for Joyce's texts, into which all the world's great texts are thrown founded alloyed and remade. There is no body proper (of our culture) without the graft right from birth.

A body, a sword, a wax tablet so old and so new, *new secondhand*, this is our culture and its writing, indeed we no longer know what old means; if Daedalus and Siegfried are in the same smithy as Stephen and ourselves, how old are we? Our culture has a strange, composed, chimerical body, encrusted and grafted with philosophies, with testaments, with laws, with genesises one hundred times regenerated, it is Neualt like a Prague synagogue and it is too jungfraud to forget and not to forget that 'there is no body proper without this graft'.[18] There is no artist without castoff feathers. Everything begins with this prosthesis.

There is no simple or proper portrait of the artist as a young man.

But rather a portrait of the Old as Young man, of the Father as Son, that is to say of the son as father of the Jung as Fraud and of the Son as Mother.

It is a prosthesis and a borrowing that bring us back to Dublin, which we have never left, to the Library.

We hear in the following passage, with more or less innocent or alert ears, the footsteps of hidden names, the footsteps of survivors, depending on what we have already read:

> Stephen looked on his hat, his stick, his boots.
> *Stephanos*, my crown. My sword. His boots are spoiling the shape of my feet. Buy a pair. Holes in my socks. Handkerchief too.[19]

The theme of the *new secondhand clothes* returns enriched by amphibologies: 'Stephen looked at his hat, his stick, his boots.' Hearing this sentence, I do not know who possesses the hat that is possessing Stephen. This hat, this cane refer to a third person; I do not know any more than Stephen himself who owns the hat itself. Indeed, this is why Stephen tries to take over borrowed attributes in a stroke of poetic magnification reminiscent of Genêt. Let this bowler be my kingdom. Now he is king. Now he is knight. Who? Hamlet? Siegfried? Ephemeral illumination: it is impossible to sublimate the boots which are blistering his feet. And it is quite beautiful: with a kick this inscribes the conflict, the hostility, the complex problematic of the hated friend, the bad brother. At the same time, this telegraphic interlude again plays out the elevation and the fall, crowning and misery. Ineluctable modality of the double carriage of the name toward the heights and toward the depths always in the same movement. 'You make good use of the name [. . .]. Your own name is strange enough' says the librarian who in the first case is correct, though in the second (your own name) he gives to Caesar what is not Caesar's. 'Own,' that is the problem. 'Ourselves we do not owe,' said brother Shakespeare already. The name in question is not in fact pronounced: so it rises and makes a ghostly apparition in the text like King Hamlet.

> Fabulous artificer, the hawklike man. You flew. Whereto? Newhaven-Dieppe, steerage passenger. Paris and back. Lapwing. Icarus. *Pater, ait.* Seabedabbled, fallen, weltering. Lapwing you are. Lapwing he.[20]

This is how one departs Daedalus and one returns Icarus, one departs hawk and *en route* one 'turns' lapwing. One departs third person and one falls into second person, that is to say first person. According to the technique of the steerage passenger. Between *A Portrait of the Artist* and *Ulysses* a voyage took place outside of books, fallen between two books. This makes of Joyce's works a play in several acts reminiscent of Shakespeare, with an unfulfilled voyage. Just like that of Hamlet who leaves Denmark only to return. But could this be the other lapwing??

At this point my grafted text speaks Latin and says: *Pater, ait.* I believe that Icarus is speaking. And that this is Ovid's voice. Yes, but in the *Metamorphoses*, I find: *Icare, dixit.* It is the father and not the son who calls softly. Indeed the son has called the father, no, *the name of the father*, but under water. They call themselves, each other. The two of them. And they do not hear each other, themselves.

But this call alerts us, we recall a younger and older mouth which says the name of the father and complains. It is Christ. *Eli Eli lema sabaqthani* he says, and there is no response. Father, why have you let me down? We are the forsaken. Who are we when this is what we call out? And we are always sounding Christ's cry.

I am darning like Stephen's mother, and I would say that this is the cry of the nursling, it is the nursling who is forsaken by the mother, who is dropped in birth, it is as if there were a sort of ancient and impossible cry of the trauma of birth. What is splendid here is that this is said to the father: why have you let me fall, while in general we say this to the mother. The sensation we have when we are abandoned, and against which we protest, affects us more as the abandonment by the mother than as the abandonment by the father. When one is abandoned, one feels one's orphanage in relation to coming into the world, in relation to the substrate, to the uterine matrix, even if it is a man who abandons.

Returning to Clarice Lispector, you will understand why I have compared *Pater, ait* to the last sentence of *The Message*: Mother, he said, *Mama, said he*. Clarice Lispector knows that it is the mother one calls, or that there is calling of the mother, she knows it with a poetic knowledge, and she knows it also because she knows Joyce very well. After all, her first text is the portrait of the artist as a young woman, *Near to the Wild Heart*, which is also a *Bildungsroman*. According to what she said, she named it thus because a friend told her that it was reminiscent of *A Portrait of the Artist as a Young Man*. Clarice Lispector says that she had not read Joyce at the time, but that the title of her book is indeed a citation from *A Portrait of the Artist*. Her first book thus calls on a *kinsman*. After the fact, she owed it to Joyce all the same to read *A Portrait of the Artist*. And for whoever has a bit of memory, the good wax, the kind which does not melt, which does not approach the sun, in this wax there is inscription, or engraving, of the artistic structures of kinship, which Joyce labored over, worked on, reinscribed so much.

Should we therefore attribute to Joyce the paternity of certain themes we find activated in Clarice Lispector? For example, the theme of initiation? of passage? of apprenticeship? No. These themes which are familiar to Joyce scholars belong – and this is what is exciting – originally, equally, but with a startling difference to the world of Clarice Lispector. We have much to learn from these differences between resemblances.

It is in this way that the story called *The Message* relates in a dense and dazzling form the experience of initiation–detachment–departure toward the age *called* man–woman, of these two inseparable entities the boy with the girl. Inseparable in what we can call the prehistoric age, so as to make themselves, to rub themselves the one against the other, leading to a separation by differentiation. Inseparable at first, and above all the two of them 'artists,' both destined for poetry, like Stephen. How each one is a bit the other, how each one takes the other a bit for him and herself, how each one is confused, is torn, in a rich sequence of alliances, of conjunctions, of disjunctions, of dislocations.

But here the metamorphosis is possible only by a dual movement.

> [. . .] they used each other to practice for initiation; they used each other impatiently, the one with the other trying out the way to beat wings so as to be able at last – each one alone and free – to give the

great solitary flight which would also signify the adieu of the one from the other.[21]

This *Message* is very much Clarice's message. The experience Stephen speaks of: 'I go to encounter for the millionth time the reality of experience,' yes it is true, every day we encounter for the millionth time the experience which is the first one, because it's the millionth, but it's the first on this particular day. Thus what Clarice's text does is to work at the message for the millionth time, it is the millionth message, but received for the first time, always just as enigmatic, and such that it will bring our characters to a moment of revelation which tears from them this unbursting cry which will not be *Pater, ait*, but rather *Mater, ait, Mama, he said.*

Clarice reminds us, after Kafka, that we cannot hope to receive the message; the person who will receive the message must not expect it; if it is waited for, it does not arrive. One cannot have a voluntarist attitude. The message arrives on condition that one does not wait for it, it arrives *unhoped-for, the goal attained unexpectedly.*

So the message arrives unexpectedly, on condition that it be unhoped-for, and on condition that the receiver be receptive, that he be ready (*pron-to* in Brazilian). But this is not to be ready like the schoolboy in the morning or like the soldier; it is to be the *place* capable of receiving, prepared, without being voluntarily prepared, but having been prepared in a good passivity, by dint of looking and of not knowing what one is looking for, by dint of stamping the ground, of getting edgy, of trampling, of knocking against things without knowing, in a sort of anguished openness, because one does not know what for, without anticipation, without forecast, without prediction, and then the message can arrive:

> And never, never did anything arrive which would have finally ended the blindness with which they extended their hands and which would have made them ready for the destiny which waited impatiently for them, and would have made them finally say adieu for ever.[22]

When I am sixteen years old, I do not know that destiny is waiting impatiently for me. But, and this is sublime, as in Brueghel's painting, while I am there with my wings, perhaps the plowman or the shepherd or I the painter see something Icarus with his wings does not see: destiny. It is destiny which waits for me, I do not wait for it. And destiny (we are speaking Greek, but how can we do otherwise), destiny will arrive, but it will arrive when I am ready. It will arrive. He will arrive. We recognize the gaping forewarning of Messianism.

> Perhaps they were so ready to detach themselves the one from the other like a drop of water about to fall . . .[23]

One must manage to detach one's selves the one from the other like *a single* drop of water. Which means that it is not easy. It is in falling that the drop of water will detach itself the one from the other. Carried by its own weight. Like a tear.

> . . . and they only waited for something which would symbolize the plenitude of *anguish* to be able to separate themselves. Perhaps, ripe like a drop of water, they had provoked the event of which I will speak.[24]

The detachment and the fall (of the tear, of the drop, of the child) happens when the subject has arrived at maturity. Maturity and anguish go together and change places.

> The message? But what message? That is the enigma.
>
> The first condition is the dispatch of the dispatch. The message is not necessarily a letter, or at least the letter is not necessarily composed of letters. There are substitutes for letters. The message arrives. It travels. It is a traveler. Let us say that the cannonade, the arrow, all that is sent without voice and by air or by sea mail, all that travels with a direction and which is at once mute and extremely eloquent, is a message. One sends messages to oneself hidden in the form of symptoms. Stephen is constantly sending himself these. For the moment I am working here rather on the message coming from a foreign elsewhere, it could be my own elsewhere, and which comes bringing what is called so beautifully in French: *une nouvelle*, news, something unknown, which at the same time ought to be decipherable in one way or another. The second condition is thus that the addressee be capable of receiving the message.
>
> This text warns us: I am sending you a message. To start with I am called *The Message*, which is already a message, and then I send you a message.
>
> In the end I also constitute the message through my own reading. If I receive, if I read, if I perceive something given to me to read in French or English and taking this form: the message, perhaps I will not react. If, however, I line up the following in a translating game: *Le Message / A Mensagem / (The Message)*, I will perhaps be sensitized to the grammatical

gender: in French the message is masculine, in English neutral, while in Brazilian it is feminine.

> And he had seen her, all full of impotent love for humanity, climbing like a monkey into the bus – and then he saw her sit quiet and composed, readjusting her blouse while waiting for the bus to start . . .[25]

Here we are with this text *The Message*, a bit in the same situation, hesitating or feeling uncertainty and the origin of uncertainty, which is the mystery of sexual differences, ever since the beginning of the text. And what's more the text is unabashed, this is not hidden, it is incessantly reinscribed, re-edited, it is constantly a question of sex, and at the same time in a slightly unexpected way, not entirely classical. When the word sex appears, neat and clean, it is not always in a form or a place that is obvious and familiar to us. There are words which make sex, brutally. Not only is sexual opposition or sexual difference or sexual indifferentiation in the text on every page, but what's more there are slightly unusual sexes, for example new sexes; sometimes the new sex is a word, sometimes the sex begins to speak. In the stroke of a wing we find our young man in the process of being born – in Brazil. In the process of being born what? Bird? Artist? Man? No. *A* man. A singular, indeed masculine individual, and a poet.

> While she went off skimming the wall like an intruder, already almost the mother of the children she would have one day, her body anticipating the submission, a body sacred and impure to bear. The boy watched her, astounded at having been tricked for so long by the girl, and almost smiled, almost shook the wings which were finishing to grow. I am a man, the penis said to him in obscure victory.[26]

One would think here that a boy is not born unto his destiny without wings. But of course, detachable wings. I will only follow here, for lack of space, the boy's voyage, because he is our Icarus. And because it is he who calls mama. He who could not be born a man without going, like Stephen, through Mother.

Here he is beating his wings like the bird at the edge of the nest. But no. It is not he. It is his penis which has wings. And what's more, the penis speaks. It speaks Brazilian, it says I and it says I in the place of and addressing itself to the I. 'I am a man,' these are the words of the penis, not of the boy. There is a group of subjective authorities which constitute the 'boy.' Joyce distinguishes soul, body, clothing. For Clarice Lispector these are *all the parts of bodies*, the sensitive interior body which expresses itself in sweat, in heartbeats, and the other one, which on its feet has size 44 shoes. And among all these emanations of the ego, there is one which is the penis, and which says: I am a man. All of the boy does not say I am a man. Clarice Lispector works on the exact location of places of enunciation. This text permits us to recall that messages are sent from, they originate in the different mouths of the different regions of the body. The penis says I am a man, with pride. The penis addresses itself to its chief. It is a very limited message. I do not know what the heart says.

But the message? Where is it? The last paragraph is going to arrive and still no message? The sublime last paragraph comes after a moment of anguish for the boy:

> [. . .] but in the end what is happening to me?, he alarmed himself.
>   Nothing. Nothing, one mustn't exaggerate, it was just an instant of weakness and hesitation, nothing more than that, there was no danger.
>   Just an instant of weakness and hesitation.[27]

The repetition almost inverts the meaning of the remark. It has passed, and it returns. It was nothing, well no, quite precisely it was *nothing*. *Nada*. *Nada*, the other name of the girl. What happens to him is this *nothing* which is everything.

> But within this system of hard last judgment, which does not permit even a second of incredulity or else the ideal collapses, he looked dumbfounded at the long road – and everything was now ruined and dry as if he had his mouth full of dust. Now and finally alone, he was without defense at the mercy of the eager lie with which *the others* tried to teach him to be a man. But, and the message?! the message shredded in the dust which the wind carried toward the grill of the gutter. Mama, he said.[28]

End of story.

But, and the message?! Whose cry is this?
Mine, yours, the narrator's, and the boy's. After all, this story was called *The Message*. It promised. And here it ends, with its mouth full of

dust, and it has not given me the message?? We're not really going to finish, to die perhaps, without having received the message?

And the message?

Alarum! we have slept five thousand years and all of a sudden the text cries: *And the message?!* The question is an answer. The form is elliptical. The *and* presupposes interlocution, presupposes dialogue, presupposes that something has preceded. But what has preceded? We have dealt with many mysteries in the story, and all of a sudden there arrives this *and the message?!* which indicates to us that the message arrives *in supplementary position.* Maybe it has always been in supplementary position in the text. I give a start because I had forgotten. Recollection is a start.

What makes me wake with a jump: 'Just an instant of weakness and hesitation.' There is a crack, it is this moment of anguish and agitation for the boy, who realizes, once he is born separate from the girl, that *he needs her*, the woman, 'sunk,' as he is, 'into his kingdom.' But we are 'within this system of hard last judgment.' It is a fortified system, which permits not an instant of weakness, 'which does not permit even a second of incredulity.' We have seen this before, it is the 'phallocratic system.' This is how Clarice Lispector, who did not think in terms of phallogo-centrism, who does not belong to what is already the heritage of thought and language of our half century, this is how she conceives of it: a 'system of hard last judgment, which does not permit even a second of incredulity.' The phallogocentric system is a fragile system, which does not stand for hesitation, for incredulity, not even for a second: a second would suffice for the entire edifice to crack. This is what is called resistance to castration, a gigantic bastion, but it can fall in a second; therefore this second must not take place. What is described rapidly for us here is the condition of the subsistence and even of the survival of the hard masculine and phallocratic system. What is it that one must never approach? What is it that causes the fall of Icarus? On what does the solidity of phallicity depend?

'Just an instant of weakness and hesitation. But within this system of hard last judgment,' which he is in, which he lives in like a fortified tower, 'which does not permit even a second of incredulity or else the ideal collapses, he looked dumbfounded at the long road.' There was a second. The road we have already seen, the road where there was the sphinx, etc., 'and everything was now ruined and dry as if he had his mouth full of dust.' There is confusion by metonymy between the road and the mouth, the road and his body proper. And we may remember 'this poor flesh of which, in climbing into the bus like a monkey, she seemed to have made a fatal path.' The path of all flesh which is dust.

Here he is with his mouth full of dust, as if that instant where he had seen the girl – who will one day be a mother – was sufficient to give him a taste of death, not of his own death, but of the destiny of every human being, which is dust. 'He looked at the long road' and 'his mouth full of dust.' He looked at the mouth full of dust. With his mouth full of dust. What he takes into his eye he takes into his mouth.

And then we have the tragic moment of this text: 'Now and finally alone,' without her, but without her he is 'without defense.' Such are the paradoxes of resistance; he defends himself from being with her, but alone he is without defense against everything, 'at the mercy of the eager lie with which *the others* tried to teach him to be a man.' In the ambivalence of solitude, he wants to be without her, but without her he is with 'the others,' whom he does not want. So what can be done?

At this very moment the text remembers in an explosion, *But, and the message?!* It is now that we must latch on and try to hear if there is a message, what message. 'The message shredded in the dust which the wind carried toward the grill of the gutter. Mama, he said.' The last two sentences of the text are nonverbal. 'And the message?' Response: 'The message shredded . . .' The message is that the message has no verb, the message does not have a word, the message is not, the message is without being, I cannot even say the message *is* shredded. The carried off message, the wind, the dust message, toward the grill of the gutter. Shades of Ecclesiastes. In linguistics, the message is the signified; now the signified is just that: shredded in the dust carried off by the wind. In the logocentric tradition, the message is pure speech, revelation. The message is treated in the poetic mode as a letter in its materiality; but in fact, in its concrete materiality a message has two meanings, it is on the one hand the content, and on the other hand the container, or else, the message, that is the content, is the shredded container. The message: the container shredded in the dust which the wind carries toward the grill of the gutter. You want a message: here it is, says Ecclesiastes: and there is no message. In other words, it's a message. And here is what it gives as a response – it gives: Mama.

Mama, said he. This last sentence is without exclamation point. It is the first time in the story that we find the interpolated clause *he said*; it is also the first word of the nursling. The last word of the text is this *he* (Mama, said he) of the narrative authority. It is the he of a dying person. The he of Icarus who wants to survive. And then *Mama*, to end with. A small boy's word. But where is mama? At the end of this text we do not know what it is the boy names mama. Mama calls what or whom? Perhaps the message, perhaps the girl, perhaps the dust, perhaps the road. We do not know. Who is mama? We are in dust. It is as if this last word were saying to us the word which is uttered both by the person being born and by the person dying. Clarice changed the message. As if finally what one could hear is that even in a civilization that wants to conform to the inflexible system which allows not a second of incredulity, and where the woman seen from behind by the man is moved to cower along the wall, even here, being alone is no solution, and what makes itself felt stronger than everything at the very last minute, is the need at least to name mama. To avow. To recognize that the *one* needs the *zero*.

This is because the zero is not the nonvalue we think it is. The originary zero (zero comes from the Arabic *sifron*, the cipher, the number) is the key cipher, the one which permits the writing of numbers with the notation of position. To write 10, 100, 1000 we use the same numbers, but the ciphers have different values according to their position in the writing. If I want to say 100 I put the 1 in third position from right to left. Thus I need a first and a second position, I need a position *marker*. The 0 was introduced at first as an empty and necessary position. It is a *space*. Originally zero is not a number, but a marker of space. I transpose my zero in the omnibus and in life. And this is what the boy called *nada*, which is the key to the world for the one. The girl is a nothing which changes the value of the 1 according to its position.

Everything began with zero. Zero is how much there is when there isn't any. When there isn't any, there is, nonetheless. This is what permits us to conceive of the father already no longer father, and the mother not yet mother.

Now I could tell you of the birth of Zero in Babylon, but that would be another story . . .

Notes

1 James Joyce, *A Portrait of the Artist as a Young Man* (New York: Viking, 1964 [1916], pp. 252–3.
2 Clarice Lispector, 'A mensagem', in *Felicidade clandestina* (Rio de Janeiro: Nova Fronteira, 1981 [1971]) pp. 140–1.

> *Ele tinha acabado de nascer um homem. Mas, mal assumira o seu nascimento, e estava também assumindo aquele peso no peito: mal assumira a sua glória, e uma experiência insondável dava-lhe a primeira futura ruga. Ignorante, inquieto, mal assumira a masculinidade, e uma nova fome ávida nascia, uma coisa dolorosa como um homem que nunca chora. Estaria ele tendo o primeiro medo de que alguma coisa fosse impossível? A moça era um zero naquele ônibus parado, e no entanto, homem que agora ele era, o rapaz de súbito precisava se inclinar para aquele nada, para aquela moça. E nem ao menos inclinar-se de igual para igual, nem ao menos inclinar-se para conceder . . . Mas, atolado no seu reino de homem, ele precisava dele. Para quê? para lembrar-se de uma cláusula? para que ela ou outra qualquer não o deixasse ir longe demais e se perder? para que ele sentisse*

em sobressalto, como estava sentindo, que havia a possibilidade de erro? Ele precisava dela com fome para não esquecer que eram feitos de mesma carne, essa carne pobre de qual, ao subir no ônibus como um macaco, ela parecia ter feito um caminho fatal. Que é! mas afinal que é que está me acontecendo?, assustou-se ele.

Nada. Nada, e que não se exagere, fora apenas um instante de fraqueza e vacilação, nada mais que isso, não havia perigo.

Apenas um instante de fraqueza e vacilação. Mas dentro desse sistema de duro juízo final, que não permite nem um segundo de incredulidade senão o ideal desaba, ele olhou estonteado a longa rua – e tudo agora estava estragado e seco como se ele tivesse a boca cheia de poeira. Agora e enfim sozinho, estava sem defesa à mercê da mentira pressurosa com que os outros tentavam ensiná-lo a ser um homem. Mas e a mensagem?! a mensagem esfarelada na poeira que o vento arrastava para as grades do esgoto. Mamãe, disse ele.

3 James Joyce, *Ulysses* (London: Bodley Head, 1960 [1934]), p. 270.

4 Ovid, *Metamorphoses*, translated by Mary M. Innes (Harmondsworth: Penguin, 1985 [1955]), book VIII, vv. 183–5. All English versions of the *Metamorphoses* are from this translation, which has been slightly modified throughout.

> *Dædalus interea Creten longumque perosus*
> *Exilium tactusque loci natalis amore,*
> *Clausis erat pelago.*

5 Ibid., vv. 188–202.

> *{. . .} et ignotas animum dimittit in artes,*
> *Naturamque novat. Nam ponit in ordine pennas,*
> *A minima cœptas, longam breviore sequenti,*
> *Ut clivo crevisse putes: sic rustica quondam*
> *Fistula disparibus paulatim surgit avenis.*
> *Tum lino medias et ceris alligat imas,*
> *Atque ita compositas parvo curvamine flectit,*
> *Ut veras imitetur aves.*
> *{. . .}*
> *Postquam manus ultima cœptis*
> *Inposita est, geminas opifex libravit in alas*
> *Ipse suum corpus, motaque pependit in aura.*

6 *Ibid.*, vv. 225–35.

> *{. . .} Rapidi vicinia solis*
> *Mollit odoratas, pennarum vincula, ceras;*
> *Tabuerant ceræ; nudos quatit ille lacertos*
> *Remigioque carens non ullas percipit auras,*
> *Oraque cærulea patrium clamantia nomen*
> *Excipiuntur aqua; quæ nomen traxit ab illo.*
> *At pater infelix, nec jam pater: 'Icare,' dixit,*
> *'Icare,' dixit 'ubi es? Qua te regione requiram?'*
> *'Icare,' dicebat, pennas aspexit in undis,*
> *Devovitque suas artes, corpusque sepulchro*
> *Condidit, et tellus a nomine dicta sepulti.*

7 Joyce, *Ulysses*, p. 270.

8 *Ibid.*, pp. 4–5.

9 *Ibid.*, pp. 10–11.

10 Arthur Rimbaud, *Une Saison en enfer/A Season in Hell*, translated by Enid R. Peschel (New York: Oxford University Press, 1973 [1873], pp. 102–5.

Adieu

L'automne déjà! – Mais pourquoi regretter un éternel soleil, si nous sommes engagés à la découverte de la clarté divine, – loin des gens qui meurent sur les saisons.

L'automne. Notre barque élevée dans les brumes immobiles tourne vers le port de la misère, la cité énorme au ciel taché de feu et de boue. Ah! les haillons pourris, le pain trempé de pluie, l'ivresse, les mille amours qui m'ont crucifié! Elle ne finira donc point cette goule reine de millions d'âmes et de corps morts et qui seront jugés! Je me revois la peau rongée par la boue et la peste, des vers plein les cheveux et les aisselles et encore de plus gros vers dans le cœur, étendu parmi les inconnus sans âge, sans sentiment . . . J'aurais pu y mourir . . . L'affreuse évocation! J'exècre la misère.

Et je redoute l'hiver parce que c'est la saison du confort!

– Quelquefois je vois au ciel des plages sans fin couvertes de blanches nations en joie. Un grand vaisseau d'or, au-dessus de moi, agite ses pavillons multicolores sous les brises du matin. J'ai créé toutes les fêtes, tous les triomphes, tous les drames. J'ai essayé d'inventer de nouvelles fleurs, de nouveaux astres, de nouvelles chairs, de nouvelles langues. J'ai cru acquérir des pouvoirs surnaturels. Eh bien! je dois enterrer mon imagination et mes souvenirs! Une belle gloire d'artiste et de conteur emportée!

Moi! moi qui me suis dit mage ou ange, dispensé de toute morale, je suis rendu au sol, avec un devoir à chercher, et la réalité rugueuse à étreindre! Paysan!

Suis-je trompé? la charité serait-elle sœur de la mort, pour moi?

Enfin, je demanderai pardon pour m'être nourri de mensonge. Et allons.

11 Joyce, *A Portrait . . .*, p. 252.

12 Etymology: Old English: *cyn.* Old Teutonic: *Kunjo* – to engender, to beget.

13 Joyce, *A Portrait . . .*, p. 169.

14 *Ibid.*, p. 171.

15 *Ibid.*, p. 168.

16 *Ibid.*, p. 171.

17 One melts what? Swords? Instruments of the mastery of phallic signs perhaps. Signatures.

18 Jacques Derrida, *Politiques de l'amitié* (Paris: Galilée, 1994), p. 213.

19 Joyce, *Ulysses*, p. 270.

20 *Ibid.*

21 Lispector, 'A mensagem', pp. 128–9.

> *{. . .} usavam-se para se exercitarem na iniciação; usavam-se impacientes, ensaiando um com o outro o modo de bater asas para que enfim – cada um sozinho e liberto – pudesse dar o grande vôo solitário que também significaria o adeus um do outro.*

22 *Ibid.*, p. 131.

> *E nunca, nunca acontecia alguma coisa que enfim arrematasse a cegueira com que estendiam as mãos e que os tornasse prontos para o destino que impaciente os esperava, e os fizesse enfim dizer para sempre adeus.*

23 *Ibid.*, p. 132.

> *Talvez estivessem tão prontos para se soltarem um do outro como uma gota de água quase a cair {. . .}*

24 *Ibid.*

> *{. . .} e apenas esperassem algo que simbolizasse a plenitude da* angústia *para poderem se separar. Talvez, maduros como uma gota de água, tivessem provocado o acontecimento de que falarei.*

25 *Ibid.*, p. 140.

> *E vira-a, toda cheia de impotente amor pela humanidade, subir como um macaco no*

ônibus — e viu-a depois sentar-se quieta e comportada, recompondo a blusa enquanto esperava que o ônibus andasse . . .

26 *Ibid.*, p. 139.

Enquanto ela saiu costeando a parede como uma intrusa, já quase mãe dos filhos que um dia teria, o corpo pressentindo a submissão, corpo sagrado e impuro a carregar. O rapaz olhou-a, espantado de ter sido ludibriado pela moça tanto tempo, e quase sorriu, quase sacudia as asas que acabavam de crescer. Sou homem, disse-lhe o sexo em obscura vitória.

27 *Ibid.*, p. 141.

28 *Ibid.*

Going off writing

8   Unmasked!

Translated by Keith Cohen

> The eagle, the vulture, the black vulture, the red kite, any kind of
> black kite, any kind of raven, the horned owl, the screech owl, the
> gull, any kind of hawk, the little owl, the cormorant, the great owl,
> the white owl, the desert owl, the osprey, the stork, any kind of
> heron, the hoopoe and the bat.
>
> (Leviticus, 11:13–19)

These are the birds that you shall revile, those that shall not be eaten, as
they are unclean for you. These are impure, do not defile yourselves by
eating them.

And the woman who becomes pregnant and gives birth to a son will be
ceremonially unclean for seven days, and she must wait thirty-three days
to be purified from her bleeding. She must not touch anything sacred. But
if it is a child of female sex that she gives birth to, even worse, for two
weeks she will be unclean, and she must wait sixty-six days before being
unsoiled from her bleeding.

'Birds, women, writing,' as I read the chapter from Leviticus, form a
series of equivalencies. A very poetic chapter from Leviticus presents me
with a long strange list of what is prohibited and what is allowed, you
are sacred, you are defiled – oh, the interminable inventory of abomina-
tions. In the anguish-producing dictionary of species of the air the
verdict is returned. Here are species that I never watched out for which
are called *unclean*.

For a long time I've been dreaming of the *uncleanliness* of the stork, am
I really going to have to stay away from it?

I'm not associating birds, women and writing because it's a game. I see
clearly that there is a no-man's-land (*imundus*), a park of the cursed, a

'Démasqués!' was first published in Michel de Manessein (ed.), *De l'égalité des sexes*
(Centre National de Documentation Pédagogique, 1995): 73–80.

reservation hated by man-made decrees where these species of birds are found that I for one honor and cherish. Birds, women and that literature I call 'writing,' the noblest in my view, a free traveler along edges and abysms, the one that confers upon the language it traverses all its primordial strangeness.

The one I love goes off willingly to travel down into what Genêt called 'the lower depths,' others say 'the grottoes,' down into the most hidden, most elusive regions, the most difficult to work, the most sensitive to the touch, down into the unconscious, and the bodily passions. They can be reached by borrowing the ladder of writing that goes down to the roots.

That writing suffers in fact the fate of birds, women, the unclean. Because it runs the risks of its truths, because it makes its way into places where danger grows – there are few people there – it is joyfully received only by 'people whose souls are already shaped,' as Clarice Lispector says: 'People who know that one's approach to each thing is made gradually and painstakingly – including the passage across the opposite of what one is approaching. Those people who, alone, will understand very slowly that this book takes nothing away from anyone. The character of G.H., for example, gave to me little by little a difficult joy; but it was a joy.'

Why is there such a great conflict between these birds and the others? The others have the feeling in fact that something is being taken away from them. While actually nothing is being taken away from them, rather one wishes to give them something. But how is that?

Let's switch continents: let's follow Gandhi. How he is *hated* in India today, as yesterday. He died as a result. It's true, he had a portion of the Indians with him, mostly those *on the bottom*. He didn't demand, he didn't request. But he did, and he showed what he did. So, many experienced this action as an offense to their non-action. Love the supposed 'lower depths' and you'll see that the words that make the law are deceiving.

But what disgust we feel upon pronouncing the word *unclean*, we who are taught disgust. And yet 'unclean' means simply (in no-man's-land) not clean. And that the world is defined as being clean. One stroke of a word, and a whole Economy has established its rigorous measures over the universe.

But what does not-clean mean? – none of these mixed dishes, undisguised, unprepared, not transformed in appearance so as to become edible. Certain things, creatures, actions have remained raw, alive, ever since the moment of creation. 'They have continued to be the root,' divines Clarice Lispector. The root is twisted, doubled up, entangled, it digs with all its force into the ground, evil and good happily mingled, before the tree with two separate halves, it is humble (*humilis*) for it knows that nothing is simple, that it is itself not simple, thought is a struggle with itself, one cannot reach, but one can stretch, from the two forces together springs forth *the moment*. And this energy is joy.

Now, it is joy that is prohibited – the thing that escapes all economies. It is with joy that I am beside myself. In the non-self ether of the earth, down in the depths.

I do not understand people's disgust for roots, or their fear of joy. I do not understand that insidious joyless thing called misogyny. I have tried hundreds of times, for hundreds of years, to understand why the eagle, woman, the stork, the poetry of upper and lower depths are things they can't swallow. In vain.

And why when the World started to recount its history there was already in the voice of narration the harsh stress on misogyny, and why there is no memory without this poison.

Who then could have invented 'justified' hatred, the right to hate? And all these churches and religions that are built on the rock of hatred, bastions of the World against everything that they (the editors of Bibles) call '*unclean.*' First there were the Bibles, fathers, sons and grandsons, those magnificent apocalyptic monsters, who do not hide, no, they pride themselves on the triumphs of unjust, criminal kings. On the one hand, they love David, the handsome king, killer, for the sake of adultery, of Uriah, the loyal soldier, and on the other hand, they stone adulterous women.

But who, then could have written their Bibles and their Korans? The book with everything mixed together, Moses and Job with David, the just and the unjust alike?

And amidst the assemblage of just heroes and criminal heroes, all male, who, then, which man – which woman – could have slipped in amidst this clash of arms, angers, incests, crimes and punishments, the minuscule and sublime garden of the *Song of Songs*? One thousandth part of the whole is reserved for indigenous love. From this garden where he and she give of each other totally, one as great as the other is beautiful, one as powerful as the other is tender, is descended the line of equally loving couples.

A thin, fragile genealogy doomed from one end to the other to a tragically realistic fate: those two are intolerable. The rest of you, strangers whom love brings into harmony, you are abominable to a world in which discord and divisiveness reign. Return then to obscurity, you Tristans and Isoldes, you Romeos and Juliets, get out, Paolo and Francesca, trespassers without visas, anomalies, mistakes, deviations of the imagination, outlaws, Bible-outcasts, return to obscurity Jan and Jennifer, there is no place on our continents for this irreducible twosome.

The Bibles never died thereafter, and they engendered most of the books we read. And today fierce hatred is still authorized and naturalized as human. 'Me, me, me, me me me,' says hatred. Or rather: memememe . . . so how could it ever get in a 'you?'

Most humans but not all, most books, except for a few. For there are 'the happy few,' a small number, the miracles, a handful of charming grains of sand in the desert of millennia. The secret guardians of the inestimable richness in being two different yet equal beings in terms of strengths and differences. Both, as much one as the other, equally mysterious. All those who love and who think, who think and who think about loving, know that there exist during every period a few clandestine beings, born to watch over the little double flame, that it doesn't go out. Sparks in the darkness. Why do you keep watch, while the human tribe sleeps across the earth, indifferent to misfortunes, to wars, to joys, to massacres? Asks the watcher. There has to be someone, Kafka answers. Watchers, prophets of the present, agents for the most arduous, most dangerous cause there is: to love the other, even before being loved. Without waiting, without counting. The cause of 'you';

No, poets – real poets – do not hate the other, it's impossible, how could they give up half their language, why would they want to cut their tongue in two and spit out one half? Those philosophic lovers who live in the forest of languages cannot be in favor of closing the borders and ejecting one word out of every two. But what about misogynist poets, are there some such just the same? Ah yes, poor guys, they are half-poets. They write Portraits of Mistresses with a suicidal ink. For one kills oneself to kill.

Stay away from us, you women, say most of those Males.

Let's stick with men, with smokers, with brothers. What clubs, boudoirs, swimming parties, pubs, reserved temples! There are even countries where the sea water is cut off to avoid contact. 'Women not admitted. Gentlemen only.' But is it love among men – or rather friendship – that weaves the bonds of these fraternities? No, of course not, it's war. Yes, but war is still an agreement among brothers to kill one another. History, as it has been proudly recounted, is the sum of all the fratricides. Women are not even counted among the dead. They were sent off every which way with the children and the sick in the genocides that History sweeps behind its door. Even death is not shared equally. Duel for men, tanks against tanks, planes against planes. For the women, the stake, just ashes in the Seine.

But that's all Helen's fault, say the Bibles.

That's what the wicked old men in the chorus of the *Agamemnon* cackle. Everything is her fault, and the fault of her name. Such is the stress of the Ancients. It is She-to-be-hated [*Elle-haine*] who sinks the ships, dooms the men, takes the towns.

Ho! Mad Helen, who single-handedly destroys so many lives in Troy.

Then we hear the immortal voice of Aeschylus (author of the *Agamemnon*) responding to the blind old men he has created:

> Direct not your curses against Helen
> As if she alone, killer of men,
> As if she all alone
> Had destroyed the lives of all those Greeks.

Thus when Theatre was in its infancy, a man who was at once woman, daughter, father, old man, God, or sister, had already given voice to the clash between Lying and Truth, between giving one's opinion and speaking what is right. And Aeschylus knew then that in the end the blood of the father would win out, with unjust glory, over the blood of the mother. He was already lifting his voice in endless mourning.

Here I am at the Theatre. It's not by accident. If I were asked: Is there a social space in this country where the disease (misogyny) is not at home? What would I say? Wherever I go it's there, in every public place. Schools, universities, parliaments, places where the words of democracy whirl about – they are all stricken with the countless symptoms, stiffness, blindness, treachery, uneasiness, hypocrisy, death and rape drives, denial.

Except the theatre. It is there, in what was once a Temple and which doesn't forget it, in the enclosure where the mysteries take place that are called: rehearsals, acting . . . mise-en-scène, incarnation – it is there that the incidence of misogyny will be the lowest, or else non-existent.

Because no one can set foot on the sacred planks of the stage, in the hopes of approaching the living heart of the mystery, without having first stripped from head to foot down to one's self: for the aim and the mission of these agents (actors as well as director and author) is to increase the odds of the birth of the You:

I shall speak about the actors. They have arrived.

Undecided, detached, undressed, without any rank, unarmed, without any particularity. Joyously prepared for fate. There are no brothers, there are no wars. He might have been born she. She will perhaps be taken for him tonight. They have come to become unknown.

This sort of abnegation can't be accomplished painlessly, He touches on She. Rubbing of shoulders. Heorshe is someone who for a certain time (hours, days) no longer is. Is no longer self. Let us follow the formidable rite: first He-she is laid bare, stripped, dis-figured, practically to the point of becoming nobody. Now before the mirror Heshe puts on a mask. This is not a metaphor: 'Persona' puts on one of those masks, magic figures that come from Bali or Italy, always the same ones. Perhaps there's only one mask produced by all these masks. The mask is very striking, with big enormous features, a long nose, protruding teeth, bushy eyebrows. This is because the mask must muster all its force to combat the actor's face, chase it away, rapidly impose a totally alien image.

When the person turns hisher mask toward the mirror, heshe no longer recognizes himherself. Heshe doesn't recognize himherself in the mask either. The mask is there to keep the self from getting its face back. It is apotropaic: it chases the self away. Later the mask might be replaced by serenely beautiful make-up. There is no one endowed with consciousness there in the mirror. The separation is complete. First phase of the child-birth. Next to take place: the magnificent and painful cominginto-the-world. The labor is long. Behind the mask, for the moment, there's a panting absence. The interior space is free for the other. For the coming into being of Henry V, Desdemona or King Lear. Yes: one woman one man or the other, the space is ready to receive them without distinction as to sex, age, race. There is no particularity.

That's the way it is for the outer shell left of Himher, a copious skin subject to the processes of incarnation. What is happening inside this sensitive shell, all ears, still uninhabited? Tense, attentive, it waits. For the character to come. Queen or assassin, anything is possible. Or a combination.

If there were a remnant of self, of identity, of worry, of memory in the actor, if there were any preoccupation, the coming-into-the-world couldn't take place. (Sometimes, uptight, gripped with anguish, inspired by the demon of impatience and mistrust, the mask cannot bear the wait and rushes to heave on to the stage a fabricated character that exudes immediately shame and deception. But a simulacrum cannot last.)

The wait is done neither sluggishly nor purposely. It is attentive, open, set. Painful because it is passion, but also a promise of what is to come. Mute invocation: Come! Come! Then into the fertile night that stretches out between the text of the play and the still uninhabited bodies, the souls of the characters step forth. They speak. I don't know exactly what happens next. The souls of the characters speak into the ear of the bodies. And then there is contact between one another, an internal contact,

which is not simply touch, but which imprints, permeates the support –
the subjectile – that affects the Truth-Incarnate of Cordelia or Macbeth in
the living cloth of this somebody who is not a woman, who is not a king,
who is an adolescent-mother, who has no historical experience and no aca-
demic knowledge, heshe is neither savant nor discriminator, nor analyst,
but rather a yes, heshe is absolute assent. Internally. Hisher inside is
assent. Hear, o hear, the Theatre is all virgin ear.

Now: the immense personage enters hisher innermost self-less heart.
And now an unknown countenance covers the actor's face, under the
influence of the character's violent passions. That's the way it works: a
transfiguration comes into the bare shell. And it astonishes us all. For
here's Hamlet, and it's the first time I'm seeing him, and I hadn't imagined him this way. I remember my surprise when I saw Orestes. He had
just made his appearance (or was just resurrected), and it was then that
I first met him. (If I unfortunately 'recognize' a character, it's because the
actor has resorted to a vulgar copy of reproductions.)

And there's nothing to stop a woman shell from receiving the transfiguration of a male character. For here, in this kingdom that stretches
beyond oppositions and exclusions, it is well known, from having had
the experience so often, that it's the soul, that is, the heart – and its
moods – that makes the face, the voice, the inexplicable and complicated
truth of a human creature. *May I* thus be another woman, another man,
who I am not myself? In this human crucible of ours, who would call
into doubt 'the equality of the sexes?' Who even thinks it? The creature
is. All creatures contain infinite possibilities of being an other. One possibility is just as good as another. If our internal world were reduced to
a single self and a single sex, what a boring scene it would be, what
sterility. It's up to us to be peoples and be placed under the spell. But to
accomplish this one must have the utmost courage to let go of the bal-
last of the self, to leave oneself unweighted on the celestial platform. Let
go of the weight of the self, but not the memory, or the trace. For heshe
becomes not simply quite-other. The most delicate and most precious
aspect of the transfiguration, without which there would be neither joy
nor learning, is that I-can-be-another (creature)-whom-I-am-not-myself:
it is perhaps the most wonderful of experiences to be able to pluck the
chance and pleasure of being another person all the while knowing that
I am not the other, only the place with the scent of the other, and that
me-my-other is taking place. For a little while, at least.

For this extreme boundary state can last only so long as it is performed, acted, created. And only so long as the actors remain within the
sacred enclosure. But during this time I am both, I am another person
who retains at the same time my not-being that other. This is why the

actor is always trembling a bit for fear of not being enough, being too much, not being quite exactly too clumsily the other. He's continually touching up the creature. It involves, in secret, a marriage, love. Between the actor and the character. Sublime respect. 'Am I sufficiently you and not too much you? Am I loving you right?' the actor asks the character. It is in this incessant effort to be exact, neither more nor less, that there appears the point of absolute inexchangeability, where sexual difference can be sensed. At the point of contact is located the tiny yet unbridgeable gap that separates and keeps us two, together, both together, two together. As when, making love, we get a taste of the unknown.

All of us have once wished in a dark recess of childhood to 'be in the Theatre': to die and be reborn Phèdre or a boy. To experience the frightening thrill of being taken over. And the only reason we didn't do it is that we were afraid of passing over into the other and never coming back. But we've remained on the borders of this dangerous and prophetic curiosity. We remember having had the desire to be You, for a whole lifetime.

That's why we go to the Theatre with the emotion of someone getting ready to be transfigured. Who knows who I shall be, a moment from now, in the fertile night?

9   Writing blind

Conversation with the donkey

Translated by Eric Prenowitz

What we call the day prevents me from seeing. Solar daylight blinds me
to the visionary day. The blaze of day prevents me from hearing. From see-
inghearing. From hearing myself. Along with me. Along with you. Along
with the mysteries.

To go off writing, I must escape from the broad daylight which takes
me by the eyes, which takes my eyes and fills them with broad raw
visions. I do not want to see what is shown. I want to see what is secret.
What is hidden amongst the visible. I want to see the skin of the light.

I cannot write without *distracting* my gaze from capturing. I write by
distraction. Distracted.

Whenever I go off (writing is first of all a departure, an embarkation, an
expedition) I slip away from the diurnal world and diurnal sociality, with
a simple magic trick: I close my eyes, my ears. And *presto*: the moorings are
broken. At that instant I am no longer of this political world. It is no more.
Behind my eyelids I am Elsewhere. Elsewhere there reigns the other light.
I write by the other light.

When I close my eyes the passage opens, the dark gorge, I descend. Or
rather there is descent: I entrust myself to the primitive space, I do not
resist the forces that carry me off. There is no more *genre*. I become a
thing with pricked-up ears. Night becomes a verb. I night.

I write at night. I write: the Night. The Night is such a great deity
that one day she ended by incarnating herself and appearing in one of my
plays. The Night is my other day. The most prodigious half of my life.
The most prodigal half. It is out of admiration and passion for her that
I make the night by day. Even with my eyes open at noon, I am able to
not see. When I am in pursuit of a thought which bolts off before me like

A first version of this translation of 'Ecrire aveugle' was published in: *TriQuarterly* 97
(1996): 7–20.

some marvelous game, my eyes see only the neutral and empty space where its shadow darts away.

There is surely a scientific explanation for the way in which my eyes are capable of non-seeing my family circle, my friends, my books, my audience, but I do not know it.

Not seeing the world is the precondition for clairvoyance. But what does it mean, to see? Who sees? Who believes they know how to see?

All human beings are blind with respect to one another. The 'sighted' do not see what the blind see and do not see. Non-seeing is also a kind of seeing. The blind person sees. I who am not blind do not see what the blind person sees. I am the blind for the blind.

To be neither blind nor very nearsighted causes a sort of blindness.

By misfortune and by secret good fortune I was born very myopic. The blind person was always my neighbor, my cousin and my terror. A little more and I was him.

My nearsightedness is the secret of my clairvoyance. (I will not speak of this today.) I owe a large part of my writing to my nearsightedness. I am a woman. But before being a woman I am a myope [une myope]. Myopia is my secret. A secret? But what if you reveal it? Even when it is avowed, the secret is not aired: extreme myopia is inconceivable to those who are not extremely myopic. I belong to the Masonic Order of Myopes.

But myopia does not suffice to make night.

Let us close our eyes. The night takes me. Where do we go? Into the other world. Just next door. So close yet so difficult to access. But in a dash we are there. The other side. An eyelid a membrane, separates two kingdoms.

My myopic name, my *nom de myope* is Miranda. I pass from the blurry to the clear crying O Brave New World. Illusion! Indeed. What is important to me is not the appearance, it is the passage. I like the word passage. *Pas sage* (ill-behaved/unwise). All the passwords all the passing and boarderpass words, the words which cross the eyelid *on the interior* of their own body, are my magic *animots*, my animal-words. My philters. We pass also by Illusion. I like the name Illusion.

At dawn, barely awake but not yet having passed to an upright position, still on all fours and on the run, still clothed in sleep, but already convoked, I put on the brakes, I slide very slowly toward the day. Between the night and the day there is a long vivacious but fragile region where one can sleep even while being awake, where even standing on two legs one is still a phantom, where the doors do not yet exist in us between the two kingdoms, where what will be past survives, lingers, *stays* (oh I lack this word in French), *Steht*. Lightest Ecstasy.

It is a fragile region that can be shattered by a too brusque gesture, a magic hour that can be chased off by too brusque an encounter with an inhabitant of the day.

What I write then knows neither limit nor hesitation. Without censorship. Between night and day. I receive the message. I receive without trembling. In broad daylight I would never have paradisiacal nudity. One can only receive nude. No, not unclothed. The nudity from before all clothing.

Then I raise the visor from my eyes, I turn my naked eyes toward the world. And I see. I see! with the naked eye, and it is exaltation itself. I pass from non-seeing to seeing-the-world. The features of the world's face rise, emerge, pass from the unperceived into presence. It is a sudden, dazzling, engendering passage. I feel myself see. Eyes are the most delicate most powerful hands, imponderably touching the over-there. From over there I feel a self return to me.

Me is thus the meeting place between my sighted soul and you? I raise the visor and behold: the world rises for me. Is given to me. The gift of the world. What is given to me in this sudden rising is at once the world and giving. I say *world*: its face: the physical world. Its landscape.

Now I write. Which is to say that in my black interior softness the rapid footsteps of an arriving book print themselves. Catch me it says

The race begins. In front of me

My book writes itself. Creates itself. (In French: *se crée*.) Secret. With jubilation and play. With French. Within French, riding French. Afrenching itself from French. It turns back to see if I am (following) it.

It makes a fool of me while creating itself. This too is its secret: the proof of creation is laughter. It is a marvel to feel the innumerable vibrations of the soul make themselves, collect themselves, crystallize themselves into words, to witness the rain of atoms Lucretius made us dream of. Millions of signs rain down and in their flood they stick to one another, they kiss. I call it 'my book' because I'd be so happy if it would let itself be caught, to caress it if it would let itself be caressed, as I say 'my love' to the beings I belong to by the love that dedicates me to them. 'Mylove' listen you know when I write my love it does not mean, my love, that you are mine but that I am yours [*je suis moi à toi*].

I note, I want to write *before*, at the time still in fusion before the cooled off time of the narrative. When we feel and there is not yet a name for it. The scene is in the entrails with turmoil, élans. Knees knock, the heart catches fire, a great repulsion, a great attraction, later it will be pacified into a name. But first it is passion. Our common fate. The tempest before fixation. The I-know-not-what-torments-me. The inexhaustible manifestation of nerves. With confusion and summits.

Furor. Heartrending joy. In the anguish, hope. I want to paint our subterranean soul. There are already words. But not yet proper names. Here,
by the way, before, nothing is proper, nothing is of its own. This is why
my books have no titles. Giving a title is an act of appropriation. The
books for which I am the scribe belong to everyone.

An employee of Air France tells me on the telephone: I like your books
because they touch me. We all like to touch – to be touched. Above all by
the books that have a soft and violent gaze. It is with emotion and nostalgia that I touch the soft and ferocious touch of my cat [*mon chat ma
chatte*], the cat whose cat I am, and between us no appropriation only
moments of grace, without guarantee without security without a glance
thrown toward the following moment. This is *jouissance*. All now.

Coming from afars and from voices that rise among the cities and
woods that grow and pass behind me the scenes press at the door of my
back, enter into the vast vestibule of a docile sensibility I am only an
ideal donkey, I carry and I hear [*j'ouïs*] I admit my work is of acceptance
my principal organs are: my ears which are spacious extensible velvety of
the necessary size, courageous also never closed and my eyes which are
other ears. The rest, heart above and heart below, is connected to the
telephone exchange. I catch everything by the ear, the murmurs, the
most enigmatic phrases and the angers also that convulse all my being
when a drop of poison is served to me on the tympanum. Be careful
because I hear all [*tout et tout*]. All that is said. All that not being said is
said otherwise.

I owe books and books to the telephone and I will give at least one
back to it. May it be this very one.

To return to my ghostly, totally invisible and unfigurable partner, but
who was a voice, at the end of our conversation during which we had only
one name for two voices and it was mine and we were both united under
this name that held us like a parasol, I thought I ought to ask her name
before separating; but perhaps I shouldn't have. What is your name I say
most softly but in spite of the softness it was nonetheless the small wound
of separation and I had not wanted it. And with timidness she went back
into her name and turned it toward me as if she felt encloistered behind
the door. And so out loud I said her name, she said that she did not have
one and I said that no one had one, there are only words and phrases with
hands and lips tears in the eyelids, while names are explosives, it ought to
be possible to disarm them, and that they are called proper and pride and
aggression, it is the names, I say, that should be chased off like honorary
excrement, and I said her name softly to her to take her by the hand with
vigor and bring her back under the two-voiced parasol. And when we
interrupted our adventure we were again together.

My business is to translate our emotions into writings. First we feel. Then I write. This act of writing engenders the author. I write the genesis that occurs before the author. How does one write the genesis? Just before? I write on writing. I turn on the other light.

This is done in the way life happens to us, by gusts, by events, depositing discontinuous elements. The link exists, however: it is the thread of breathing. It continues to discontinue.

To write by shreds, by storm clouds, by visions, by violent chapters, in the present as in the archpast, in pre-vision, in the true chaos of verbal tenses, crossing over years and oceans at a god's pace, with the past on my right and the future on my left – this is forbidden in academies, it is permitted in apocalypses. What joy it is. All those who secretly have not broken with the earliest times are so happy when they find the giantities [*géances*] of their magic stage under the policed mask of a volume.

It is always there, just behind thought, behind the eyelids, the kingdom whose queen is poetic freedom, and where all these values that do not have civil rights in reasonable and so-called democratic society are reaffirmed: there we can say: justice, truth, love, forgiveness, responsibility, we can speak a language that is laughable in the city governed democratically by law, Realpolitik, conflict, hate, lies, irresponsibility.

No, I am not painting for you the picture of an ideal kingdom. On the other side there is good *with* evil. Good in evil, evil in good, and above all: difficulty. Life on the other side is difficult, you feel somewhat alone or very alone, climbing the slopes of what the philosopher Kierkegaard calls the absolute.

And if there were not the donkey to keep Abraham company it would be infernal. But there is the donkey. The animal – I will come back to this – who puts a limit on abandonment. The Bible does not report the conversation Abraham had with the donkey on Mount Moriah. And this does not surprise me. Nevertheless, it is enough to follow them. And we hear them talking. I would like to give the donkey with Abraham a chance to speak. I want to give the donkey the floor. One does not say foolish things [*bêtises*] to a donkey, do you agree? Nor to a cat. It is only to another human that one says foolish things, that one chats, that one strays from the point, that one lies.

With the donkey, we ride straight to the essentials, and right away.

I write on the donkey.

(Duncity & donkey. Duncity is a human, not a donkey.)

I am trying at this moment to capture the mysteries of passage so as to confide them to you, this is an attempt to note down what goes much faster than my consciousness and my hand. But the passage, luckily, leaves traces. One must act fast. And no time to learn.

I do not command, I do not concept, I chase after what goes beyond me. On occasion I try to go after four hares at once and it makes me all out of breath and contorted. So I stop and I get back my breath.

When I write I do nothing on purpose, except stop. My only voluntary intervention is interruption. Breaking. Cutting. Letting go. Cutting is an art I have acquired. Nothing is more natural and more necessary. All living beings, mammal or vegetable, know that one must cut and trim to relaunch life. Nip the quick. Harm to help.

In language I like and I practice the leap and the short-cut, ellipsis, amphibology, speed and slowness, asyndeton. Speed is a means of defending oneself against dishonesty. An actor who plays too slowly (lies) [*lentement*]. But of course an actor who plays too fast, in a single tone, swallowing the words, also lies.

One must play language quick and true like an honest musician, not leap over a single word-beat. Find the slowness inside the speed.

Language, bless it, has innumerable resources of acceleration, and this is how it gets close to the vital processes that go faster than lightening.

This speed is not superficial. It strikes deep. It is grace. I have an idiomatic gift of grace. I do not know why or how it was accorded to me. I receive it and foster it.

The text comes over me too fast for my slowness in recording. What to do? I take down the squall in notes. My sentence retains something of this telegraphy.

A book writes itself quickly. How long did it take you to write this book? There is a long time and a short time. Add my whole life.

There is gestation and giving birth. The book is written at full speed when it is ready. I have always given birth quickly and without pain – at full term. A detachment. Maturity.

But beforehand, where is it, that which will come into the world, how does it prepare itself? I do not feel it. The womb is all the world. The child is made from all sides. Throughout months, years. It is not me, it is at the crossing of my thinking body and the flux of living events that the thing is secreted. I will only be the door and the spokesperson supplying words. The linguistic receptor. The scribe.

There comes the time of imminence. A desire to write rises in my body and comes to occupy my heart. Everything beats faster. The entire body readies itself. I say to my daughter: 'I feel like writing.' Thirst cannot be refused or rejected. I do not say: 'I have an idea.' I have no idea what this book will be. But very quickly scenes, sentences press forth and scarcely have I noted down twenty pages or so when I discover not the content but the direction, the ways and the song of the book.

At times I prepare myself to say: 'I have some things to say' I say to myself. This is how I prepare my seminar during two or three days. When the day comes it does not at all happen as planned: what I say is infinitely far from what I had counted on saying.

At times I want to say essential, complex things to someone I love. I note them down. I will say them later on the telephone. Our telephone is our donkey stopped and placed on the table near my hand. It is the shell of our common saintliness, the supersonic car, it is our personal animal, the being called-telephone it is very corporal and very spiritual, in short it has a mind to be our exterior hut while being our miracle mount and our most internal cavity of good fortune. There is no more living more ordinary more divine more adorable-and-terrifying more familiar and less familiar than this instrument-that-allows-a-conversation between two distant people. The object itself resembles the shoulder bone of an ox. Between caller and called [*abonné demandeur et abonné demandé*].

Now the telephone rings. And it's you. With you I always avoid chatting because it falls dead before life. To say what is essential, I hurry, I launch a phrase of great density which burrows into your deep mysterious internity [*internité*]. With all the weight of a prayer. There. The phrase now voyages in your internal silence.

We never reach a goal *hoped for*. But we can reach a goal unhoped for. At times this can hold good surprises for me.

It was an hour very agitated with winds and alone, ears buffeted by the wind's great kicks, I made my way head lowered on the paper. I was in the process of writing: But the telephone rings. And I wrote: and it's you. (I mean the telephone itself.) It was then that the telephone rang, this one here, and it was you. It was you! And I burst into laughter. (I must say I was not waiting for you.) And it was you and I say to you: o my love I was in the process of writing: but the telephone rings. And it's you. And you say to me: no way! – I swear! I say with fervor. And you say to me: but are you sure this happens outside, or is it in the text?

Here, I cannot continue. I do not know where outside happens or if the text is inside, inside outside or if the text is itself outside, or if outside is in the text. This is what happens when one writes what happens. But I can say here that I am sure. Yes I am sure that I am sure.

A book does not have a head and feet. It does not have a front door. It is written from all over at once, you enter it through a hundred windows.

It enters you. A book is just about round. But since to appear [*paraître*] it must adjust itself into a rectangular parallelepiped, at a certain moment you cut the sphere, you flatten it, you square it up. You give the planet the form of a tomb. The book has only to await resurrection.

Quickening.
They have to be written to the quick, on the now,
Live,
All these scenes, all these events which only happen once. All the rebeginnings which are new beginnings. Garden moments in springtime: the walks in the garden with my daughter and my mother remain unforgettable. Ten-years-ago grows back today. My mother my daughter and I, in the garden we engender ourselves reciprocally.

If you do not grab them in the instant they pass, these pulsations are lost forever. In the moment where in passing they brush by us, they whisper in our ears, knocking at the doors of our senses, at our ears, at our nostrils, they wake in us thoughts never yet formed. If you do not grab them 'in flight,' by the fringes of their dresses, by the edge, by the verbal traces, by the tips of the fingers.

So, have on hand a notebook, a bit of paper, and capture the rapid traces of the instant. That the past which arrives at full speed will engulf in a few minutes. What has just happened will perish. Strange and exultant encounter of the quick and its end. One moves ahead while leaving behind. Human destiny: to be flesh of forgetting [*chair à oubli*]. And to have no more vivacious desire than to wrest one's prey from forgetfulness, to keep the passing in the present.

A combat with bereavement. One must forget in order to re-present oneself virgin, to offer oneself virgin to the new year.

One must make allowance for death.

We die very much. We bury a great deal. We cover the tombs and the burials with fertile earth.

Take the living instant with the closest and the most delicate words. Without words as witnesses the instant (will not have *been*) is not. I do not write to keep. I write to feel. I write to touch the body of the instant with the tips of the words.

Above all do not waste time passing from the outside to the inside. Don't waste time wiping your feet before entering. The first sentence takes off like an arrow and sticks in the heart of internity. It plants the earth of internity. Before it there was no earth. And already, right away, under its feet (the feet the hooves of the sentence) bursts forth the expanse of a land to discover.

Neither preamble, nor antechamber. A foreign tongue must ring right from the first words.

Enter a sentence [*une phrase*]. And there was the book. And it had never before been seen.

From sentence to sentence we leap.

I adore the multiple powers of sentences. Often the events of my life come in sentences or are sentences.

But no manufacturing, no mechanical fabrication. Astounding or stunning sentences come by surprise. Like divine messages: prophecies of the present. If only we heard ourselves! If only we saw ourselves! If only we read ourselves. A comma is worth Cleopatra's nose. And vice versa. My destinies overbalance on a word. On the unfathomable ambiguities of a verb in the present tense, the present that is the future: I call you: *je t'appelle*.

Words – what chance and what energy!

However much we may forget where we come from, from what distant foreign countries, they remember in our very mouth.

They say everything, in Gothic and in Greek, they make us spit out language. They avow our hidden worst thoughts, our unknown thinking. It suffices to listen to our politicians: the twisted use they make of words. The words denounce them. So many people imagine that words are teeth in a pair of dentures. Or fossils.

But not at all. Words (I saw them with my eyes when I was three years old) are our dwarfs, our gnomes, our minuscule workers in the mines of language. They perforate our deafness. They forethink. And at times they are the Scandinavian tomtes or else the imps. Naturally they know what goes on in the more or less well-tended corners of the back of our mind. As everyone wants not to know, we all have the words we deserve. These little so ancient agents never stop joking and bringing us gifts in secret. Too bad for those who consider words to be worn down pebbles. An etymological presentiment guides me. Call it a good nose. I smell the odor of origins on the most familiar words. At this very moment I am addressing you in Indo-European. Words go half the way for us, they do half the transportation, rushing from the Scamander and from the Rhine and from the Ganges they launch forth and with a hard-wearing foot they come to strike the earth of the text.

I sense that in each book words with roots hidden beneath the text come and go and carry out some other book between the lines. Suddenly I notice strange fruits in my garden. It is these verbal dwarfs who have made them grow.

And what words do between themselves – couplings, matings,

hybridizations – is genius. An erotic and fertile genius. A law of life presides over their crossbreedings. Only words in love sow [*Seul les mots qui s'aiment sèment*]. Clandestine semantics.

Language is not finished. We can all be provisional demiurges by creating newborns. Language lends itself willingly to these genetic miracles.

I love what grows [*croît*]. All that grows grows to ripening and dying. But dying is not what we think. I love the word *croître*, mother and daughter, I love the daughter words [*les mots filles*] that carry their mother in their womb. I love the old women who engender. Language is an old woman who brings into the world

A newborn word moves us. A word born out of the love of two words is not a concept. *Pfeilige. Internity.* It is only a poetic individual.

Models? No models: there are none where I go, the wild earth is still being invented. But while I move ahead alone in the mobile night, I perceive the signals of other nocturnal vessels passing under the same sky. It is because there is always that famous secret society, the Masonic Order of the Alert, the entirely diasporated people of border-jumpers. No one of them imitates another. But each one recognizes that the other is also called. And we hear their passwords resonate. There is not a unique password, one shibboleth. Each one has his own according to his language, and it is all the language of each that is shibboleth. The sonorous night is a caravan. Kayrawan came from Persia in the thirteenth century. And to sense that dead and surviving star-searchers share the solitude is reassuring. The solitude of each writing is always shared [*partagée*], partaken.

About the author:

It is undoubtedly the death of my author that grafted in me the obligation to make sentences. I must write, or else the world will not exist. I must make, I must do everything: the morning, the world, the night, the day, the garden, the shopping, the childing, the countries; and I myself depend on this gesture.

I write to replace the deceased author. I do not say 'disappeared,' because he is not entirely disappeared: he returns. I cannot not write: I must weave the (new) year's days [*jours de l'an*]. Planting, constructing, raising . . . All of this is to keep death at a respectful distance. Death and I, we dialogize.

It is not a desire for mastery or for triumph. It is the fabrication of the raft on nothingness.

I have often said that my father, in going off precipitately, took with him the floor of the world and all the temple. It was terrifying to see that ruin. And what then happened to the family? Each one made a gesture to saturate the abyss. My mother became a midwife. My brother is almost a midwife, he is a pediatrician. Each one of us got busy around the process of bringing into the world. I set myself to weaving time. A year without a book – this has never happened to me, a year without the fabric of life. But I can go for as much as eight months, nine months without putting into the world a world where I can put myself. But not longer.

But this world is first of all an emergency stage, so that the characters of the play can make their entrance.

A book and I are the hen and the egg. A self-fertilizing, dense, precise, polyglot and polyphonous language – in who engenders whom, who engenders who.

But how is it that I do not speak that language of writing when I speak? I cannot write in the air with my voice? When I speak – no writing, only discourse.

Answer: the text needs the paper. It is in the contact with the sheet of paper that sentences emerge. As if coming out with great wing-strokes from a nest hidden beneath the paper. Maybe the sheet of paper is Khora?

It is not *written* in my head. There must be the contact between my hand and the paper. I am not an intellectual. I am a painter. No computers. You do not paint with a computer. I paint, I draw the sentences from the secret well. I paint the passage: one cannot speak it. One can only perform it. No, never computers. The idea of the machine-that-is-not-me and that looks at me with its eye and reflects words in my eye reminds me of Polyphemus. Straight away I slip under the belly of a sheep and body to body with the animal, my face buried in the wool, I flee the Computer that stares at my Night.

No, no eyes facing my blindness. I write without seeing that I write, what I write. As when we make love. It is a making with perfect dexterity and necessity, but we close our eyes so as not to distract our body, not to divert it from its intimate course.

As when we make love with the loved one, the only one, the one who – is to me,

the one we trust as our own mother, the one I believe with my eyes shut, and I close my eyes so as better to believe, and so that the exterior will not exist, and so that we will be the two of us together in the hand of one same Night.

About the person whose name is You:
I write you: I write to you and I write *you*. I will never say enough what (I) my writing owes you.

I address myself to you. You are my address.

Each book is in a certain way a letter that wants to be received by you.

But it is not *for* you that I write: it is *by* you, passing through you, because of you — — — And thanks to you each book takes every liberty. Crazy liberty, as you say. The liberty to not resemble, to not obey. But the book itself is not crazy. It has its deep logic. But without you I would be afraid of never being able to return from Mount Crazy. But I can lose myself without anxiety because you keep me. This book is not a narrative, it is not a discourse, it is a poetic animal machine, the grain of its skin is pure poem. Because you keep watch, this book gives itself the freedom to escape from the laws of society. It does not fit the description. It does not answer the signals. It does not get a visa.

For the policeforce reader it seems to be an anarchic thing, an untamed beast. It incites the reflex to arrest. But the freedom my book gives itself is not insane. It exercises the right to invention, to research. We only search for what no one has yet found, but which exists nonetheless. We search for one land, we find another.

The word *God* in French: *le mot Dieu: le mot d'yeux:* the word (of the) eyes. Melodious. The name God: *le nom Dieu*.

Whom do I call God, what do I call god? Necessity of the word god. No language can do without a word god. I like the French word god. The word–god: *le mot–dieu. Le mot dit eux:* the word says them. *Le mode yeux. God* is *dog* in the English mirror.

This page writes itself without help, it is the proof of the existence of gods.

God is always already *di-eu*, di/vided, aimed at by us, hit, split. Lips open in his absence of face. And he smiles on us. The smile of *Dieu* speaks of the wound that we are to him.

I have never written without *Dieu*. Once I was reproached for it. *Dieu* they said is not a feminist. Because they believed in a pre-existing God. But God is of my making. But god, I say, is the phantom of writing, it is her pretext and her promise. God is the name of all that has not yet been said. Without the word *Dieu* to shelter the infinite multiplicity of all that could be said the world would be reduced to its shell and I to my skin. *Dieu* stands for the names that have never yet been invented. *Dieu* is the synonym. God is not the one of religions, the one that is attached like Samson the donkey to the wheel of religions.

His true name? We will know it on the last day, it's promised.

The force that makes me write, the *always unexpected Messiah {Messie toujours inattendu}*, the returning spirit or the spirit of returning – it is you.

Everybody knows that one must not wait expectantly for the Messiah, he can only come to leave, by leaving, from [*il ne peut arriver qu'à partir*].

You have always just left, you come from leaving: *tu viens de partir*. Leaving is the condition for returning. Then an 'I believe-you-will-return' begins. It is always accompanied by a But if . . .? *Mais si* . . .? *But if* you did not return??

It is an I want that does not dare believe it. Not-daring-to-believe is a very delicate form of belief.

The temptation to not believe and belief breathe in the same breath.

I *believe* that you will come and this belief is accompanied by its indissociable double which is (a) *but-if*: a *mais-si*.

Just before you arrive, when I almost hear your footsteps, I am *struck with belief*, even though I *knew* you would come. I did not know. And I begin to tremble.

Knowing is not *believing*. Knowing does not believe. Knowing is without fever and without life.

My thinking self waits for you. And there is another myself who trembles.

I myself, I do not believe in miracles. One must not believe in miracles. If you believe in miracles, then there are none.

I have a cat who took me so much by surprise that she is named miracle.

In my writing night I am subject to the laws of hospitality. I welcome newly arrived terms. And if they want to leave again, I do not hold them.

I have a submission for what arrives, and a submission for what returns. This is why I tremble and fear. I fear that the Messiah will arrive and I fear that the Messiah will not arrive.

If I had known that I would come to (have) a cat or that one day a cat would come to me, I would have said no. I would not have wanted it.

This is how she came. Unwanted. Entirely unexpected. Never desired beforehand.

And I love her. We cannot not love the found child. What we love is the undesired. The arrival of what is desired satisfies but does not fill with enthusiasm. Enthuse says god. The word enthuse(s) . . .

More than everything in the world we love the creature we would never have expected. Never thought of loving.

Me, a cat?

This is a chapter of a book that could be called the imitation of the cat [*la chatte*].

How does a book arrive? Like a barely weaned cat who sticks a small paw-hand out from under the wood-stove. And a few days later it is she who explains humanity to you.

Who would have believed that I could *love* an animal and imitate a she-cat? And now I believe.

I have already learned a lot from her. She brings me closer to the formation of the soul.

I will stop shortly.

The sense of the ridiculous is the first difference between a god and me. The sense of the ridiculous is my modern comic dimension. I burst out laughing in the tension between the two measurements of our own character. Between the giant and the dwarf that we are. When the dwarf puts on a dress that is too big and the giant a shoe that is too small, we stumble. Walking is difficult, uneven. Freudian slip, subconsciously deliberate mistake, lapsus, disjunction, inadequacy – my story is ridiculous as is yours. The smallness of the great character is multiplied by his greatness. Those political men are very ridiculous. Their tongue forks and they claim to command us.

The Fall is ridiculous. But in the Bible one does not laugh. The sense of sin keeps God from laughing. It is coming up against the limit that makes us laugh.

In my Bible, one has the sense of the ridiculous. It is a great liberty. We enjoy it when we do not have the constraint of contrition. So chased from paradise, I go off precipitately and concretely without having had the time to take my shower. Then I spend the whole day looking for a bathroom. In complete contravention of the sense of epic decorum.

And glasses? Can we imagine a literature without glasses today? How did the myopic heroes manage before the walls of Troy?

We cannot imagine Phaedra entering on stage with glasses. And yet? Cleopatra with glasses is an act of violence. I want Phaedra not to be ashamed to wear glasses.

My effort in language and in thematics is to break with interdictions and false modesties. This is why I go so willingly into the house of dreams: I admire them for their aptitude for nondiscrimination. It is in their house that the equal light from before the guilty feeling reigns. Neither pride, nor shame. It is only in dreams that we are strong and generous enough to look God in the face while he bursts out laughing. That creation, really! Those creatures! It takes some doing! And I also laugh to have caught God doing what he has never done elsewhere.

10 My Algeriance, in other words: to depart not to arrive from Algeria

Translated by Eric Prenowitz

To Doctor Pierre Cixous

My way of thinking was born with the thought that I could have been born elsewhere, in one of the twenty countries where a living fragment of my maternal family had landed after it blew up on the Nazi minefield. With the thought of the chanciness, of the accidence, of the fall. Lucretius's Rain of atoms, in raining, the atom of my mother had met the atom of my father.

The strange molecule detached from the black skies of the north had landed in Africa.

In the smiling and happy little girl I was, I hid (from others and from myself) a secret, restless, clandestine little girl, who knew well that in truth she had been born elsewhere. The obscure feeling of having appeared there by chance, of not belonging to any here by inheritance or descent, the physical feeling of being a frail mushroom, a spore hatched over night, who only holds to the earth with hasty and frail roots. Another feeling in the shadows: the unshakeable certainty that 'the Arabs' were the true offspring of this dusty and perfumed soil. But when I walked barefoot with my brother on the hot trails of Oran, I felt the sole of my body caressed by the welcoming palms of the country's ancient dead, and the torment of my soul was assuaged.

Two cemeteries

The path to school went by the cemetery of boulevard Bru. The Catholic cemetery. The concrete historical résumé of our accidence in Algeria.

'Mon Algériance' was first published in *Les Inrockuptibles* 115 (20 August – 2 September 1997): 71–4; this translation first appeared in *TriQuarterly* 100 (1997): 259–79.

November the cruelest month: we get off at the cemetery stop, arms full of enormous golden chrysanthemums and the latest dahlias, posthumous victories of my father who had hastily planted a magnificent garden, then died. We lived off these plantings of the one who was dead. We ate those vegetables and those fruits that he had prepared for us. But the worst was the flowers. We sold them.

Humiliated furious docile we bore them like convicts. We went on foot, carrying great pails full of tall flowers. At the entrance to the cemetery the black little Spanish Catholic merchant women selling flowers for the tombs of the enemy dead. Right out of a tale by Hoffmann, they felt the heads of the golden chrysanthemums and paid us a hundred centimes. And we had time in fleeing to hear them instantaneously resell our flowers become merchandise for five times a hundred centimes to the widows veiled in black. The shame that reddened us was copious: it was a mixture of maledictions for our mother who, for lack of money, made distressed merchants of us, and love for our courageously realistic mother, and disgust for the action that made the beauties consecrated by the hand of my father into butcher's meat. We ourselves soiled with an ancient defilement. To sell flowers! Here died our sense of commerce. But the true cemetery, the Jewish one, called by the way Saint-Eugène, was on the other side of the city. I left my father there to mix his dust with that dust, a tribute paid to a borrowed land.

To leave behind the grave of one's father: through dust I acquire a sort of invisible belonging to a land to which I am bound by my atoms without nationality. Because of the phantom of my father I cannot be patriated anywhere. An abandonment retains my memory on the unvisited heights of Algiers. The Jewish cemetery had a superb view over the bay, if the dead had only been able to contemplate it.

Passport: I cannot look at it without trembling for fear of being unmasked, because it is a fake, always has been.

Lie, forgery, use of forgery, in spite of myself with my consent.

It is this verb *to be* that has always bothered me. What are you? Are you French? Who am I? Am I her? And to answer with a word or a cross in the box, when I would need one hundred or a blank.

To be French, and not a single French person on the genealogical tree admittedly it is a fine miracle but it clings to the tree like a leaf menaced by the wind.

Deep down I myself never believed it, and I confess I never even dreamed of desiring it nor of course of rejecting it.

And yet I must say that in the uncontrollable fall of which I am the result, I have the feeling that I had a lucky landing. And subsequently, as if there were a fatality of good fortune for me, that I have not stopped landing luckily and also just in time, just before the abyss or the prison wall.

Lucky landing: this is also due to a geographic and symbolic openness of France, a country which always seemed to me to manifest a porosity – country with maritime and voyager shores, escaping by chance the enclaved structures of Mitteleuropa for example, a traveled, passed-through, invaded, crossbred country, a country with ports, and not interned or withdrawn. I rejoiced in French passporosity.

*

The paradox of this passport: having it always closed me in a double-bind.

On one hand 'I am French' is a lie or a legal fiction.

On the other to say 'I am not French' is a breach of courtesy. And of the gratitude due for hospitality. The stormy, intermittent hospitality of the State and of the Nation. But the infinite hospitality of the language.

No coincidence between the identity papers and the intimate feeling.

My history is held between a double contradictory memory:

– on one hand my German family which moved to German Strasbourg at the beginning of the twentieth century was granted French nationality by a France victorious in 1918, yet this did not keep the family from returning hastily 'home' to Germany and it subsequently turned out to be salutary for my mother and my grandmother, when death became the master of Germany, as Celan says.

– on the other hand the same France, if it is the same – which saved my German grandmother at the last minute in 1938 by its gesture of 1918 – threw us out of French citizenship in 1940 in Algeria and deprived us of all civil rights, beginning for my brother and me with the right to go to school, and for my father to practice medicine which he had just practiced in 1939 as a lieutenant on the Tunisian front in the French Army.

Neither France, nor Germany nor Algeria. No regrets. It is good fortune. Freedom, an inconvenient, intolerable freedom, a freedom that obliges one to let go, to rise above, to beat one's wings. To weave a flying carpet. *I felt perfectly at home, nowhere.*

Wars

North Africa was an arid and perfumed theatre, salt, jasmine, orange blossoms, where violent plays were staged.

The scene was always war, they only changed wars, and above the pink and brown Tell plains and table-land the rainbow was *bleu-blanc-rouge.*

We always lived in the episodes of a brutal Algeriad, thrown from birth into one of the camps crudely fashioned by the demon of Coloniality. One said: 'the Arabs'; 'the French.' And one was forcibly played in the play, with a false identity. Caricature-camps. The masks hold forth with the archetypal discourses that accompany the determined oppositions like battle drums.

The Chorus of the French hurled out with a single voice that the Arabs were: dirty-lazy-incapable-thieves.

It was the reign of the insult and the *apostrophe.*

The characters were simplified and purified ethnically grouped people, one said: the Arabs and the French, and also the Jews and the Catholics (and no Berbers) (and no Protestants). But in our families concerned with others one used words pronounced above the mud and the gutter: 'Israelites' 'Muslims' or '*Indigènes.*' A great-uncle once removed owned a small clothes store down rue Philippe called 'Le Pauvre Indigène.'

The noun 'Algerian' was born very recently. Previously, 'Algerian' was only an adjective.

*

During the war (the war ordered all thought, as time's pivot: one thought before-the-war, during-just-after-after-the-war) the word that begins with 'j' was not spoken it was a forbidden, dangerous poisonous word like the word 'pederast' that creeps under a veil of antonomasia in *Sodome et Gomorrhe.*

My mother, in the double grip of Nazi Germany and Vichy Algeria never said the word *Jew* in the street. Naïve, she said that's a *J.* Exorcism. Taboo. I knew well the subtle poisons of interdiction: interdictions interdict themselves. They self-mutilate themselves. All that was left of us was the letter J. J. became my first favorite letter: with great energy I said *je.*

In the cities the familiar presence of the war, a life with war, the explosions, the true ones, from 1939 to 1942 the air-raid sirens at night in Oran we somnambulated enveloped in our alarm dressing gowns to the humid cellar of the building next door. Candles, howls from the sky roaring Anti-Aircraft Defense. And in the front door of my aunt's apartment the black muzzles of two bullets stuck there for ever – which bore witness to a great event, twisted and ambiguous like all the events over there: the '*North African landing.*' The entrance, for us magnificent, of the Americans, the arrival of the regiments in the *Place d'Armes* was saluted by the Oranians – in truth Vichyist – with shots fired from buildings to which showers of bullets were returned by the liberators received as invaders. Encrusted in the door the little black heads, like minute and fearsome Giacomettis and they were American. I cried at the death of Roosevelt.

*

The name of Aïcha

In Oran families had Spanish maids.

'*Mauresques.*' In Algiers, they had Moorish maids. *La Mauresque* was even a synonym for maid. At the Clos Salembier, we had a complex relationship with Aïcha and all her family.

Aïcha was an attractive woman, gentle and strong, femininity itself always pregnant and smiling. Ripe and big. The husband, whom I never saw, was eighty. Later on I learned that she had been Ouled Naïl. Aïcha was replaced, at each pregnancy, by one of her daughters. There was Bahia who limped and whom my father treated. Zouina who was ugly, black, alarmed. All the children different, blond ones, brown ones, black ones, Aïcha entered the garden, like a vine laden with bunches of children in her arms, at her skirts, at her breast.

Her gentle and caressing name.

Whereas all maids in Algeria were called Fatma. But not us. Aïcha was unique. Until the day, very late, after independence, when I discovered: Aïcha was named Messaouda. What? And for twenty years we had kept calling her Aïcha? That's right. There had been I know not what initial error, a parapraxis and Messaouda had docilely let herself be expropriated and reappropriated. She had not dared. We who had wronged her and Fatmatized her for twenty years. We want to avoid causing damage, it catches up with us. When Rosa entered the service of Freud's sister, she had to renounce her name and be called Dora. Freud was greatly saddened by this. 'Those poor people, they are not even allowed to keep their names . . .' he thought.

The name of Cixous

My wild bristling sexual name unclean improper cutting like a Barbary fig, vulnerable, attacked, barbarian.

What kind of a thing is that ?

What's in a name?

Still today the way it is treated flayed mispronounced spat out the reactions, the projections, the deformations. An impossible name.

And something in, or coming from, the French language that makes it unpronounceable and unspellable: even dictated it is inaudible and inadmissible. A non-French name. A bizarre, and unknown name. Without origin. Neither French, nor even Jewish. An ugly duckling among the Jewish patronymics of Algeria. A name worse than Jewish, or still more Jewish than a familiar Jewish name. A sort of 'foundling.' Almost an anonymic. Even Algerian Jews don't know what to do with it. 'A name to be left outside at night.' We were turned away into the night. One evening my brother climbed on to the roof. From there you could see the new little church built at the edge of the Arab shanty-town, to scoff at it. A young priest came out surrounded by a little French flock. The little Frenchmen shouted Dirty Jew! seeing my brother on his own roof. The little priest began to laugh, my brother tells me.

Then slowly very slowly through our surprise a rumor rose to my ears: one day someone tells me: Cixous is an Arab name. Arab? Then the rumor left again. To return in a firm tone: some Berber friends recognized the barbarian duckling. Cixous, they say is the name of a Berber tribe.

How, by what story of love, of conversion, of war, of passion, how my formerly Spanish family was or how it became or ceased to be Berber – only forgetfulness knows.

I almost sacrificed it: when my first book was going to come out, I was advised to use a less apotropaic one. I considered Jonas, the maiden name of Omi, my maternal grandmother. The names of my German Jewish family: Klein, Meyer, Ehrenstein, Jonas or Feuchtwanger. Easy names.

I caught myself just in time: my name, my nose too big too aquiline, my prominences. My excessive traits. At the last minute I renounced renouncing my marks. Accept destiny. What I kept away from, in keeping my name and my nose, was the temptation of disavowal.

In Algeria we lived in the proximity of disavowal: it was always the temptation above all with those who are persecuted, re-marked. Above all for the Jewish boy whose sensitive soul was tortured by the violence and vulgarity of part of the Jewish community itself, and who would have given dearly to escape circumcision, the ineluctable and intolerable election that nails the Jewish boy's body to an identity he has not chosen.

The exasperation prompted him to change sides, to make a break with endogamy, to reject the fate that had anticipated his word and his decision. I will never marry a Jewish woman said my brother. And I who was not a Jewish (and tattooed) man, I understood this revolt. I, who had not been marked by the knife, and whose body had not been decided before me, I could choose.

(The extent to which the Jews of Algeria, save exception, were altered, amnesiated of their own culture, illiterate in their own language Hebrew was always a painful experience and one that would require the long analysis Jacques has achieved, but which I could measure at my house in the difference: my maternal family came from Germany, etc . . . having lost everything but with a baggage of memory tradition knowledge, language – which was secular and entirely intact in spite of the devastation.

While the Jewish community of Algeria seemed to have sold its soul to France and for nothing, no longer being either this or that and living in its majority of cultural makeshifts and of simulations. It was my mother who informed my father about the meaning of Jewish ceremonies, of which he knew only the names and the obligations.)

I was afraid of listening to a fear. The fear of my brothers.

I was afraid also of cunning, and of temptation and of the temptation of cunning.

I wanted to remain faithful to chance, to mystery and above all to difficulty.

*

'*My house is encircled*,' is the first sentence of my first fictional text, *Inside*. It swooped down on me when I started writing.

The first garden out of which I was expelled was the 'Cercle Militaire' in Oran. In 1940 we were thrown out as Jews.

The encirclement, the Circle, the siege, are primitive figures of my Algerian scene. Our familial and social movements were attempts to enter, to be admitted, to go through the doors, to pass the thresholds of intolerance. One had to beware to the right to the left ahead behind. The *numerus clausus* (a restricted admittance quota) was the familiar demon of all our exclusions. It had a modest name, a Latin loincloth. One had to become seaweed to pass through the mesh of the fishing net or to rise a knight in armor.

The circles intersected. To be inside was also to be outside. Entering gave on to exclusion. This is the logic of the *Numerus Clausus*.

After the war in 1946 to escape the traces of the Military Circles of Oran my father brought us to Algiers. We lived in the Clos Salembier, at the edge of the city, neither inside nor outside. The Clos Salembier was our uninhabitable. Under its very French name it was a very Arab and very miserable neighborhood.

Living in the uninhabitable Clos Salembier was a gesture of great freedom on the part of my father
– one did not live in the Clos Salembier it was not done, the Europeans the French lived in town
one lived in Bab El Oued, in Belcourt, rue Michelet, or in the more reputable neighborhoods, El Biar or Hydra
but beyond the bd. Bru, no, it was not done there was only us and across the street a fallen French count, the son of a fallen family of the nineteenth century a sturdy man who buried the dead cats and dogs that were regularly thrown into our garden to rot and whose stench kept him from sleeping –

– but this gesture only had meaning for my father the doctor of the poor, my father who moreover did not survive.

For never were we 'inhabitants' of this neighborhood, we never managed, on the right hand begins the Ravin de la Femme Sauvage and we never entered there, the 50,000 indigenous people fifty meters from us remained impenetrable. In three meters our poverty was wealth.

When my mother who had become a midwife after my father's death went to deliver babies in the shantytown, she was not admitted either, she only crossed the thresholds briefly and often performed deliveries 'under the sheet.' But on the other hand, my brother tells me, during the war for independence the French houses in our street of the Clos Salembier were burnt down (by the FLN). Except my mother's house. She was the midwife after all.

– But it's *only* because she was the midwife I say.

Each scene always had other contradictory sides.

But

To live in the Clos Salembier was an impossibility, it was to live on the ramp of the abyss

But there was nothing higher and more difficult.

It gave us an uncalculated destiny. The destiny of hemmed-in isolated people and which, strange miracle, resembled us. That was it.

Without meaning to, we were not on the planet, and we lived by force and willingly on another planet.

Every day we came down from Mars to the streets of Algiers.

We went out of the encircled house. To catch the trolley bus K we had to cross the vacant lot encircled with barbed wire. The crossing at the mercy of chance: sometimes the band of little Arabs threw itself on me during the race and we rolled screaming with double rage in the dust. Once I was covered with spit and I wanted to die. Sometimes I passed among the indifferent band.

Do you remember Cinna the poet? For me it is in Algeria about 1950, in the Clos Salembier perhaps, that he was assassinated. It happened like this: early one morning he goes out. It is the ides of March, act III scene 3 of *Julius Caesar*. This man, whom no one knows (who knows the poet?) takes one step in the street: I dreamt he says that I did feast with Caesar . . .

Cinna: I dreamt to-night that I did feast with Caesar . . . something leads me forth of doors
(Enter the Algerian plebeians)
– What is your name? Whither are you going? Where do you dwell? . . .
Cinna: I am going to Caesar's funeral.
– As a friend or an enemy?
– As a friend.
– Your name?
– My name is Cinna.
– Tear him to pieces.
– I am Cinna the poet!
(They tear him to pieces)

This little ephemeral character, the poet who paid with his life for the misfortune of being the namesake of Cinna the politician friend of Brutus and Cassius, this was us. The Cixous children those not really Jewish false French odd inadequate people who loved the Algerians who spurned us as enemy Francaouis, Roumis and Jews.

At the Clos Salembier it was in vain that we cried Friend, Friend, the shibboleth did not pass. But blinded with anger and for so long the inhabitants of the Ravin de la Femme Sauvage strike wildly. The name French and, even more, French Jew rings exactly like the name Cinna the murderer. How could we hold it against the crowd? One has such rage, one would drink any blood, drought drives one mad.
– But on the other hand, my brother says, there was that Kabyle boy, who protected you, remember.
In the distance I remember: from the other side, at the end, there came a blond and gentle schoolboy, too gentle to be true. I was fourteen. A Kabyle boy, light, peaceful. A messenger of the future. Such kindness

was not of this world, not one of the three of us dared think of it. We do not recognize messenger angels, isn't that right? But we sense that their light is soft. He came to our house. It almost resembled a secret. We had such modesty

– I think his name was Idir, says my brother.

– You think so?

His true name left again with him. It was too early to stay. Perhaps he too dreamed of a world above hate.

Two hates shared the hearts differently between themselves. One of them, which I will never forgive, the colonialists' hate, was made of the scorn from which thieves and usurpers, like all despots, forge deceitful arms. In response there was the other one, which I forgive, even until today, the hate with eyes burning with tears of the humiliated and deprived, the hate of the 'Arabs' for all that was collected in the 'F' group. I was the first person to side with that uprising hate, I cried Friend! Friend! and they tore me to pieces.

Friend or enemy? And of whom? Algeria land of friendship and enmity, ferocious, the one and the other.

Who has right? Rights, laws, vacillate, pivot. What is the law? How is it, I asked myself, that the 'Arabs,' the earliest 'arrivals' in this land, are precisely those who were excluded from citizenship? *The illegitimate.*

Ah that 'legitimacy' what a story!

That French nationality granted to the Jews of Algeria by the Crémieux decree and which was a true *Gift* an example of the gift-poison of which Jacques Derrida has recounted the perversities.

It begins like this: early in the year '70 Napoléon III offers French nationality to the indigenous Jews and Arabs. 400 Arabs took it and 900 Jews out of 100,000. At the end of the same year, the Republic that emerged from the ruins of the Empire attributed French nationality to the Jewish community with the Crémieux decree of 24 October 1870 (Crémieux was a Jew). It is clear that the Jews were not asking to be French. From this extremely contradictory mix of Empire and Republic, of colonialist integrationist destructive spirit, of good will and profound misunderstanding, arose intercommunal antagonisms that were never extinguished. In spite of themselves, The Jews had become a political card used sometimes by the right sometimes by the left, etc.

N.B.: The *'républicains,'* animated by the spirit of the French revolution, wanted to extend secular French citizenship to the colonies, irrespective of autochthonous socio-cultural specificities.

N.B.: My own paternal family had itself asked for French nationality well before the Crémieux decree, in the spring of 1867. I discovered a year ago there were only 144 Jews in Algeria who had asked for it in the four years before the decree.

I have a copy of this certificate by which a certain Jonas Cixous native of Gibraltar and interpreter for the French army was made and unmade 'French,' a certificate signed by Napoleon III. This is how some Jews had a despotic Emperor as godfather for their historic baptism. People on the left never forgave them for this upstage entrance. Gambetta whom I liked did not like us. The right hated us as is its wont. Stage left stage right there was hostility. Never did the anti-Semitisms wane in Algeria. The Arabs reproached their fellow creatures for treason. To the French these Jews were venal electors. Yet certain Jews truly wanted to love France. But it was love by force. We wanted to love Algeria. But it was too early or too late.

And we the Jews, the forever-illegitimate, we were legitimate? unstably but all the same legitimate? Confusion and violence. In the Clos Salembier I lived the horror of those who know and *want* themselves to be illegitimate, who want to affirm their right to illegitimacy and who find themselves by mistake, when irony shuffles history's deck of cards, mixed at times with the pack of the legitimate.

'*The legitimate*': the French from Algeria, much more rigidly legitimate than the 'French from France' who often disengaged themselves from that malediction. (We spoke of the 'French from France,' the 'veal from France,' still more sub-groups that increasingly broke up moral and political judgement.)

The 'French' or the 'Catholics.' I do not know why those two designations merged narrowly in a colonializing militancy and a right-wing genealogy that repeated itself. Vichy, for example, was Catholic, the Pétain Youth Brigades had that navy blue color of the Catholic Youth which I have never since been able to liberate from those associations.

Still today I do not like Church proselytizing. The figure of this: how I passed before St Anne's Church in Algiers as before the secret temple of the conquistadors. I always directed an exorcising thought at the edifice. So the 'Catholics' had seized the country to establish there an occupation impenetrable to the other inhabitants. A typical phenomenon of colonialization: closed circles, clubs, beaches, swimming pools. All reserved for the French. (Jews excluded.)

And in the end a certain writing is engendered that does not settle in, it does not inhabit its house, it escapes, it goes off without turning back . . .

*

Impressions, imprints, mirrors

It was possible to not see, to have never seen anything to not see the misery, to not see the women, to not see the syphilitics and the tubercular patients the puss and the spit.

For me it was the land of the eyes: we sent looks at each other, we saw, we couldn't *not* see, we knew and we knew that we knew we knew, we were nude, we were denounced, threatened, we flung taunts, we received glances. It was the land of the other, not of the fellow human being. The other: foretells me, forewarns me, forecasts me, alerts me, alters me. Impresses me, as Montaigne said, 'I seize hold of the evil that I study and I lay it down in me' (*De la force de l'imagination*, I, 21). As soon as I went into the street I caught Algeria.

I was nearsighted, but I lacked blindness. I would indeed have liked not to see. It was impossible. The anguish of my fellow people pierces me. I was struck, wounded, marked, scarred.

I would have liked not to see the beggars, the children in rags, the blind people, the legless cripples but I saw them and I was haunted.

The bitter taste of my snack that the little Arab demanded of me and to eat outside without sharing was impossible.

But the truth is that I did not share: I was constantly paying the interest on an enormous and interminable debt, there was no gift, only the loathsome impotence of the child who has a house and a school bag.

In Oran I lived at 54 rue Philippe. A narrow urinated street that led to the port through all sorts of insinuations. It went down hill. By following it one arrived at the school of the convent, but I did not know it, I do not remember. Further on it flowed into the Naval district. The world of sailors and the great bodies of the boats, that went off, strangers that they were. At times a few little human characters made their way up, charming under the pompon berets, messengers from afar. They suddenly surfaced at the top of rue Philippe and springing from the somber gully entered the thick layer of sunlight. We saw a few of them like flowers on their stems dot the Placedarmes. They went to my aunt's tobacco shop on the corner of the Place d'armes and the rue du Cercle Militaire. It was an Ali Baba shop and on its brow was its name: *Aux Deux Mondes,* The Two Worlds. So the boutique was dedicated, and I with it, to a universe with two worlds. But I never knew in a clear, explicit or decisive way which the two were. The world was two. All the worlds were two and there were always two to begin with. There were so many two-worlds.

It is through the candy sailors that I was naturally allied later on with

Jean Genêt. The sailors were one of the species proper to rue Philippe. They were French, i.e. they were foreign visitors, elegant nomads who put in at my aunt's to stock up on marvelously refined objects: stripes they used to decorate their costumes, and glazed pink postcards. Because the sailors were fiancés who sent pink hearts in the form of Mickey ears to French fiancées.

The autochthons of rue Philippe were in every way different from the sailors. Come from grottos and caverns they rose slowly still unseparated from the earth and the cobblestones, the water carriers, laden with their goatskins. A wind carried off the sailor petals. But the water carriers were the ancient gods with two bodies a man's body and a goat's body without whom the City would not have been able to live, they gave us water to drink since the Bible, and heavy tired condemned calm heralds of potable water they announced themselves by their name called wearily in French in the somber street: 'porteur d'eau.' Passersby stopped them to buy a bowl of cool water. (One day I will speak of water, the need, thirst, the verb *désaltérer* (to quench, to slake), this land source of sources that was not called Algeria but France.) The desire for the bowl of cool water. The water gushing from the goat in a promising jet. Water promise and fulfillment.

In rue Philippe, fluxes were mixed. The body of Oran composed of Arab, Spaniard, Jew, Catholic, soldier, Frenchman was not free. It was a political, tumefied body, inflamed joints, a monster people, its mouths panting its tongues loaded with gobs of spit ready to spit them in its own face, its knees swollen, its throats big with ulterior motives, foreign to itself, furious. Joy stayed on the mountain. Below, it stank, it could not be ignored, that hate, that flagrancy which broke out between all the two worlds.

The whole history of the century was already written, the date on the walls, in the public squares, in the stairwells was 2000, but the inhabitants did not want to read it, they said they were in 1940.

Shoeshine

It was in 1941, my father was no longer either doctor or officer or French or anything. That we were pariahs relieved me obscurely, like being true, like being barefoot on the paths of Planters' hill among the Muslim graves. To survive, my father became a podiatrist. Vichy which had forbidden him the treatment of bodies had nonetheless abandoned to him the corns of the feet. He officiated in a clockmaker's booth no bigger than a standing clock situated next to the Two Worlds. At last we had fallen into the just: we were no longer among the oppressors. I knew the peace of the poor and the exultation of the outlawed. Without fatherland, without awful inheritance, with a hen on the balcony, we were incredibly happy like savages absolved of sin.

There appeared in the house a pair of white leather sandals. It was a woman from rue des Jardins, her daughter did not wear them, they were new.

There I am in rue Philippe, feet shining as if my brow were crowned with laurels, as if I had grown spurs and two cockscombs. At this drunken pace I am going to show off my glory to my father chained in the neighboring clock. Because for a triumph to be triumphant it must be reflected in the light green eyes of the father.

It was then that the noise of the Supreme Judge's hammer resonated dry and ominous, in the middle of rue Philippe. The littleshoeshines (in a single word: *petitscireurs*) did not hurl their cries toward the windows like the water carriers. They did not cry, they did not call. They banged. They knocked their wooden boxes in little dry blows with the heads of the brushes. The box gave a stubborn, imperative sound. The box barked: here! And the shoe obeyed, nose lowered. Come here! Lie down! – Stop! Here! The order hit me. I was struck with obedience. But why? Without having wanted to, I had read the whole book written in advance on the walls, and never again could I act as if I did not know what should happen and what would happen. And I was not the only one. The little boy who played the role of the littleshoeshine in that children's play, and I was not yet four and he was not yet seven, already rehearsed the role he would play when they would put on the End of the Two Worlds. I knew. But I was too young to believe that a child of four can have read the whole Book and I did not dare believe myself.

Suddenly I was an adult woman and I hastened to hide that enormous unseemliness even from my own eyes. I pretended resolutely to be the little girl I had been ordered to be.

I saw the face of the littleshoeshine and in his eyes I recognized the scintillation: it was the lust of hate, the first glimmer of desire.

Trembling I put my foot on the box as I was ordered by a violent stroke of the brush. I avowed. I was guilty. Before his tribunal, the acquittal I had enjoyed in my eyes since Vichy had no value. I lived in rue Philippe on the second floor and I had sandals given to me new. I avowed.

We knew everything. I could have run away. I could not run away. If I had been innocent I would have shouted, I would have run away. I could have denounced his hate, unmask the man who pretended to be a six-year-old littleshoeshine. I could not accuse him without accusing myself. How was it that I recognized so well the scintillation? I was not innocent.

I knew. But how could I accuse a six-year-old child of wanting to assassinate? I accused myself of harboring such a thought. It was spring in rue Philippe; and I struck the child on his knees on the cobblestones?

With dread but without surprise, I stayed, mute, because I could not ask him: why do you hate me?

What I did not know was the form that the blow would take.

Then the littleshoeshine took out one of his boxes of wax, opened it, rubbed his brush on the bright red cream and coated my white sandal with a heavy layer of thick blood. I was convulsed with horror. I suffered terribly from a wound. The red awoke the revolt in me.

At last I could stand up for myself. As if my sandals were of flesh. And I would not let my other hand be cut off. Yet I was not capable of measuring the size of the enemy. In hand-to-hand combat would it not be easy for him to mutilate me all in red? I chose guile. I acted infantile, distinguished. I told him I had to go home for the money to pay him. I got myself out of the trap, and I went off at a dignified gait, the foot red as a cry.

In Algiers at the Clos Salembier Madame Bals the Spanish grocer looked like a pig. One day I will recount how Mme Bals united us little Jews and little Arabs, with blows from a ladle and a broom on the head Mme Bals small stocky in slippers 'the kind of woman one had to be in this place, no point using kid-gloves with those rascals!' said my mother.

Or else did she take us for Arabs?

She bellowed, she cursed, she taught us the four-letter words.

*

When I was three, the age of decisive experiences and of analysis, I knew that I was destined to leave. Of course it would be later on, but it would be as soon as possible. That destination, destinality, decision, was so strong that I have been able to say: when I was three I left. It was pure departure. I had no aim or vision of an arrival, no goal, no desired country, I was in deferment and flight. In quasi-original detachment. Where to land? My first visited country was England. I was thirteen. I went there two times, Algiers–Marseilles, crossing all of France, from the South to Paris from Paris to Dieppe without stopping, without tasting it, without taking it or receiving it. I passed through France.

My own maternal family, the German one, had already detached itself from its earth (Strasbourg, Budapest, Osnabrück, Bratislava, etc.). The possibility of living without taking root was familiar to me. I never call that exile. Some people react to expulsion with the need to belong. For me, as for my mother, the world sufficed, I never needed a terrestrial, localized country. (In the family mode of dwelling there remained a nomad's simplicity: never any furniture. Always the backpack.) I did not lose Algeria, because I never had it, and I never was it. I suffered that it was lost for itself, separated from itself by colonialization. If ever I identified it was with its rage at being wounded, amputated, humiliated. I always lived Algeria with impatience, as being bound to return to its own. France? I did not know it and I knew no one there. My German Jewish family had emigrated to twenty different countries but not France.

I was a French person without France and I was the first of the family to take it as goal or as recourse. My brother believed he was a future Algerian and for eternity. But what does France mean for us, the Algerian Jews who had the strange adventure of being expulsed without moving driven out and forbidden by the anti-Jewish laws of Vichy in 1940? In 1941 in Oran my mother brought me to my first school which was the size of a dining room. It *was* a dining room, Mme Bentolila's dining room, which the Jews of the neighborhood had quickly called a school when they were excluded by Vichy from French citizenship, from education, from their professions, from everything.

There we were like the Arabs identical twins in deprivation, were we conscious of this? It was in the un-Frenchified Jewish dining-room-school that I had my first francolinguistic ecstasies. The room contained seven classes. The first row was the big kids. In the last row where I sat with my brother it was the level of lines and circles. From the back of the room I intercepted the magic that awaited me when I would be in the first row. I heard these prophetic words: '*adjectif qualificatif*' (qualifying adjective). Ah my God is this what you announced to me? One day I will have the keys to the qualifying adjective! I shivered on my chair and meanwhile the Qualiph Haroun Al Rachid made the rounds in the first row of the dining room, in the streets of Oran. So there were caliphs who slipped into the language of this France that repudiated us? It was the height of the subversive enchantment. In rue d'Arzew (one of Napoleon's victories) the Pétain Youth brigades marched in vain. I had the language and its subterranean passages.

Or rather I had:

My languages.

We played at languages in our house, my parents passed with pleasure and deftness from one language to the other, the two of them, one from French the other from German, jumping through Spanish and English, one with a bit of Arabic and the other with a bit of Hebrew. When I was ten years old my father gave me at the same time an Arabic teacher and a Hebrew teacher.

That translinguistic and loving sport sheltered me from all obligation or vague desire of obedience (I did not think that French was my mother tongue, it was a language in which my father taught me) to *one* mother-father tongue.

And History which made its voices so loudly heard in hypallages at the time I entered into languages between 1937 and 1940 transmitted the same message to me in the tragic mode.

My languages slid into each other's ear from one continent to another.

For a long time I asserted – but I did not believe it – that my mother tongue was German – but it was to ward off the primacy of French, and because German, forever distanced from the mouth of my conscience by the Nazi episode, had become the idealizable language of my dead kin. These excluding circumstances made French and German always seem to be coming to me charming like the foreign fiancée. But at school I always wanted to beat the French in French, to be the best 'in French' as they said, to honor my father, who had been driven out.

Passance

I did not believe that a creature with a soul could remain under the yoke forever. I never doubted that at the first opportunity, when it was eighteen or nineteen years old, like my mother leaving Nazi Germany, Algeria was going to rise and affirm its own destiny.

The strange thing is that this coincided with my own chronology. In 1954 Algeria and I went to sea in the same year. I waited for it, I knew it, it was the movement of life itself.

I took my leave like a bird, like a liberation: to drop pretense, errors, pains and penalties. Given wholly over to my momentum.

I went toward France, without having had the idea of arriving there. Once in France I was not there. I saw that I would never arrive in France. I had not thought about it. At the beginning I was disturbed, surprised, I had so wanted to leave that I must have vaguely thought that leaving would lead to arriving. Just as beginning would lead to ending. But not at all. Everything has always done nothing but leave and begin. In the first naïve period it is very strange and difficult to not arrive where one is. For a year I felt the ground tremble, the streets repel me, I was sick. Until the day I understood there is no harm, only difficulties, in living in the zone without belonging.

For a long time I thought it was my Algerian accidence that had made me into a passerby. I do not know how and when all this began but it was by 'arriving' in France without finding my way or my self that I discovered: the chance of my genealogy and history arranged things in such a way that I would *stay passing*; in an originary way for me I am always passing by, in *passance*. I like the progressive form and the words that end in *-ance*. So much so that if I went toward Fr*ance* without mistrust, it is perhaps because of this ending which gives the present participle its lucky chance.

To depart (so as) not to arrive from Algeria is also, incalculably, a way of not having broken with Algeria. I have always rejoiced at having been spared all 'arrival.' I want arriv*ance*, movement, unfinishing in my life. It is also out of departing that I write. I like the phrase: *j'arrive* (I'm coming, I manage, I arrive . . .), its interminable and subtle and triumphant messianicity. The word *messiance* comes to me from Algeria.

France was never the Promised Land. The sentence 'next year in Jerusalem' makes me flee. The desire, the necessity of arriving 'home,' I understand them and do not share them. What loss! What renunciation of the marvelous and infinite human condition. Zionism appeared to me in 1948 as a figure of tragedy. According to my mother, as I learned very late, my father the socialist, the atheist scalded by Vichy, expulsed, expatriated and dead in February 1948 before Israel, was tempted to go to Palestine. The idea of arriving in Israel, the death of my father spared us from having to think about it. Because if by misfortune I had been brought there, if out of obedience I had been obliged to choose a country, and what is more, a country of refuge, a country of defense, the question *What next?* would have been extinguished. The living fable would have left off without sequel. A finality would have swooped down on my free existence. I am on the side of Moses, *the one who does not enter*. Luckily.

Entering has never been my forte. I was a good student, and yet, by an action of the demon of the exit, I almost did not get into the Algiers secondary school. Once in secondary school I was not in the center. I was seen to be on the edge. It was a combat. I resisted the false communities, the false fusions. I fought and I was fought. I smelled the strong odor of racism and I rebelled. Algeria was soaked, woven, nourished, tattooed with violently racist signals. In the supposedly non-religious and republican public institutions this was not said it was lied and acted.

I tried to pull off the masks.

At the end of secondary school, from '51 to '53, in my class where I was the only Jew, there were three Muslim girls. Their way of being in the last row and half smiling. My way of being angry and in the first row. I knew immediately that they were the Algeria that was in store. I held out my hand to them, I wanted to ally myself with them against the French. In vain. For them I was France. They never opened. I understood their caution.

In the Clos Salembier at night, I heard the music of Arab weddings in the city, I adored it, it was the rhythm of the blood. But we were never invited. The war had begun long before the war.

One cannot imagine the toughness, the depth, the height of the silences in Algeria. A land populated with cries and with the deaf. Algeria was a million 'French' *among* ten million 'Arabs,' some shouting, others impassive. One did not say ghetto, apartheid, slavery.

Moreover we were not separated, no, we were *together in hostility*. Gathered together in hostility by hostility.

I would like to speak of hate in Algeria (but not enough time here) of a certain quality, of a certain composition of the hate that united us, for it was also made of hope and despair.

I did not hate and I was *obliged* to let myself be hated, I let myself be hated by the Arabs and it was the smoothest, the most mute the most passive form of love I have ever known. Body against body. In a complex process of struggle, bodies united in the clutch of separation. And I was eager for the birth to happen. For Algeria to come into the world.

*

In 1954, in summer, I was already engaged that is to say ready to slip on the wings of escape, in a café at the beach resort of Madrague, an older French man as 'French' as they can get, that is to say tall blond and Corsican, a man who had taken us to have a coffee, which I never did, pushed an Arab who was having a coffee at the bar saying: *Toi, pousse-toi!*[1] For me those words and that tone prophesied my rupture with those Frenchmen. I wished I were a man and I could push him out of the world. But for the first time in history, I saw the scene turn completely around on itself. Call that revolution. The Arab, a handsome little brown man looked the Corsican in the eyes and said: 'Why do you say *tu?*' In French. It was the first shot of the war of Independence. I had the impression of being transported into the following era. I was happy. Let me explain: before that sentence, an Arab had never revolted straight ahead in French because there was not yet hope. The Arabs accepted being theed and thoued (being *tu*ed and *toi*ed) and bit their lips.

There was no hate in the sentence, there was triumph.

I only thought of leaving. Escaping. In the meantime I escaped without moving, in books. Above all the most universal ones, those that spoke 'in our name,' in the name of humanity.

This is how I explain today my non-attraction for 'French' literature, the distance I kept from the authors I saw as being close to the court, my lack of taste in spite of admiration for Racine etc. and my intuitive kinship with Montaigne.

Even the Enlightenment was too French for me and I preferred the Anglo-Saxon penumbra.

I left. The certainty I would never return. Without regret. But it's that there are no grounds. Without hoping to be able to return.

Algeria of my foreboding doomed to the violences that had been sewn there,

Enemy of women

I will never return

Algeria returns . . .

To my great surprise it returned to me, but abroad in France the Algeria I desired in vain when I was ten the one of Messaouda, of Hamida, of Kassia, of Jamila, the Algeria with women's arms. It returned to me but in grief, threatened, trembling. I did not expect it at all. And she addressed me, for the first time since I was born, as if we had never left one another, in a movement of recognition that not a single time did I foresee or hope for.

As if there were something stronger than wars, repression, forgetting, resentment, the centuries of misunderstanding, something gentler, more ancient, more immediate, more fleshy, more free, a force independent of all struggle that laughs at championshipings, claims and reproaches, and which I would call Algeriance.

My unexpected sisters and I give each other Algeria and for the past we have the future without violence of which we dream together.

Translator's note

1   Roughly: 'You, move out of the way!' but employing the informal, in this case disrespectful, second person singular objective personal pronoun, *toi*, which corresponds to the nominative *tu* much as the English 'thee' does to 'thou.'

parallax, issue 7, Translating 'Algeria', includes texts by Hélène Cixous, Réda Bensmaïa, Jacques Derrida, Jacques Rancière, John Mowitt, Anne E. Berger, Emily Apter, Assia Djebar, Nabile Farès, Hafid Gafaïti, Couze Venn, Françoise Vergès, Assedine Haddour, Tom Conley, Winnie Woodhull, Patrice Bougon, Rebecca DeRoo, David Macey, Nancy Wood and Ronnie Scharfman.

Available from the Editors, *parallax*, Centre for Cultural Studies, University of Leeds, Leeds LS2 9JT, or Taylor & Francis Ltd, 1 Gunpowder Square, London EC4A 3DE.

From my menagerie
to Philosophy

11 Shared at dawn

Translated by Keith Cohen

We search in vain for quiescence. My cat and I.

The house is full of remnants, it emprisons us in its memory of sorrows – they are on the entryway carpet, on the floors, in the corners of the living room, in the kitchen right up to the sink; they stop there, then they start off again toward the balcony, and there, stuck for eternity, between the eleventh and twelfth banister: minuscule, powerful claws caught in the little squares of lattice-work. In vain we return there. Everything is there still, the strong smell like an unforgettable name, phantom vision; it's as if I saw you, I see it again, we see it. The whole house is now a mausoleum. Thea has found resignation but not quiescence. Resignation is an exhaustion of the heart. By dint of rubbing her heart against the banisters, she finally reaches the exhaustion of hope. Then, in the pitiable comfort of fatigue, she collapses on her bed of paper, possessed by the sorrowful specter, her body flattened, her paws opened wide and unfurled like wings.

It all started at dawn. It was gray and bitter at six o'clock. I saw it as I was leaning against the morning window: a large black dead leaf caught in the lattice-work of the balcony, upright, its round head inert, its beak sunken in, its body obliterated – on second look I felt the force of this black inertia to be heavier, bulkier than that of a leaf, and then I saw: caught there by the network's fine invisible pincers was a sort of bird stuck upright in the spaces. Oh no, I wished I hadn't seen it. And now what should I do? Now I was trapped in the vision of that immobile thing in my lattice-work. Horrified. A dark, maddening dialogue started between me looking at the thing and its threatening strangeness. For it had thrown me instantaneously into a state of irresolution. What unimaginable accident might have precipitated this presence which, as it

Original title: 'Aube partagée.'

was dying, wouldn't let go of the lattice-work, as if, dying, it had refused with its last movement to fall into the void? And it had gotten its body stuck, with a kind of buoyancy, in between heaven and earth and death and demolition. Where did this apparition fall from? What might have crushed it? Another bird? A lightning bolt? And it stopped, for no reason, in the midst of its fall. For my torment. On my balcony. For now I had this big, heavy, somber thing, the size of my hand, caught in my breast like a ghoulish broach. And I thought of Thea. The problem was as follows: I had to get rid of the dead body before the cat had the chance of catching sight of it. Otherwise, the cat would naturally want to make its acquaintance and then . . .; but as the bird was clinging to the outside of the lattice-work, Thea would want to pass over it, and that must not happen. From behind the window I couldn't possibly imagine myself making the thing go away – its claws would be hardened, and I was going to have to struggle with death. My hands turned dry and cold up to the shoulder – I said no.

So I thought, I'm going to ask my daughter who's sleeping, but no use, for I know that it's the mother who is supposed to struggle with death. And I couldn't, I can't. So I tried to make myself think. But my hands weren't willing. There was this mystery of horrified refusal in the skin of my fingers, *I am not capable* of touching the dead body, what's impossible is the touch, the tangibility of death. There I was holding the impossible in my hands, the impossible caught by invisible little black claws. So I thought, I'm going to ask my mother, at nine o'clock I'll phone her up and, as I know, she'll say show me, and she'll do it, the mid-wife, without the slightest apprehension or phobia. But afterwards, I'll be ashamed – forever – before death, and that will be serious right up to the end, I will have lost something necessary to life, and will I still be able to assert that I'm your mother?

I also thought of my love, since he would be coming that afternoon, but I didn't dare distress him with this, for I believe my love suffers from the same phantasmal afflictions as I do, even though he's a man and I'm a woman, before death our hands grow dry the same way. And also I wouldn't want to scare him with my fear. Meanwhile an hour has gone by, and here's Thea posted on the table in sphinx posture not knowing if I know the answer to the riddle, and I can no longer get off the hook. Now I've got to answer. There's no backing away.

So I think of gloves, the rubber gloves that are in the bathroom, I'll go get them, I hunt, but they've disappeared because I didn't need them. But then I think of my leather gloves.

Now was the moment to bring my daughter in on this. Instead of waking my daughter with the luminous smile as every morning for so many years – I couldn't help myself – I blurted out the phrase quickly like something that was burning me; I said: I have a problem; she let out a little cry of alarm. And I told her it's a dead bird. It was in this way that I placed on my daughter, whom I love like myself, a little burden of affliction. Now you're the one who's suffering. But I can re-group and go into battle.

Concerning the dead body, I have the feeling of being violently attacked. Everything is aiming at me: stability, solidity, the creature must have spent the night lying in wait for me, nothing could make it let go, not even a storm, and death gives it a monstrous force, stands up to us, knowing no time, no fatigue. What it inflicts on me is the strangeness of the other side. Faced with a dead creature, there's nothing we can do, right? Which is stronger? Then I think of a stick, what a relief. I'm going to go get the bamboo stick. It won't be me, it'll be this wooden thing that will push up against that ferocious little black breast and press harder and harder until the thing snaps and falls. I go into the living room, gloves in place, the stick pointing out, and now, without trembling, I open wide the French doors and move forward, going resolutely in front of my daughter who is trembling on my behalf.

That's when the cat pounced. And what do I see? The creature is not on the other side of the lattice-work, it's on this side. Clinging, stiff, bulky – the stick is useless against it. I'll take it with the gloves then. But Thea turns it into her own serious business. Oh I can't separate those two without getting cruel. The cat sucks in her breath, mildly astonished. Me too, I can't figure out why the presence of this specter seems even more uncanny inside than out. And then.

Things start happening fast, at Thea's pace. She takes the thing in her mouth, the wings open out – she does all this effortlessly – and she brings it over and puts it down on the carpet. Death is now inside the house. It lies on its stomach, wings slightly opened, head scarcely discernible, eyes lifeless, the size of peppercorns. Uncertainty, astonishment, mourning fill Thea. Three times she walks around the body. She's not sure. Is it dead or alive, the thing doesn't answer. Then Thea moans softly. So I'll never get to meet you alive? Ah, my friend, another missed encounter, she rubs up gently against my knees and we both carry out a gentle, uncertain mourning, for now that the creature is lying down and no longer a fright up against the banisters, it elicits sorrow and compassion. We both add a dash of pity. Though the mistrustful Thea delivers a sharp blow to the body. To make sure. The bird is dead. Its two wings lift and fall back down. It's worse. If there is still a breath, some remnant, a memory, reflex. Thea: uncertain. The experiment starts over. No response. I go to get some newspapers. Because we're not going to spend any time with a corpse in here. It's bad for the living. But I don't want to rattle Thea, I let her suck in her breath and turn around, moaning tenderly. She mourns the one she never knew. It's a moment of communion.

It's not good to remain living for long with a dead body. Now is the moment when we must close up the grave book. Now is the time for burial. We are going to bury it in the garbage pail, says my silent thought, and there is a hint of vengeance in its violence. I delicately spread a piece of newspaper over the little body, for once it *was* alive. Wait, says the cat, one more good-bye. And she lifts the newspaper without violence. Now is the moment for the bird to pass over into nothingness. Say I. But I don't dare go ahead of the cat. For I recognize the rights animals have among themselves.

When at last I think that it's my duty to put an end to the story, with a rapid gesture I seize the thing. At that moment the thing springs away from death. And it rises a few inches, then lifting off flies around the room. I'm left not knowing what to expect. Thea takes off. It's a miracle. Now she is given the unexpected chance to fight. What's going to happen? Is she going to kill the bird in the living room, in the kitchen, in the bathroom, draw blood on my bed and wipe it on the carpet, on the tiles? Fortunately my daughter, my better half, is my witness, for otherwise the devil would have made off with me. But she is there, bent over, the same wind blowing the same panic across our faces.

What's in your heart? Submission to horror: we were dragged from our beds early so we could be party to a little assassination. Your horror gives me the force I'd be lacking if I were alone.

An instinct coming over me makes me throw myself at the bird, quickly I grab the wings as I would a chicken, I don't want something to die in my house, where am I going to throw it, I run to the window, instinct guiding me, we're on the balcony, instinct, the wings, the dead creature darts forward in a burst of flight and makes it all at once to the other side of the city. It's not what I wanted.

In the house it's a tragedy; Thea my dear one my love runs all over Egypt land picking up traces, all the little fragmentary odors and events, goes back over a hundred times where she's been, where the creature was, gathers together everything, but the essential is missing – the main event, the magic morsel without which life will never return to the disseminated god, the bird is missing, she cries, she digs her claws into her fine face, she digs into my guilty heart, in vain she tries every sort of animal magic, letting out shrill entreaties in the corner of the kitchen, beseeching the carpet, running sobbing to the banisters, raising the eyes of a supplicant to the deserted lattice-work, hoping beyond hope, scanning from end to end the guileless sky; the entire world has stolen her love away, and no one is giving it back to her. Ah, in vain she cries, and I too utter a great cry in secret. My daughter my sister my love, what sorrow the sorrow I caused you causes me!

And why all that?

Instinct! That cursed human instinct, that nastiness, that phobia, ah what wicked cowardice is lurking in my bones, and now I understand why Moses didn't receive anything from God up there. That human prohibition was in his bones. Thou shalt not kill in my home. That fear of defilement. No, it has nothing to do with morality. It was in my bones and before I knew it, I threw that thing that was moving into the air, because I didn't want any blood on my bed. What impurity, my god who will ever forgive me?

Knocked out, exhausted, shunned by that self-respect that forms the abandoned prop of our soul, my daughter and I lean heavily on the breakfast table and do not eat.

The cat's sorrow is that of a mother who can't find her baby in the house any more, it drives us crazy, all the orphan mothers spring from our flesh raising cries to a derisive heaven; it's that of a lover whose heart has been stolen while he's asleep, and there's no desire to live, no desire to die, because it's got to be found.

Fortunately, we are together, thinking together, we'd like to eat the little morning buns but our body filled with tragic emptiness cannot eat a bite of food, fortunately we're all three together. It's my fault. I had it in my bones. And so do you.

That day never ends. Gentle and sick with hoping, Thea gets up every hour and sadly goes to make the rounds of Egypt, for it is great and courageous not to give up on the miracle one has given up on. Hopelessly she runs around fields and gardens and without a word she lies back down in the form of a bird on her dried-out bed.

And I weep.

Oh my god, what have I done!? I've betrayed my counterpart, my betrothed, my little bride with the boundless heart; oh my god if that bird comes back I will give it to her, I swear – yes it's better that I swear, surer that way, yes, if it came back, I too would play with its lukewarm little body, I'd give it sharp little blows with my paw and I'd slit its throat cheerfully.

Besides, didn't it deceive us? Being alive playing dead.

Thea waits on the balcony, sitting in front of the lattice-work, her face stamped with the patience of our race, we who were born to await home-comings, even if we know: it's not the dead who do not return, it's the living.

She comes to get me so I will open the French doors of her church for her. I open, I who do not believe, I open for her who believes, for I bow down before faith.

She goes toward the lattice. What has come one time just might come a second time. All the faith that's not in me is in her. Holy little mistress of humility.

Penitent, I follow Thea on to the balcony, my head bowed: another human sin.

It's evening.

Now I am very tired, many tears have flowed under the bridge of time. I would like to write down that terrible thing that came to pass among us this morning, a shipwreck in my head, lumps of paving stone rattling around in my head, but I see that almost everything that we went through has been carried away by time. What came to pass has gone away, I've forgotten it all.

Thursday, May 23, 1996

12 Stigmata, or Job the dog

Translated by Eric Prenowitz

It all begins with a *Felix Culpa*. A happy fault, a blessed wound. Blessèd. This is what St Augustine tells us in his *Confessions*. The remarkable fortunes of this thematics of the wound are well known in the work of the other Augustine, James Joyce, but maybe less perceptible or explicit in other notable texts. In Proust it is buried, one must exhume it. For Genet the wound is the founding secret of all major creation.

> You will remember that I said, above, that my dearest friends took refuge, I was sure of it, wholly in a secret wound. Now I wrote soon after '. . . in a very secret domain, perhaps irreducible . . .' [. . .]

> It is possible that his immense grief – the death of Saskia – turned Rembrandt away from all the daily joys and that he filled his mourning with the metamorphosis of gold chains, feathered hats, swords, into values, or rather, into pictorial feasts. I do not know if he cried, [. . .] but toward '42 he will experience his baptism of fire, and bit by bit it will transform itself, his prime nature, vain and bold. [. . .]
> From the death of Saskia on – I wonder if he didn't kill her, in one manner or another, if he didn't rejoice in her death – at last his eye and his hand are free. From this moment on he undertakes a sort of licentiousness in painting: Saskia dead, the world and social judgements have little weight. One must imagine it, Saskia dying and he in his studio, perched on ladders, dislocating the order of The Night Watch. [. . .]

This translation of 'Stigmates' was first published in *Philosophy Today*, 1997 (Spring): 12–17.

> It goes without saying that all I have just said only has a bit of importance if one accepts that it was all pretty much false. The work of art, if it is finished, does not permit, based on itself, insights, intellectual games. It even seems to muddle intelligence, or bind it hand and foot. [. . .]
> And it goes without saying that all the œuvre of Rembrandt only makes sense – at least for me – if I know that what I have just written was false.[1]

I was young and inexperienced the first time I saw this theme appear as I was working on Joyce, it struck me as foreign, very 'Catholic' or very masculine. It recently emerged in some of Derrida's latest works. As it became visible in 'Circonfession', it wasn't Catholic. This text is about circumcision, a wound inflicted on someone who is not present at the scene of his own mutilation. With Derrida the wound is concrete, it is a violent event that took place in reality; Joyce's story of the rape of Shakespeare by his own wife, is a more or less distant metaphor.

James Joyce's *Ulysses* can be read as a portrait of the artist as an old dog:

> Belief in himself has been untimely killed. He was overborne in a cornfield first (ryefield, I should say) and he will never be a victor in his own eyes after nor play victoriously the game of laugh and lie down. [. . .] The tusk of the boar has wounded him there where love lies ableeding. [. . .] There is, I feel in the words, some goad of the flesh driving him into a new passion, a darker shadow of the first, darkening even his own understanding of himself. [. . .]
> – The soul has been before stricken mortally, a poison poured in the porch of a sleeping ear. [. . .] Ravisher and ravished, what he would but would not, go with him from Lucrece's bluecircled ivory globes to Imogen's breast, bare, with its mole cinquespotted. He goes back, weary of the creation he has piled up to hide him from himself, an old dog licking an old sore. [. . .]
> – You are a delusion, said roundly John Eglington to Stephen. [. . .] Do you believe your own theory?
> – No, Stephen said promptly.[2]

Is the fertile wound, I wondered, part of the masculine phantasmal makeup? and is there anything analogous in women's texts? What about my own relation to the inscription on the body of psychomythical events? I wrote a text called *Stigmata*, or *Job the dog*. Or else *The Origin of my Philosophy*. Or else *First Symptoms of Writing*. Or *The Opening of the Mouth*.

It is an autobiographical narrative, which does not mean very much, because an autobiographical narrative is at the same time a creation.

The scene is Algeria where I was born and where I lived as a child, in a neighborhood in the city of Algiers which had a glorious name: the 'Clos Salembier.' The tale must be understood in a socio-political context. The neighborhoods of Algiers often had 'Arab' names, some famous, like Baбеloued. It happens that this neighborhood with such a French name, Clos Salembier, was located on the heights overlooking Algiers and that it was 'Arab.' (*Arab* is what one said at the time, though it was in no way the appropriate word, no one said Algerian, but rather Arab without any distinction. The Arabs. The word Arab belonged to French colonization.) In this neighborhood 50,000 people lived in slums, in the most abject misery. The slums were one hundred meters from our house. My father was a physician, a politically conscious 'humanitarian,' and a poor man; for all these reasons he chose a house and a life not in one of the 'French' neighborhoods (that is also colonial vocabulary) of Algiers, but in this destitute neighborhood. We had hardly moved there, after the war, when my father died; whereupon my tale begins. It was as if our house was at the joint, at the articulation of Algeria. Down the hill you would go into the city and enter the French world, while up here the future Algeria was smoldering. We lived at an utterly unworkable junction. For the Arabs, and in spite of my family's commitment to the Arabs' cause, we were French. This was an absolute misreading: on the one hand we had only just re-become French: indeed as Jews during the war we were thrown out of French nationality, we became nothing. Besides, although French since 1867, my family was originally Spanish on my father's side, and German on my mother's side. But the history of nationalities had made us in turn French, de-French and re-French, and we were Jewish. Yet we did not identify with any nationality. For the Arabs this jewfrenchness was a double original sin. So long as my father was alive, because he was a doctor, we lived in peace, we were tolerated by the world of misery. As soon as he died, the depths of the rage surfaced.

This story ends as a tragedy. We were doomed by disjunctions and anachronisms, as if the partners who should have been partners in love were constantly separated by a chronological discrepancy. There was not enough time. (If there had been time between the Arabs and ourselves, which is what is happening now, the two destinal durations would have found themselves in concordance at a certain moment.) Discord orders the tale of Job the Dog. There was no time.

*

At present when I return to the age of the Clos Salembier, to which I have not come back for forty years and I will never come back, where conserved in the blue amber air of the immemorial past, the house awaits me in the garden where still each year rows of flowers and vegetables that my father had planted grow, of all the animated beings that pursue their immortal life in the enclosed dwelling of my childhood, the one that remains the most alive, the most intensely vibratile, powerful, agitated, the one that also takes the most space in the garden that contains my meticulous memory, yes, I see the one that is incomparably the biggest, an effect of perspective naturally, the one that comes before me like an arrow, when having made the corner of the boulevard Laurent-Pichat at the pace of a dream I devour the dozen meters that lead to the portal, the portal with rusted bars from the first day, the one that awaits me the first and that I find standing at the entrance and immediately everywhere, is neither the phantom of my German grandmother who stays in the background, nor any of the inhabitants, who were nonetheless strong, of that era kept like an ancient century, all are there but a bit faded by the light of the times, a bit slowed in the immobile air of memory,

the only one of the strong animated beings that still inhabit Bd. Laurent-Pichat, and among whom I am myself, the only one that is not affected and weakened by the great distances is Fips the dog. The most miserable of the gods and the most divine of the miserable.

To see him burst forth yelping like the spirit of survival, not like one of the slightly effaced phantoms that we ourselves are, but like a unique case of triumph of life over all the conditions and customs of gradual lessening of the things that were, I marvel, my heart is loaded with a bitter joy and with shame, and I admire this dog, with the humility that in the past I was never able to feel, because a sacred terror prevented me. I admit, Fips you are unforgettable, you have attained the rank that was always denied you while you lived, you are the most living of the departed. The manifestation of Fips is the proof that there is no universal or absolute law of effacement. At this very moment he is piercing the frail but solid cloud that separates our now from before, and I see him as if I saw him right here in reality, as if he saw me, as he looks at me, cast up more than standing, violently addressed, as if he could throw his eyes at my eyes, in the superhuman effort that thrust him almost to the point of killing him, well beyond his dog's border. Just revenge, I say to myself, just reward. Fips, you wanted so much to cross, all your forms outstretched every day to try to pass through, to shatter the walls, you wanted to break the prisons, lacerate the skins, your soul called for deliverance, never have I seen a being in such furious rebellion against the ancient fates that fix our bounds right from birth, the polices, the stupidity, *les bêtises* that have debasing powers over every creature who goes beyond. The eyes almost torn from their orbits, the soul darted as an arrow, the entire being in a flash, the ultimate groan with naked teeth, the nose soft imploring, he stands up to the attacking worlds.

Behold a being that would not be tamed living and dead for a very long time he resists every attempt of nothingness.

Today when I return home to 54 Bd. Laurent-Pichat, the one who comes out to meet me, the one who calls just as I turn the corner, fawn-threats on me, the one who reminds me of myself and who turns out to be the character the most secretly necessary and marking of the flesh of my soul, I see him, it is he. I am the result of his visit. Indelible are the traces of his cruel stay in my flesh and my soul. It is to him that I owe my scars. He is the innocent author of the signatures that inaugurated my book on my feet and my hands.

I have his teeth and his rage, painted on my left foot and on my hands, I never think about it, because the little mute lips of the wounds have traveled, what remains of them on my feet and my hands is only an insensible embossment, the marks of the cries are lodged on the sensitive very sensitive membranes of my brain. I have that dog in my skull, like an unrecognizable twin.

You who know my bursts of rage, the sudden moments when the door of my calm opens to give way to a very ancient furor, you do not know that then I am Fips, I leap out of myself called by his gallop that hoped to pass in a prodigious bound over the spikes of the portal, barking I follow his hope I am his extravagance, he invented invisible wings for himself, it was miracle to see him fly over the obstacle, belying the envelope that made him small and dog. But as for me when without thinking I wanted to escape I failed, I fell back on to the spiked portal and I impaled my obstinately human thigh. He was god and I was realistic.

All that I manage to think today, the awful complexities that make love twisted bloody and criminal up to the belated hour of softness, I learned from him without knowing that I was and would be his disciple while we lived tempestuously together;

At the time, the suffering that came to us from the suffering that we inflicted on ourselves each one by the other was so great that in the great obscure silence into which one descends to dream of evil, in our last times I was able to desire that he should die. But I could not say it to myself. But I remember having felt the obscure and impossible desire-without-words. And this desire opened other very nasty wounds behind my heart.

We never had the joys, only the hope of joys always haunted us and united us to deceive us.

At the bottom of the bottom of all my ignorances, I must have had a prescience inaccessible to myself, that this mydog was something else, that he *was*, much more than I, and that I do not know what a dog is nor what being a dog is.

Essential, urgent, that he was, expectantly desperately unexpectedly. A dog guards the entrance. If he barks so loud it's so you won't see he's the lamb. Sir Lamb barks in vain. But we begrudge him for having instituted the reign of love that costs us so dearly. Because as a lamb the dog is born to give his life for us. Which entails that in return we be ready to give our life for him. But we did not want to give our life to the dog. We wanted the ideal dog, the all powerful, the assistance, the idea of dog in the heavens. This is how his misfortune began even before he appeared preceded by our desire. As for me, I am ready to give my life for my cat but it was necessary that Fips should first have given his life for me.

For our inevitable misfortune, I the child-of-man, I considered him in the beginning as a dog of man, and *bêtement* ineluctably like every child-of-man I spoke to him as we do inadvertently with foreign visitors up to the day I stopped addressing him forever.

He was the hero of misfortunes and contretemps.

On the one hand he came too early: we the children were not ready, we were far from having the animal height and even from imagining that it existed, which is the trait of human immaturity. It is only for having gone through his resurrection which took place dozens of years after his death, that I made the unexpected discovery of those heights so near and so denied. And even his resurrection I nearly missed it, because it took place so accidentally, it could have not taken place, and it was accomplished in an oblique form, as if in order to happen it was obliged to deceive my old vigilances, take the most cunning detour. For dozens of years his death was well guarded. Mixed with the past earth to which we will never return, his rot buried in the flower bed to the right on entering where there were dahlias with voluminous red nudes, we had left him behind us, abandoned soul representing thoughts we would never again come to visit. Not forgotten, but seized by a manner of fatal repudiation. The guilty feeling we keep closed in a cage concerning beings of our own blood who, their body closed in the tomb, cannot follow us on our distant exportations – and so as to snuff out the flame, we murmur quickly that they cannot feel it since they are dead and we feign to believe that we believe in the extinction of the dead and we feign to be convinced materialists, an elevated but unsteady lie that is, and we live all our life – with those dead that we have not been able to avoid condemning; under the red earth they voice soft mews so light that we do not hear them.

Thus my father and Fips, their death kept very far behind me.

Admittedly my father found in me the force to cross stone and earth and to return several times a year to see me in dream as an attached parent and we never spoke of that bad thing, i.e. his completely deserted funerary residence, we said nothing about it, I infringe, with his consent I hope, the silent laws of the family, I do not go to see my father, it is he who comes. But Fips never. I never even persuaded myself that Fips had any mortal remains. I assigned him the terrible role of holocaust. So it was, and in the notebooks where I consigned the surprises, almost all cruel, that life reserves for us as it unfolds, I noted down the case of F next to that of Michael Kohlhaas: in life things are so tortuous, it can happen that the most innocent of beings finishes as a quartered criminal and we can do nothing about it; and it can happen that we betray father and son compulsorily.

And suddenly, the resurrection. Of which I had never thought. It happened one morning, and it had the features of a cat. Consequently I did not pay attention, at first. Two years, my dreams had to repeat the same message for two years for me to finally wake up from my deafness after so many absent-minded years and for me all of a sudden to hear my former and first animal yapping. My cat came from my dog, which explains the singular power of my cat over my heart, an absolute power that makes of this young and childish beast my daily prophet, like the small subjectile creature in which the Tibetan oracle recognizes the successive reincarnation of the Buddha. And that is why my cat still barely larger than a mouse reigned already. A minuscule imperceptible never-awaited messiah who would have thought?

We who had always waited in vain for a third child my brother and I were transported with fervor when, the world-war over, my father announced the impending arrival of a babydog. This is how he completed the era of regrowing and blossoming: my father needed to plant trees with his hands, a supreme attempt to hold life back by the roots. After the plantation came the hour of the garden's inhabitants. And it was a dog. During the wait which was long we kept busy. The cradle occupied all our thoughts. We chose a shoe box. For the mattress we sewed two small pieces of cloth, which we then filled with bougainvillea petals. This filled us with excited satisfactions. We could already see the little one sleeping beneath our zealous eyes, answering all our wishes. None of the cradles of the children we engendered later on ever filled us in its emptiness with such pressing emotions. Crouched before the box we brooded.

The sex did not interest us. What we wanted was the child.

Fips did not let himself be laid in the bed of all our cares. We fought for several hours or several days. We caught the little one we laid him out, we flattened him, we ironed him, we held him in place while we covered him with the sheet, and immediately in a start he overcame the box. Our advances were not understood and we did not understand that they were not understood. This caused tension. Not for a minute did he sleep under our tender eyes. The dethroned cradle. We lost our sublime parents' heads. Fallen from the window of a high dream, we looked like dolls broken on the rock. And no one had warned us of the danger. The donkey and the ox chased off with a blow of his paw.

So it was a dog. Yet on the other side, us. So he was not born to us, and he did not even conceive of our bond. There was not even a rupture. We were sent off to a distant planet of penitence, we who had already loved him so much even before his birth. And he had no idea of what he inspired in us. The twinge of loss of this thing we had never had and for which there was no consolation. We were very small and we were the place of inordinately large feelings. We suffered enormously, but from what. Those feelings in fusion that no name comes yet to contain – it is an inundation. We unloved him a bit and we did not approve of this retreat, we found ourselves less beautiful, less radiant, he careless leaping, he was a little piece of furry light, but there was cloudiness in us, a closed gate, a bit of sediment. And this decrease in clarity, our fault. Our fault weighed heavy. It must have weighed a kilogram, we felt its inert and inaccessible body lying like a stone on our heart. And it was his fault. But since he suspected nothing it was even worse our fault. The poison we secrete on the occasion of the innocence of a being who has done nothing to us – we lay it to his face. In spite of ourselves and without our knowing we were becoming a little bit mean.

(And now I understand that all we did not understand was not taken from us but on the contrary entrusted to us to keep in the shelter of a non-understanding that conserved future treasures frozen until our spiritual coming of age. All that remained painful closed, foreign, is in truth our dowry. A lode of torments, we think, mistaken. There comes the day when these sleeping clots wake into revelations.)

The dog was there and it wasn't right. I wanted him to love me like *this* and not like that. (I would have liked him to obey me like a dog. But if they had told me I wanted a slave I would have responded indignantly that I only wanted the pure ideal dog I had heard of.) He loved me as an animal and far from my ideal. It was a creature of small size intoxicated with life and in that way much larger than itself. And who would never have been able to squeeze into a box.

It was my father who was his father without images and without ideas. He cared for his health. It was a natural obligation and my father the doctor fulfilled it in a movement that he performed equally for all his fellow creatures. He put drops in his eyes. Of Fips and my father, in their contact, there was born a point of resemblance. Both were carried inwardly by the breath of a song. Fips was happy to be. They both had those feverish eyes.

Suddenly our father died, I did not think then what this must have meant for the dog.

The family that rose trembling from the ruins of the deceased family was entirely different. Commanded by my German Jewish mother commanded by my German Jewish grandmother. I did not think about it. By an ancient unwritten but all the more solid tradition it was understood in the maternal generations that to have feelings for an animal 'is not recommended.' The maternal millennia naturally treated animals like mere animals. The interpretation of the tradition went without commentary because it was confused in the distance with the white sun of the evident. A dog is fed. Dogfood. Feddog. Instantly our dog withered but the tradition did not see it.

It was then that from outside the garden the hunt was unleashed against us. Our Arab neighbors encircled us in a daily siege.

So the hunt was unleashed. The acrid war that had been held back until then in the face of my father the doctor swoops down on the family. We live besieged as diminutive soldiers inwardly undermined by a just and bitter sympathy for our Arab assailants. We defend ourselves like inhabitants who are forbidden by everything to attack the enemy. They called my father 'my brother.' Dead with him was this privilege, this love. Now we were Jews. Now we were French. Now we were Jewfrench, the worst in their eyes. Now we were insulted and I often bit the dust mad with rage. At least *we* did battle. My brother and I. But the dog was hostage. And we did not let him fight. It would have been a carnage. It was a tragedy.

Here begins the agony. How remote the time when implacable-I wanted him enclosed with love in his box and I begrudged him for not giving me any of his freedom. At present he suffered our enclosed fate. Ten times a day there rained on the family a hail of stones. In no time, the volleys that wounded our spirit made Fips into a mad dog. By a horrible turn of wars, he was punished because of the misfortune he suffered to be us. He did not have the time to come back to himself between two offensives the froth never dried, besides it was for us the besieged together that he groaned, I too foamed and he ran for me howling toward the gate where the rose rosebushes and the hostile packs climbed. The dog began to suffer in me from these lapidations. It was the dog in me that suffered. If only they had shot at us with bullets. But the choice of the assassination, they threw stones at us and we were three severly wounded beings who ran bristling in the garden transformed by the assault into obligatory box. The sun of war rose and set in the garden. Ancient and hoarse tribe. The dog no longer slept skin taut fur sticky throat full of knots one morning he had an effusion of hate eyes drowned in the black juice brain inundated by the flood that unhinges, life became nocturnal and nightmare the sun is for nothing, and the postman who opened the portal was the messenger of the apocalypse. Like one in ecstasies who throws himself into the furnace Fips enthused with terror fell on the postman his teeth in flames and the error was fateful.

We put the dog on a leash and tied the leash to a wire and the wire to an iron post so he would not kill, we ourselves chained up our own incarnation, we ourselves put my father's heir in irons.

Fips descended into hell like those that a just cause led to blood. There is no more law. We beat the innocent. I am so alone thought the one in chains. And the only one to be repelled on both sides. No doubt he understood the enemy better than the friend. This world is upside down and the dog is betrayed. I should have spoken to him, I should have, if I had been able to understand him but I thought him perhaps incapable of understanding for I was not then capable of understanding the profound animal humanity, if I had not said to myself as we precipitately lie to ourselves, that a dog does not understand our bad complications and that he is a dog. I stopped thinking. I stopped feeling. After all I could not take on to my back this chained-up cross that waited for me in the garden, his feverish eyes that searched for my fleeing eyes as soon as I set foot on the earth of the garden. I did not speak to him. Am I Jewish? he thought. But what does that mean Jewish, he suffered from not knowing. And me neither. And I did not make light in his obscurity, I did not murmur to him the words that all animals understand.

But the obligation to love the prisoner has the taste of bitter herbs, it was Easter and we were in the square desert, forbidden not to love the prisoner, I loved Fips by force, according to the laws of captivity. But it was a love on this side of breath, never did I exclaim: my love. I did not tell him that injustice hate cruelty had all the rights and that the wars devoured the living by breaking their bones and their souls interminably, only until the day when all of a sudden it stopped, I did not tell him that to live was to survive in chains until the day you know not why they fall, and if you are still living. I did not tell him that the massacres exhaust themselves. He knew only horror without hope. I did not put drops in

his eyes. Moreover he had ticks. I did not speak to him, I forgot to speak
to him. Moreover we were all in the process of becoming mean dogs each
one for the others, as it happens when the war raging outside begins to
gnaw at the hearts to better propagate itself inside. Then one bites one's
brother and one bites oneself. Oneself the barbed proboscis attached to
the warmblooded vertebrates. The excitation of fear, rancor, acid indig-
nation up to the smooth foliage of the banana trees. The great baleful
glass of persecution: all is deformed. We were fuming. Our movements
brusque, our ears pulled back in waiting.

Someone rang. I was twelve. I was way in the back of a book reading.
The bell of the portal was it the knell, no one hears it, no one hears
anyone any more in this house, it is always I who must open. I emerged
from my cave and I brought my dreamy foot down on the ground before
the kitchen.

As it is told that at the corner of a street a Mercedes rolling heavy and
mad cuts down with an enormous and heavy scythe the unfortunate
passing woman nose to nose with death that she had not seen coming,
what I had not foreseen happened. I did not see my dog coming. I did
not see my dog see me jump wild-eyed with feet together on the bruised
ground. I did not see my dog see me come on to his tumefied body with
the brutal stroke of the alien executioner. No doubt I drove him mad. It
seemed to him that it was hate. It seemed to him that now I too. And
that there was no crime nor any betrayal that his own family was foreign
to. In his extreme abandonment. And you too. Et tu quoque. It seemed
to him that I was not his sister and I was his assassin. And in a great
hoarse shiver as if he were breathing his last he leapt on the foot that I
lifted close to him. It seemed to me that from that bite I would die
because it no longer released me, it sank in, it was penetrating it planted
all its teeth in my heart.

The teeth lingered. We entered sobbleeding the mad eternity. The dog
could let me go no more. Hideous attachment, an ecstasy held us him-
to-me under the yoke. We moved no more harnessed to pain, aghast. The
Earth turned over.

What could have separated us?

From the laundry basin boiling in the courtyard Aïcha took a sheet
that she twisted into a hard damp cord and fell full force on the back of
the beast, her arms so round, very strong, she brings the flail down ten
times on the backbone.

The washerwoman cried to the sky climbed the incense mixed with
cries tears groans. Where was I, in a gaping elsewhere, expelled from
myself and held back by the fangs. No hate sadder than that of furious

love. I understood that there is no worse enemy than the small brother enemy, I cannot want to kill you who are my own raving twin, the bearer of bitterness.

At the thirteenth stroke the muzzle cracked, I removed my frightening foot from the jaws. I saw the meat we are. We came out of the mortal spasms broken lame and delirious. Unrecognizable.

Because it could not be me. Because it could not be him.

As always in these apocalyptic moments, the sky was extremely blue. The geraniums brightly red.

We let out sacred howls: supernatural terror on both sides.

When at last we were separated the one from the other, it was too late. The root had been reached. On the inside of my brain the very slight bleeding of a small lack of forgetting, a minuscule wound would not close its eyes. The five scars on my foot like a clumsy star had closed. I even saw it as an ornament. But in the depths of my thoughts in the shadow and the silence, with the secret heart of an evildoer I hid myself and I said to him: no. It was a no so sad and so secret, it was shameful and never did I avow it. There was nothing to be proud of. It was laziness. It was not vengeance. It was a lack of strength. I should have taken Fips in my arms and rocked the innocent. Why I did not do it. And I will never have children I thought. Until suddenly later I wanted just the opposite.

Subsequently I knew the lowest form of family life with him: silence under the same roof. The poison is not hate it is weak love. We were poisoned. I poisoned him. My good will did not turn itself toward him. I passed before him with at my sides the high severe silhouettes that guarded me at my right Terror at my left Pity. Between us the days were nights with separate bedrooms. We acted as if there were two moons. But he had ticks big as chickpeas. This gave him saintliness.

Job was that dog I am sure. The scourges were sent to him, god was well hidden, the father dead, the house ruined and now the plagues and the ulcers. And without being conscious of it I did not love the leper like myself. With terror I tore off the monsters that devoured him and not with joy. The suffering of the beast made me suffer for myself. I did not stretch out my hands to bless the tortured victim. I was not his knight at arms, he hurt me on the wrong side and I did not rush into the flames to save my child my dog which today I do, I was powerless to do it I felt the bitter pain of those who are denied the all-powerful sainthood of love. I was the non-keeper of my dog, I crossed the garden suppurating, trying to go by the body eaten with ulcers and grief without stopping.

They ate him alive, those blood drinking inventions created to kill a victim entirely lacking in possibilities to escape them, those proofs of the existence of the devil soft vampires that laugh at the dog's lack of hands, they suckle it to death, Fips feels his life flow into their tribe of stomachs and without the chance of a combat. The agonizer perished living. I succumbed myself amongst them. It was every day as a pulling of teeth swollen with the mush of his blood. A nightmare demography, the same night I saw them reproduce themselves they were on the bars of the gates, on the door frames they were born from everywhere and out of nowhere and they descended in slow frenzies to sit on his ears on his neck on his flanks and they introduced their jaws of stomachs into the necrosed purple of his veins.

All the DDT in the world for nothing, the muzzle full of powder and the blood on top of it all. I succumbed myself beneath the purplish thoughts and I did not save him.

It was the end. I received the dispatch: we were condemned. All constructions destroyed, works suppressed, research burned. The bad news kept coming; the expiration was announced.

We were on the bridge of the boat, the enemy's breath blew at our back. We barely escaped, when at the moment of landing I saw Fips before my eyes disarticulated, it was a dislocated spine, between the open legs the soft and white stomach stretched the body in a cross, the tender fright seized me, I saw the danger, an inexpert hand could break my beast. What had to be found in the foreign land was the being called veterinarian. Quick, I cried to my brother, get on the motorcycle, I straddled the machine, there was only the handlebar, the motor had stayed behind on the bridge. Between my arms the animal as between life and death I cried: the motorcycle! go look for the motorcycle but I did not believe it. Surely they robbed us up there, and I did not know where to go to prevent death from arriving. I dreamt this dream and it remained without end.

I did not accompany him. A foul fear of seeing the one I did not love strong enough die, and as I would not give my life for him I could no longer share his death.

When at last what was left of him departed watched over by my brother I was not there. Moreover never, by chance or will, was I present at the departure neither of my father nor of my son nor of my grandmother nor of any being of my flesh. The mouths sewn shut on my foot.

And even so I loved Fips but not then, not there in the garden of war, not yet, but later.

Notes

1 Jean Genet, 'Ce qui est resté d'un Rembrandt . . .,' *Œuvres Complètes* (Paris: Gallimard), pp. 24–8.
2 James Joyce, *Ulysses* (London: Bodley Head, 1960 [1934]), pp. 251–74.

Bibliography

Hélène Cixous's book-length publications 1967–1998

Place of publication is Paris unless stated otherwise.

Books published in French

Fiction

(1967) *Le Prénom de Dieu*, Grasset.
(1969) *Dedans* (Prix Médicis), Grasset; second edn, Des femmes, 1986.
(1970) *Le Troisième corps*, Grasset.
────── *Les Commencements*, Grasset.
(1971) *Un vrai jardin*, L'Herne.
(1972) *Neutre*, Grasset.
(1973) *Tombe*, Le Seuil.
────── *Portrait du soleil*, Denoël.
(1975) *Révolutions pour plus d'un Faust*, Seuil.
────── *Souffles*, Des femmes.
(1976) *La*, Gallimard; second edn, Des femmes, 1979.
────── *Partie*, Des femmes.
(1977) *Angst*, Des femmes.
(1978) *Préparatifs de noces au-delà de l'abîme*, Des femmes. Excerpts read by
   Hélène Cixous, La Bibliothèque des voix, Des femmes, 1981.
(1979) *Vivre l'orange*, Des femmes; second edn in *L'heure de Clarice Lispector*,
   1989.
────── *Anankè*, Des femmes.
(1980) *Illa*, Des femmes.
(1981) *With ou l'art de l'innocence*, Des femmes.
(1982) *Limonade tout était si infini*, Des femmes.
(1983) *Le Livre de Promethea*, Gallimard.
(1986) *La bataille d'Arcachon*, Laval, Quebec: Trois, collection Topaze.
(1988) *Manne aux Mandelstams aux Mandelas*, Des femmes.
(1990) *Jours de l'an*, Des femmes.
(1991) *L'ange au secret*, Des femmes.

(1992) *Déluge*, Des femmes.

(1993) *Beethoven à jamais*, Des femmes.

(1995) *La fiancée juive, de la tentation,* Des femmes.

(1996) *Messie*, Des femmes.

(1997) *Or, les lettres de mon père*, Des femmes.

Theatre

(1972) *La Pupille, Cahiers Renaud-Barrault* 78, Gallimard.

(1976) *Portrait de Dora*, Des femmes; reprinted in *Théâtre*, 1986. Opened 26 February 1976 at the Théâtre d'Orsay, directed by Simone Benmussa; a radio version was broadcast on France Culture, 'Atelier de Création Radiophonique' in 1972.

(1977) *L'Arrivante*, unpublished (adaptation of *La*). Directed by Viviane Théophilidès, Théâtre Ouvert, Festival d'Avignon, July.

(1978) *Le nom d'Oedipe: Chant du corps interdit*, libretto, Des femmes. Music by André Boucourechliev, directed by Claude Régy, Festival d'Avignon, 1978.

(1982) *Je me suis arrêtée à un mètre de Jerusalem et c'était le paradis,* unpublished. Reading at the Théâtre Ouvert with Hélène Cixous, Michelle Marquais and Bérangère Bonvoisin, 7 June.

—— *Amour d'une délicatesse,* radio play, unpublished. Radio Suisse Romande, Lausanne, 28 August.

(1984) *La prise de l'école de Madhubaï, Avant-Scène du Théâtre* 745 (March): 6–22; reprinted in *Théâtre*, 1986. Opened 13 December 1983 at the Petit Odéon directed by Michelle Marquais.

—— *Celui qui ne parle pas,* unpublished. Théâtre Tsaï, Grenoble, T.E.P., Paris, June.

(1985) *L'Histoire terrible mais inachevée de Norodom Sihanouk, roi du Cambodge*, Théâtre du Soleil; new, corrected edition, 1987. Opened 11 September 1985 at the Théâtre du Soleil, directed by Ariane Mnouchkine.

(1986) *Théâtre*, Des femmes.

(1987) *L'Indiade, ou l'Inde de leurs rêves, et quelques écrits sur le théâtre*, Théâtre du Soleil. Opened 30 September 1987 at the Théâtre du Soleil, directed by Ariane Mnouchkine.

(1989) *La nuit miraculeuse*, television screenplay with Ariane Mnouchkine, Théâtre du Soleil. Broadcast on FR3, La Sept, December.

(1991) *On ne part pas, on ne revient pas*, Des femmes. First reading 24 November 1991 at (La Métaphore), directed by Daniel Mesguich and André Guittier.

(1992) *Les Euménides* by Aeschylus, translation, Théâtre du Soleil. Opened 26 May 1992 at the Théâtre du Soleil, directed by Ariane Mnouchkine.

(1994) *L'Histoire (qu'on ne connaîtra jamais)*, Des femmes. Directed by Daniel Mesguich at the Théâtre de la Ville and (La Métaphore).

—— *Voile Noire Voile Blanche/Black Sail White Sail*, bilingual, translation by Catherine A.F. MacGillivray, *New Literary History* 25, 2 (Spring), Minnesota University Press: 219–354.

(1994) *La Ville parjure ou le réveil des Erinyes*, Théâtre du Soleil. Opened at the Théâtre du Soleil, 18 May 1994, directed by Ariane Mnouchkine.

Books of criticism

(1969) *L'exil de James Joyce ou l'art du remplacement*, thesis for Doctorat d'État, Publications de la Faculté des lettres et sciences de Paris-Sorbonne, Grasset; second edn, 1985.

(1974) *Prénoms de personne*, Seuil.

(1975) *Un K. incompréhensible: Pierre Goldman*, Christian Bourgois.

—— *La jeune née*, with Catherine Clément, U.G.E., Collection 10/18.

(1977) *La venue à l'écriture*, with Madeleine Gagnon and Annie Leclerc, U.G.E., 10/18, (title essay reprinted in *Entre l'écriture*, 1986: 9–69.)

(1986) *Entre l'écriture*, Des femmes.

(1989) *L'heure de Clarice Lispector, précédé de Vivre l'Orange*, Des femmes.

(1994) *Hélène Cixous, Photos de Racines*, with Mireille Calle-Gruber, Des femmes.

Books published in English

(1972) *The Exile of James Joyce*, translated by Sally A.J. Purcell, New York: David Lewis; London: John Calder, 1976.

(1977) *Portrait of Dora*, translated by Anita Barrows, *Gambit International Theatre Review* 8, 30: 27–67; reprinted in, *Benmussa Directs*, Playscript 91, London: John Calder; Dallas: Riverrun 1979: 27–73; translated by Sarah Burd, *Diacritics*, 1983 (Spring): 2–32.

(1979) *To Live the Orange*, translated by Ann Liddle and Sarah Cornell, in *Vivre l'orange* (bilingual), Des femmes.

(1985) *Angst*, translated by Jo Levy, London: John Calder; New York: Riverrun.

(1986) *Inside*, translated by Carol Barko, New York: Schocken Books.

—— *The Conquest of the School at Madhubaï*, translated by Deborah W. Carpenter, *Women and Performance* 3 (Special Feature): 59–95.

—— *The Newly Born Woman*, with Catherine Clément, translated by Betsy Wing, Theory and History of Literature, vol. 24, Minneapolis: University of Minnesota Press. 'Sorties: Out and Out: Attacks/Ways Out/Forays,' (pp. 63–132) reprinted in Catherine Belse and Jane Moore (eds), *The Feminist Reader: Essays in Gender and the Politics of Literary Criticism*, Houndmills, Basingstoke, Hampshire: Macmillan Education, New York: Blackwell, 1989: 101–116.

(1988) *Neutre*, translated by Lorene M. Birden in 'Making English Clairielle: An Introduction and Translation for Hélène Cixous's "Neutre,"' M.A. Thesis, University of Massachussetts at Amherst.

(1990) *Reading with Clarice Lispector* (seminar 1980–1985), edited and translated by Verena Conley, London: Harvester Wheatsheaf.

(1991) *The Name of Oedipus*, translated by Christiane Makward and Judith Miller, *Out of Bounds: Women's Theater in French*, Ann Arbor: University of Michigan Press.

——   *The Book of Promethea*, translated by Betsy Wing, Lincoln: University of Nebraska Press.

——   *'Coming to Writing' and Other Essays*, edited by Deborah Jenson, translated by Sarah Cornell, Deborah Jenson, Ann Liddle and Susan Sellers, Cambridge, MA: Harvard University Press.

(1992) *Readings, The poetics of Blanchot, Joyce, Kafka, Lispector, Tsvetaeva* (seminar 1982–1984), edited and translated by Verena Conley, London: Harvester Wheatsheaf.

(1993) *Three Steps on the Ladder of Writing*, The Welleck Library Lectures, Irvine (June 1990), translated by Sarah Cornell and Susan Sellers, New York: Columbia University Press.

(1994) *The Terrible but Unfinished Story of Norodom Sihanouk, King of Cambodia*, translated by Juliet Flower MacCannell, Judith Pike and Lollie Groth, Lincoln: University of Nebraska Press.

——   *Manna, for the Mandelstams for the Mandelas*, translated by Catherine A.F. MacGillivray, Minneapolis: University of Minnesota Press.

——   *The Hélène Cixous Reader*, translated and edited by Susan Sellers, London: Routledge.

(1997) *Rootprints,* translated by Eric Prenowitz, London and New York: Routledge.

(1998) *FirstDays of the Year*, translated by Catherine A.F. MacGillivray, Minneapolis: University of Minnesota Press, forthcoming.